Presidential Rhetoric and the
Public Agenda

Presidential Rhetoric and the Public Agenda

Constructing the War on Drugs

Andrew B. Whitford
   and
Jeff Yates

The Johns Hopkins University Press
Baltimore

© 2009 The Johns Hopkins University Press
All rights reserved. Published 2009
Printed in the United States of America on acid-free paper
9 8 7 6 5 4 3 2 1

The Johns Hopkins University Press
2715 North Charles Street
Baltimore, Maryland 21218-4363
www.press.jhu.edu

Library of Congress Cataloging-in-Publication Data

Whitford, Andrew B.
    Presidential rhetoric and the public agenda : constructing the War on
Drugs / Andrew B. Whitford and Jeff Yates.
        p.   cm.
    Includes bibliographical references and index.
    ISBN-13: 978-0-8018-9346-9 (hardcover : alk. paper)
    ISBN-10: 0-8018-9346-1 (hardcover : alk. paper)
    1. Presidents—United States.   2. Political leadership—United
States.   3. Rhetoric—Political aspects—United States.   4. Political
oratory—United States.   5. Presidents—United States—
Language.   6. Drug control—United States.   I. Yates, Jeff,
1965–   II. Title.
    JK516.W487 2009
    363.450973—dc22   2008052444

A catalog record for this book is available from the British Library.

*Special discounts are available for bulk purchases of this book. For more
information, please contact Special Sales at 410-516-6936 or specialsales@press
.jhu.edu.*

The Johns Hopkins University Press uses environmentally friendly book
materials, including recycled text paper that is composed of at least 30
percent post-consumer waste, whenever possible. All of our book papers are
acid-free, and our jackets and covers are printed on paper with recycled
content.

Contents

Figures and Tables

TABLES

Preface

All research projects are complicated, and this book is certainly no exception. We began this fully understanding neither the causes and consequences of the war on drugs nor the demands imposed by book projects like this one. We had certain factors on our side, though. We drew on two powerful and richly developed literatures in the social sciences. The first was on presidential rhetoric, populated by the work of eminent scholars recognizable by their last names alone: Tulis, Kernell, Edwards. The literature they helped establish, along with other students of the presidency, provided a theoretical base on which to develop and refine our primary argument.

The second literature centers on social construction and leadership in large, complex organizations. Here the names are also renowned: Kaufman, Selznick, Weick. We specifically drew on studies of presidential leadership and management of the bureaucrats that support their administration. We pulled these two literatures together to show how an executive can use the spoken word to lead those who implement his policy vision and positions.

Also facilitating our research was that our primary thesis—that presidents lead and manage by policy signals sent from the "bully pulpit"—was part of the conventional wisdom about the presidency, though systematic testing of this premise was scant. Rather than offer anecdotal evidence from American political history, it is more useful to point out that the idea of leading large numbers of agents by direct signaling and symbols predates both the American founding and, indeed, most of European history.

Consider how one leadership scholar expressed these ideas long ago in a place far away from American politics:

> Fighting with a large army under your command is nowise different from fighting with a small one: it is merely a question of instituting signs and signals.

This is one of the principles found in Sun Tzu's classic statement on leadership and management, *The Art of War*, first described in 6th century B.C. China (chap. 5,

"Energy," principle 2, from Lionel Giles's 1910 translation). For Sun Tzu, though, this idea is not just a platitude but has real implications for leading and managing large numbers of battle troops (perhaps the ultimate agents of policy implementation):

> On the field of battle, the spoken word does not carry far enough: hence the institution of gongs and drums. Nor can ordinary objects be seen clearly enough: hence the institution of banners and flags.
>
> Gongs and drums, banners and flags, are means whereby the ears and eyes of the host may be focused on one particular point.
>
> The host thus forming a single united body, is it impossible either for the brave to advance alone, or for the cowardly to retreat alone. This is the art of handling large masses of men.
>
> In night-fighting, then, make much use of signal-fires and drums, and in fighting by day, of flags and banners, as a means of influencing the ears and eyes of your army.   (CHAP. 7, "MANEUVERING," PRINCIPLES 23–26)

Well over two thousand years ago, the principles of leading and managing large numbers of implementation agents through signaling and symbolic communication were well understood. Of course, Sun Tzu's troops are different from modern-day, street-level American bureaucrats, but they also have important commonalities. The president wants to keep policy agents in tune with his policy vision despite the potential for discord on policy within the bureaucratic ranks; Sun Tzu's general, fearing discord among his officers during battle, employed signals and symbolic communication to keep the ranks in line with his vision for battle strategy. A president may use rhetorical signaling to focus field agents on his primary mission and motivate them toward attaining executive goals; Sun Tzu's general may have used signals and symbolic communication to focus soldiers on their tasks, discipline them in their efforts, and inspire them in their mission in the face of adversity. There are distinct differences in how they used communication and attained their goals, but the mechanism is the same.

We know that our book is certainly not the first to investigate this principle, and we hope that it is not the last. We began thinking and writing about this concept in American governance in the late 1990s. We sincerely hope scholars will find our approach useful for thinking about the phenomena and interpersonal dynamics across a wide range of policy topics. Wrinkles and twists remain to be uncovered about how this theory applies to different interpersonal relations, leadership situations, and institutional contexts. Clearly, the idea applies to American presidents and Sun Tzu's generals, but we guess there are applications in a variety of governance, business, and other settings. This principle probably is useful in certain situations and is not as relevant for other interpersonal relations. We encourage those who work in the area of leadership and management of all sorts to consider how this intriguing concept applies to their own work, especially those working intensely on one policy area (as this book does in the case of the war on drugs).

In large research projects like the production of a book, for better or worse authors receive inordinate credit for what is, in many ways, more appropriately considered a group effort. Academic authors are like actors in movies (usually on a smaller scale, often with lower remuneration). At the end of a movie, the credits roll and as viewers exit the theater they may catch only a glimpse of the names of all of the people who contributed to the production. Actors who win Academy Awards typically use their acceptance speeches to thank a list of people who were involved in making the movie. They benefit, though, from the orchestra's cue music that makes sure the actor does not dwell on listing everyone from their yoga instructor to their agent's cousin. Acknowledgement sections in books offer the same opportunity, and so we will balance completeness and brevity.

We want to express our appreciation to everyone who helped us complete this book; some helped without even knowing they did so. Just as directors and lead actors take the brunt of criticism for their films, we willingly accept criticisms of this book.

Andy Whitford thanks two political scientists for the way they have shaped his view of presidents, bureaucracies, and the power of prosecutors. Many of the ideas on leadership expressed here can be traced to conversations with Gary Miller over the past fifteen years. The intense focus on prosecutors and law enforcement agencies this book represents started during that time, but was only sustained by constant encouragement from Matthew Holden. Finishing the book project was another matter. He thanks (and here, apologizes to) Jan Whitford and his children Anna and Max for the time they gave him away from the family in order to get this thing done. Ideas are great, but as John Sprague often says "we all live by the law of the 24-hour day."

Jeff Yates thanks two political scientists for helping him sort through ideas and discuss matters that probably bored them to death, but were helpful, either directly or indirectly, toward completing this project. Paul Brace provided encouragement to study the presidency and has provided sage guidance all along the way. Jamie Carson was kind enough to review early drafts of most of the chapters in this book and has always been a dependable person to turn to for advice on important topics such as social science theory and what is worth watching on television. Last, but certainly not least, he thanks Rebecca Yates for her patience and willingness to endure (for quite a long time) a dining room table covered in books on the presidency. He dedicates this book to mothers: his mother, Bobbie Jean Yates, and his mother-in-law, the late Betty Sue Heybruch.

We would like to thank the Johns Hopkins University Press staff, including Henry Y. K. Tom, Suzanne Flinchbaugh, Juliana McCarthy, Courtney Bond, Mary Mortensen, Kathy Alexander, and Robin Rennison. Thanks, too, to copy editor Martin Schneider.

Presidential Rhetoric and the
Public Agenda

CHAPTER ONE

Presidential Leadership and Policy Construction

When Americans discuss national politics, their conversations about the president and the executive branch often turn to perceptions of "leadership"—of the path the president has chosen for guiding American policy. This is perhaps as it should be. Presidents are ultimately judged as leaders, and their ability (or inability) to provide effective leadership largely determines their mark in history. It also offers a way to compare them with other presidents. Scholarship in political science on the presidency suggests a good deal of consensus on the importance of executive leadership, not only for assessing and comparing presidents but also for gaining a foothold on understanding the political dynamics of the executive office and presidential policy making in general (Edwards and Wayne 1994).

Usually, however, we are not clear on the meaning of "presidential leadership," in part because the phrase lends itself to competing definitions and meanings. Certainly, specific instances of executive leadership stand out. Franklin Delano Roosevelt offered the country inspiring words and wise guidance during the Great Depression and after the Japanese attack on Pearl Harbor. In an era of public doubt about government and the proper actions for presidents, Jimmy Carter assured the country that he would "never tell a lie," bringing a new hope for a trustworthy executive to a skeptical and disillusioned nation following the Watergate scandal. More recently, George W. Bush's steady words and demeanor helped a shocked and distraught nation recover after the devastation of the terrorist attacks of September 11, 2001. These instances, among others, lead some to argue that with regard to presidential leadership they "know it when they see it." But presidential leadership undoubtedly involves much more than just managing crises or assuaging the concerns of the public during troubled times.

Consequently, studies of the presidency have sought to define the overall shape of presidential leadership as well as provide innovative ways to assess accounts of executive leadership more systematically. Of course, when we begin to develop a systematic analysis of presidential leadership, we tend to refer back to the proper role and powers of the president. In this regard, we often juxtapose competing historical views on the appropriate role of the president, for example, the "constrained president" advocated by William Howard Taft versus the "president as steward" view set forth by Theodore Roosevelt. Taft drew on a legalistic approach that befitted his post-presidency position as Chief Justice of the United States Supreme Court. He concluded that the executive post had a highly structured and limited function, arguing that "the true view of the Executive functions is, as I conceive it, that the President can exercise no power which cannot be fairly and reasonably traced to some specific grant of power or justly implied and included within such express grant as proper and necessary to its exercise" (Taft 2005, 67).

In contrast, Teddy Roosevelt claimed that the silences of the Constitution regarding presidential powers indicated an expanded role. He asserted:

> My view was that every executive officer, and above all every executive officer in a high position, was a steward of the people. . . . I declined to adopt the view that what was imperatively necessary for the Nation could not be done by the President unless he could find some specific authorization to do it. My belief was that it was not only his right but his duty to do anything that the needs of the Nation demanded unless such action was forbidden by the Constitution or by the laws.   (ROOSEVELT 2005, 63–64)

One view sees a circumscribed role for the president in which the president is not specifically granted authority; the second sees opportunities for executive power in the absence of specific restrictions. With rare exceptions, modern presidents (and many scholars of the presidency) have favored Roosevelt's expanded version of the role of the president. Indeed, it is hard to imagine a presidential candidate advocating Taft's vision of the executive office ever being elected today.

The differences between Taft and Roosevelt on the appropriate powers of the executive mirror a change in how scholars of the presidency have approached their studies of the executive branch over time. Traditional studies of the presidency focused primarily on the president's formal powers and the limitations of the office, not unlike Taft's outlook regarding the office. In the 1940s and 1950s, Edward S. Corwin's seminal works on the executive branch reflected the tone of most studies up to that time in his focus upon the formal constitutional and statutory parameters of the executive office (for example, see Corwin 1957). On one hand, Corwin's classic treatment of the powers of the executive provides an excellent account of the development and history of executive power within a constitutional system and how the presidency fits within the broader framework of American democracy. On the other hand, Corwin's approach largely ignores the less tangible aspects of presidential power and leadership. In essence, scholars at that time left presidents' capabilities to govern through means not formally prescribed largely underexamined.

This began to change following the publication of Richard Neustadt's influential *Presidential Power* in 1960. For Neustadt, understanding the presidency necessitated an expanded approach to assessing the opportunities for presidential leadership, one that focused on powers that were not necessarily constitutionally or statutorily specified. His main premise is seen best in his axiom that the president's power is the "power to persuade." Neustadt found ready examples in the administrations of Harry S. Truman and Dwight D. Eisenhower that illustrated the core problem of coming to terms with the nature and dynamics of presidential power. Presidential power—the ability of an executive to influence the paths of other political actors and policymakers—boils down to persuading political actors that what the president wants them to do is the same thing that their public responsibilities and duties dictate they "ought to do" anyway (Neustadt 1960, 34, 46). A classic example is Truman's quip on the executive experience: "I sit here all day trying to persuade people to do things they ought to have sense enough to do without my persuading them. . . . That's all the powers of the President amount to" (1960, 10).

Executive power emanates from the relative bargaining capabilities of presidents, their reputation with other political actors, and their reputation with the public. While certain things beyond the executive's control may affect his or her political power, it is his or her *choices* regarding these sources of power—what he or she says and what he or she does—that give him or her some ability to control, to manage the ebb and flow of his or her power (1960, 179). For Neustadt, a president's power is his or her unremitting quest for personal influence; how executives manage their resources of bargaining, attention, and reputation are the main ways we can assess presidential leadership.

Since Neustadt's seminal work, scholars (including Neustadt himself in later editions of *Presidential Power* and in other scholarship) have built on these themes to consider increasingly innovative ways of defining and assessing presidential leadership. A profusion of studies followed in his footsteps to expand our interpretation of presidential power and provide many insights on the limits and dynamics of executive leadership. In practical terms, one of the core consequences of this move to redefine how presidents work in a system of implicit powers has been the development of more precise definitions and measures of presidential leadership success, as well as a move beyond the president him- or herself to explore increasingly complex explanations for effective executive leadership. And there are many paths presidents can follow when they try to enhance their effectiveness as leaders: they take positions on bills before Congress; they attempt to set the agendas of other political actors by proposing legislation; they struggle to gain control over a large and complex federal bureaucracy; they endeavor to frame public opinion by getting ahead on issues or redefining policy debates; and they try to influence the courts through their appointment powers and making nominations to the Senate.

Two examples help to show how these studies advance our knowledge of presidential leadership and expand how we conceptualize executive influence—of how presidential leadership is *forged*, not owned. In 2000, Charles Cameron offered a nuanced treatment of the executive veto power that departed from the prior exclusive focus on the influence of actual vetoes on congressional behavior. For Cameron, presidents can use veto threats to exact policy concessions from Congress. This means that studies that concentrate solely on how the president invokes the veto do not adequately account for the full array of weapons in the president's political arsenal. Similarly, Canes-Wrone and de Marchi (2002) argue that previous studies have not appreciated the complexity of the relationship between presidential public approval and congressional influence. Specifically, they show that public approval can shrink or expand the president's policy influence in Congress, that the link between a president's prestige and his or her policy success depends on the salience of the policy issue and the complexity of the legislation.

Our understanding of the presidency as a primary institutional player in the American political system has been constantly stretched by novel ideas about how presidents—through their choices and actions—exercise influence over the Congress, the courts, and the bureaucracy. Since Neustadt, political scientists have moved our understanding of presidential leadership beyond a construction dependent on powers to one in which presidential leadership depends on the executive's ability to make claims on the attention and duties of other actors in the system. Americans in conversation actively engage this question by asking, "How is the president leading the country?" Historians grade presidents on their relative effectiveness at proposing a direction for the country and then carrying through on that promise. Political scientists ask how presidents construct that vision and then what strategies they use to reach their goals. In the end, the choices presidents make about what they want and how they are going to get there have real consequences—for policy, for society, and for politics.

Our Approach

Our view is that presidents make choices on how to allocate the resources at their disposal, such as time, attention, and credibility, and that those choices provide vital information about the construction and implementation of presidential leadership. Presidents have many resources at their disposal relative to other politicians, but these assets are not boundless. A president who chooses to spend a significant amount of time promoting one policy in effect pushes all other policies (in relative terms) to the back burner. Those constructing a president's policy focus and approving his or her expenditure of leadership resources face opportunity costs.

Among the most important of the president's institutional resources is his or her capability to build and carry out a policy agenda through relatively well-publicized policy rhetoric. In American politics the executive has unparalleled access to media attention for making public pronouncements. He or she also has the advantage of speaking with a single voice, unlike the other two branches of government.

Our purpose in this book is to move forward the study of a largely hidden, yet important, facet of presidential rhetoric: the president's ability to drive American policy by using rhetoric to set the policy-making agenda. Specifically, we do this by examining the chief executive's ability to lead the agents of American policy implementation, the federal and state bureaucracies, through rhetorical leadership. Our central question is: can the president, by signaling his or her policy preferences through the use of rhetoric, get the agents charged with implementing policy to do what he or she feels that they (by virtue of their responsibilities and duties as public officials) should know that they "ought to do" anyway?

Our approach to analyzing presidential leadership through policy rhetoric takes us down a less conventional pathway of executive influence on the direction of American governance. A wealth of prior work has explored the president's ability to influence policy making in Congress by making rhetorical appeals to citizens: this is the well-known strategy of "going public" (Kernell 1997). In contrast to many studies on presidential rhetoric and congressional-executive relations, our focus is squarely on the president's powers and responsibilities as the primary enforcer of the law (as "chief administrator") in the separated powers system of American government. As presidents have come to find policy influence via legislative avenues often vexing, a strong literature suggests that executives have turned to gaining policy leverage through government agencies—hence, the well-documented "administrative presidency" (see Durant 1992; Durant and Resh forthcoming). In this view, presidents can affect the direction of American life by influencing the government agents at the front lines of national policymaking; through agency rule-making, reorganization, and other management strategies, he or she can shape the bureaucracy to achieve his or her political and policy goals. Durant and Resh see this perspective, one that focuses on how presidents achieve their policy goals by leading the bureaucracy through formal and informal mechanisms (including rhetoric), as one of the key missing pieces in the modern study of the presidency. We believe that one reason presidents value their rhetorical agenda is that it enhances their leadership and control of the nation's bureaucracy, especially the enforcement agencies. Our focus on this "power of the pulpit" helps move the literature on the administrative presidency forward and fills one of the missing pieces in modern presidency studies.

Presidential Rhetorical Leadership in the Policy Arena: The War on Drugs

Can presidents use words to change how policy is implemented by executive agencies? Can they change how the states—which do not fall under their immediate purview—implement policy? To answer these questions, we examine presidential leadership in one of the most compelling Oval Office policy initiatives in post–World War II America—the war on drugs. We focus on the long-term effect of the president's involvement in defining and constructing this policy issue, because perhaps more than in any other policy agenda in the postwar era, this effort has captured the attention and focus of the media, the public, and politicians. More important, narcotics control policy has significant impact on many areas of American life—on families, in the workplace and schools, in our prisons, on responses to terrorism, and on urban renewal.

Yet, the "war" on drugs is ultimately carried out by field agents, both federal and state, over whom the president wields only limited formal control. We ask whether the president's policy involvement in the war on drugs—especially, through his use of the "bully pulpit"—has changed how enforcement agents like the Drug Enforcement Administration, the United States Attorneys, and the states have sought to limit the production, sale, and use of illicit drugs. Can the president exercise policy leadership by using rhetoric to change the focus of field agents and get his or her policy preferences implemented? Did rhetoric enable the president to send a message to the front lines of the war?

We argue that presidents use their power of rhetoric to change how public agents implement public policy, to send leadership signals, and to set the public agenda. Specifically, we argue that presidents, through their use of rhetoric, help fashion a social construction of a public problem, a construction that focuses the attention of bureaucrats looking for guidance about how to allocate their own enforcement agendas. The president, as executive, tries to control bureaucrats by encouraging coordinated action on the part of both career service and appointees by "communication, exhortation, [and] symbolic position taking" (Miller 1992, 217; see also Bennis and Nanus 1985). He or she seeks to forge a common goal, provide direction for appointees struggling to identify their agency's critical tasks, and infuse his or her "subordinates with a sense of mission" (Wilson 1989, 364; see also Doig and Hargrove 1987). Establishing these policy themes and initiatives helps appointees in their management of agencies and signals civil servants about the "responsible" implementation of public laws by forging a social construction of the problem. How executives construct the sense of mission has consequences for what agencies do. Selznick saw this as an essential task of leadership: to help define an organization's "distinctive competence" in order to communicate values and mobilize and direct the future behavior of bureaucrats (Selznick 1957; see also Weiss and Piderit 1999).

This rhetorical mechanism is especially relevant in the war on drugs. The American experience is partly defined by the moral construction of public problems like narcotics (Meier 1994; Morone 2003). As James Morone notes, in this construction "dangerous others" threaten the polity: they are lazy, they drink or take drugs, they threaten violence, and they challenge self-control (Morone 2003, 16). Of course, we recognize how construction permeates policy in many areas (Schneider and Ingram 1993; Lieberman 1995).

Perhaps more than any other public problem, narcotics have troubled society for generations, and presidential rhetoric appreciates (and extends) this construction of threat. It does so because narcotics help define morality, and they threaten values like hard work, self-control, and stability. In sociological terms, narcotics are the core of a "moral panic," the shared perception that helps define what is "deviant" (Goode and Ben-Yahuda 1994). Under Schneider and Ingram's policy schema, presidents can make political gains through narcotics enforcement prioritization and rhetoric by simultaneously addressing two socially constructed target populations in their rhetoric. They can position themselves as symbolic protectors of "dependent" populations—most notably, teenagers—while at the same time rebuking and punishing negatively perceived and politically weak "deviant" target populations—hard core addicts and dealers (Schneider and Ingram 1993, 336–338). Prioritizing narcotics enforcement and drug rhetoric allows presidents to construct the perceived role of government in addressing social problems and move the administration's agenda forward.

Of course, the social construction of target populations (and the problems associated with them) is just another version of the age-old game of "problem definition" in the policy process. For Deborah Stone, problem definition is a matter of strategically representing situations. Actors use different types of language to define and portray those problems, including symbols (including words and other "literary devices"), numbers ("the language of counting"), causes ("origin stories"), interests ("of heroes and villains"), and decisions (that rationality leads us to the "single best choice") (Stone 2002, 133). The social construction of policy problems like narcotics, then, reflects how actors manipulate and use symbols, how interests are portrayed, and how we have arrived at the point where we must take tough societal actions; furthermore, they importantly reveal the rationale used to arrive at these points of decision. Throughout this book we try to offer a view of the president's role in the war on drugs that reflects these processes of construction and definition in order to show that those who implement narcotics policy have changed society by how they translate those constructions into action.

Study Structure and Framework

In the next chapter we examine the role of public rhetoric in presidential policy leadership and begin building a case for its viability as a means of influence on other political actors. We briefly trace the lineage of the rhetorical presidency, consider the relevant literature on presidential policy leadership via public appeals, and develop a theory of executive influence on policy implementation by way of rhetorical agenda setting. We also document how political scientists have studied the presidential use of public rhetoric in advocating and signaling their policy preferences and use this general theoretical framework to consider the role of presidential rhetoric in policy leadership. Our focus is on critical themes in the president's use of rhetoric to define and control public perceptions of national problems.

In chapter 3 we describe the political history of narcotics enforcement in the United States, focusing mainly on federal initiatives and the president's involvement in the era after World War II. We describe the president's political incentives to focus on narcotics and the implications of that focus for the evolution of narcotics control policy in the United States. Specifically, since the mid-1960s presidents have increasingly defined narcotics policy by offering legislation, reorganizing the agencies that enforce that legislation, and intermittently engaging treatment and demand reduction as ways of reducing the presence of drugs in society. This historical analysis provides important insight on the evolution of the social construction of the drug problem and the political implications of that construction.

Chapter 4 extends this discussion to show, primarily through a series of graphs, how the use of narcotics and public responses to that use (both real and perceived) have evolved over the last several decades. This chapter also focuses our attention on the president's rhetorical agenda. We show that the president changed his relative attention to narcotics policy over time; as he allocated his rhetoric, narcotics policy passed through phases of attention and inattention. We are especially interested in the relative disconnect between this allocation and factors like actual drug use or health consequences like overdoses. We argue that this disconnect shows that the president sees political incentives for engaging in rhetoric about narcotics.

Three analytical chapters follow. In these chapters we assess the influence of the mechanism we are interested in as an explanation of outcomes in the war on drugs—presidential rhetoric—on three levels of implementation of the war in the field. In the first analytical chapter, we examine the influence of presidential rhetoric on the policy agenda of the frontline actor in the federal drug war, the Drug Enforcement Administration (DEA). However, while the DEA stands on the front lines in carrying out federal enforcement priorities, it does not represent the final and conclusive decision point in the executive branch enforcement process: in the end, cases must be prosecuted, and the DEA is only an investigatory body. For this reason we show in the second analytical chapter how the federal prosecutorial agenda (reflected in the priorities shown in decisions of the U.S. Attorneys) is influenced by the relative emphasis in presidential rhetoric on narcotics policy. In the third analytical chapter we move from this focus on federal actors in the war on drugs to the state and local level, the main implementers of most criminal justice policy. We believe that this last chapter represents an especially hard test of the potential effect of the president's use of rhetoric on the agendas of field-level agents.

In our concluding chapter we reflect on the constraints on the president's policy agenda initiatives and how these attempts to set the public agenda help define the powers of the presidency. Debates over the efficacy of the war on drugs notwithstanding, narcotics policy offers a unique lens into presidential policy leadership. Our central claim in this book is that while the president can, to a degree, use rhetoric to set priorities of the front lines of the war on drugs, his or her power to do so is limited by competing constraints and varies by context. If the power of the president is the power to persuade, then we believe our book's contribution moves our focus beyond getting legislation passed to how the president gains as both politician *and* executive by changing policy at the street level, where the war on drugs affects real people, their communities, and the health of the nation.

One final point is that we mainly see this book as helping answer questions about presidents, policy, and governance. Inevitably, the book also makes statements about the past and future of American policymaking in the war on drugs. The war on drugs has become one of the most contentious arenas of policy in American political life, at least in part because society continues its struggles with narcotics as an aspect of human life. Our focus here is intentionally positive (for example, Friedman 1953), although we fully understand how blurred the line between positive and normative can be (Hanson 1958; Kuhn 1962). We return at the end of the narrative to discuss the consequences of the war on drugs for both the president and society, and we recognize that its impact has probably been greater on society than the chief executive. It is that mismatch that drives some of our interest here: that the president can do so little and have such impact. In the end, though, this is often how policy moves forward.

CHAPTER TWO

Presidential Rhetoric as Policy Leadership

C‍an the president, as the American executive, exercise policy leadership through public speech making? In this chapter we describe the state of scholarship on presidential leadership through rhetoric and show that only recently have scholars paid significant attention to presidential oratory. As such, we do not yet have a comprehensive understanding of how public appeals help the president gain policy influence.

Our first purpose in this chapter is to offer a lineage of the rhetorical presidency. We then consider the emphasis shift in academic work from describing presidential policy leadership through public appeals to forming theories of why and when the president acts. We argue that an important missing piece is a strong understanding of how rhetoric changes the behavior of those agents that carry out policy on a day-to-day basis. Our final purpose in this chapter is to offer a theory of how the chief executive influences policy implementation by those agents when he or she uses rhetoric to set the policy agenda.

The Development of the Rhetorical Presidency

A main concern of the Founders during the early years of the nation was the possibility of and potential damage from demagoguery, so they sought to limit popular democracy as a way of limiting the ability of a widely admired executive to usurp power from the other branches by appealing directly to the public (Tulis 1987; Cohen and Nice 2003). Among these limits were the basic checks and balances of the separated powers system as well as indirect election of the executive through the Electoral College. As the fledgling democracy matured, many considered these formal and informal checks to be valuable for protecting governance from the caprices of popular opinion and the demagogues who might rise to power by "paying obsequious court to the people" (*Federalist* No. 1). Indeed, the Founders understood well human nature and the delicate balance between popular representation and tyranny:

> In framing a government which is to be administered by men over men, the great difficulty lies in this: you must first enable the government to control the governed; and in the next place oblige it to control itself.
>
> A dependence on the people is, no doubt, the primary control on the government; but experience has taught mankind the necessity of auxiliary precautions. This policy of supplying, by opposite and rival interests, the defect of better motives, might be traced through the whole system of human affairs, private as well as public. We see it particularly displayed in all the subordinate distributions of power, where the constant aim is to divide and arrange the several offices in such a manner as that each may be a check on the other that the private interest of every individual may be a sentinel over the public rights.   (*FEDERALIST* No. 51)

It was the vision of the Founders that the executive branch would be "carefully limited, both in the extent and duration of its power" (*Federalist* No. 48). The president was to be a leader of the people, not a populist reduced to channeling (indeed, exacerbating) the often ill-conceived opinions of the masses. While some exceptions to this anti-populist conception did arise, most notably Andrew Jackson, who believed that the president, as the only nationally elected official, was primarily responsible for advancing the will of the people, its continued pervasiveness in the first hundred years of the new nation is evident.

Perhaps a collateral consequence of this norm against populism is that up until the end of the nineteenth century, presidents were less inclined toward public rhetoric than the modern executives we observe today. When they did address the public, their speech was generally less policy-oriented. When early administrations wanted to communicate with Congress, they did so by written correspondence rather than by public oration: the State of the Union message was delivered to Congress in writing rather than as a speech. On even more informal occasions, such as tours of the nation by the president, his speeches were not intended to take positions on specific policies but tended more toward general discussions of patriotism and language instructing citizens about republican government and constitutionalism. In his well-known book on presidential rhetoric, Tulis notes:

> Rhetoric that was directed primarily to the people at large developed along lines consistent with the case against popular leadership. Nowhere are they mentioned in the Constitution, but the practices of issuing proclamations and offering an inaugural address were instituted in the first presidency with attention to their constitutional propriety. The inaugural address, for example, developed along lines that emphasized popular instruction in constitutional principle and the articulation of the general tenor and direction of presidential policy, while tending to avoid discussion of the merits of particular policy proposals.   (1987, 47)

During this era, though, a highly partisan press was an expedient way for the president to tout his policy stances indirectly, usually through surrogate writers, in order to inform and persuade the public about his ideas. Accordingly, the growth of newsgathering organizations and the decreasing partisanship of the press over time meant that presidents had to find other ways to relay their policy positions to the public (Edwards and Wayne 1994; Cohen and Nice 2003).

By the turn of the twentieth century, the nation was ready for a presidential style of leadership, one practiced by the man most scholars consider to be the first rhetorical executive—Theodore Roosevelt. Specifically, Roosevelt made unprecedented use of the office as a platform for marketing his positions on specific policies to the public. His approach laid the groundwork for the notion of the executive office as a "bully pulpit." For example, he was the first president to hold regular meetings with the press and the first to provide reporters with a room in the White House (Edwards and Wayne 1994, 10). Roosevelt saw an approach to governance built on a stewardship role for the president: the president should be a catalyst for ensuring the nation's well-being and should use the "bully pulpit" to take policy proposals directly to the people.

Woodrow Wilson intensified and expanded on Roosevelt's rhetorical leadership style. Wilson hoped that he could take his bold plans for the country to the public, his message serving as the mechanism through which those policies would be brought to fruition. He reinstituted the practice of delivering the State of the Union message to Congress orally, a practice abandoned by Thomas Jefferson. Moreover, he made speeches before Congress on key measures taken by his administration and used stirring rhetoric in public forums to promote those policies (Pious 1996). For Wilson, the president's use of rhetoric to influence policy was fundamental for American democracy. On the subject of presidential use of rhetoric to influence policy, Wilson commented:

> His [the president's] is the only national voice in affairs. Let him once win the admiration and confidence of the country, and no other single force can withstand him, no combination of forces will easily overpower him. . . . If he rightly interpret the national thought and boldly insist upon it, he is irresistible; and the country never feels the zest of action so much as when its President is of such insight and calibre. Its instinct is for unified action, and it craves a single leader. It is for this reason that it will often prefer to choose a man rather than a party. A President whom it trusts can not only lead it, but form it to his own views. (2005, 409)

Of course, this strategy was not always successful, as shown in Wilson's well-known disappointment in failing to win support for the League of Nations through massive public appeals. Yet, his administration stands as a key turning point in the development of executive rhetorical leadership in the American political system.

Taking up the rhetorical mantle after a respite was another Roosevelt, this time Franklin Delano. He revolutionized the format of news conferences: unlike past presidents he allowed the press to quote him, with some reservations, during such meetings. He also employed his famous radio "fireside chats." Moreover, he was the first president to deliver the State of the Union Message live during prime-time radio to the American public, rendering obsolete the previous practice of delivering the speech during working hours with no broadcast at all (see Canes-Wrone 2006). This proactive style of executive governance, carried out in part through his extensive employment of public rhetoric, has come to help define the modern presidency.

Since then, presidents have made varying use of rhetorical leadership, but all have governed with the tacit understanding that public rhetoric is not only a resource for them to use but is also to some degree an expected component of executive performance. Certainly, the progression of technology has facilitated the increased use of rhetoric by executives as communication mediums have evolved, from the wire services to radio to television—and next to the Internet. These developments allow, perhaps even compel, the president to take their ideas directly to the citizenry and take a leadership role in the marketplace of ideas. Indeed, Richard Nixon declared, "As far as the general concept of the Presidency is concerned then, I believe the President must lead. He must set the moral tone of the country" (quoted in Zernicke 1994, 40). In a 1983 meeting with high school students, Ronald Reagan offered a central insight into how presidents see public rhetoric as underpinning executive policy leadership: "Well, what I have used to get much of what we want is taking the case to the people. I once said about legislatures and Congresses that it isn't necessary to make them see the light; make them feel the heat" (quoted in Cassell 1984, 131).

We have also come to realize how far the public relations campaign attached to presidential elections carries over into the administration's policy program as presidents continue to take their policy issues and political rhetoric public in a seamless crusade designed to sway the national sentiment (see Edwards 2003). For example, reporters asked about Bill Clinton's extended travel after the 1996 presidential election, and Clinton's press secretary, Michael McCurry replied that "campaigns are about framing a choice for the American people. . . . When you are responsible for governing you have to use the same tools of persuasion to advance your program, to build public support for the direction you are attempting to lead." (quoted in Kernell 1997, 34).

Describing the Rhetorical Presidency

As we discussed in chapter 1, it was after World War II that scholars began to study the presidency in ways that appreciably moved beyond a focus on the executive's formal or legal powers and constraints. They shifted their focus toward studying how and when the president tries to influence other political actors in our system of separated powers. Because of this shift, we now have a broader and deeper understanding of the president's powers of personal politics and persuasion. Specifically, scholars spent some time examining the president's plebiscitary activities. In this manner, the president's power was not defined by strict legal parameters or circumscribed by the continual checks of the other branches but rather was steeped in the executive's personal authority, which in turn was drawn from his backing by the electorate; in essence, an "imperial presidency" (Schlesinger 1973). While Corwin warned against turning the study of executive power into a "personalized presidency," a number of other important scholars, such as Clinton Rossiter and Richard Neustadt, developed meaningful insights about the president's manipulations of his public rhetoric in order to enhance his leadership position. Rossiter argued that the president acts as the moral spokesman of the people, yet he did not develop that insight into a statement about how and when public rhetoric supported presidential political influence or leadership. Neustadt saw public rhetoric as supporting the president's role as a "teacher to the public," but unfortunately the American people are largely inattentive to the president's declarations; they only pay attention to the executive when events and personal concerns compel them to do so (Rossiter 1960, 100–107). But these early insights provided a basis for other scholars to move beyond statements about why presidential public oratory was important to construct arguments about the tenor, tone, construction, and impact of executive speechmaking.

First and foremost, scholars want to assess the influence of presidential statements on politics, both inside and outside the Beltway. But at the same time, many are quite reasonably skeptical about its impact, that is, skeptical about its centrality as a way for presidents to enhance their ability to govern effectively. Finally, some scholars have normative concerns about a democracy in which presidents exercise leadership by talking directly to the public. Our position is that presidents like the strategy of talking directly to the public (or come to like it due to strong political incentives) and that the onus is on scholars to understand why and when it is effective for enhancing their leadership. We build on this position first by examining three seminal contributions to the presidency literature that frame how we understand executive rhetorical leadership.

The first claim, advanced by Jeffrey K. Tulis in *The Rhetorical Presidency* (1987), is that the advent of the rhetorical strategy pins the presidency between two constitutions. The first one was framed by the Founders, who were wary of a demagogic executive, and is characterized by its carefully constructed system of checks and balances available to Congress and the Supreme Court. However, this constitutional model presents policy-making problems for the executive as he or she tries to lead a sometimes unwieldy bureaucracy toward his or her policy vision in the face of constraints presented by the other branches, which often have competing views about the direction of American governance. The American public expects to see its presidents lead the country to prosperity and well-being, so this model can work to frustrate executive attempts to meet the perhaps unrealistically high expectations of the populace.

In contrast, in Tulis's second constitution, twentieth-century (and later) presidents "go over the heads" of the other branches and lead the direction of American policy by taking initiatives directly to the people by way of public appeals. He explains: "This new understanding is the 'second constitution' under whose auspices presidents attempt to govern. Central to this second constitution is a view of statecraft that is in tension with the original Constitution—indeed, is opposed to founder's understanding of the political system. The second constitution, which puts a premium on active and continuous presidential leadership of public opinion, is buttressed by several extra-Constitutional factors such as the mass media and the proliferation of primaries as a mode of presidential selection" (Tulis 1987, 18). We are left, he argues, with a fusion or hybrid presidency of sorts in which executives try to lead the nation while living within the formal constitutional framework on presidential power. It is the push and pull between these two conflicting constitution visions of the executive role that has come to be a defining aspect of the modern presidency.

For Tulis, "direct popular appeal has been the central element of a political strategy that has produced a stunning string of partisan successes, including budget cuts, tax reform, a large military build-up and accompanying social and diplomatic policies" (1987, 4). Unfortunately, he offers no systemic empirical evidence to support this assertion. He does, however, point to many examples in which the president has attempted to lead through rhetoric, including the administrations of Teddy Roosevelt (the Hepburn Act), Woodrow Wilson (the League of Nations), and Lyndon Johnson (the war on poverty). These examples highlight and illuminate the powers, limitations, and dynamics of the rhetorical presidency. Overall, Tulis sees some virtue in the rhetorical presidency, especially in times of crisis. But on the other hand, he is troubled by the prospect that presidential rhetoric, by focusing or narrowing policy attentions, reduces carefully informed policy deliberation and oversimplifies complicated issues. Moreover, it can make the president too dependent on sometimes ill-informed public opinion, even during noncrisis times.

The second claim, as observed by Samuel Kernell in *Going Public: New Strategies of Presidential Leadership* (1986, 1993, 1997), is that the president can use public rhetoric to change the structure and process of democratic deliberation over public policy. This observation is rooted in the rise and impact of the rhetorical presidency and the effect of context on this strategy. For Kernell, the trend in presidential plebiscitary activity over time and contextual considerations help us evaluate the power of and prospects for rhetorical leadership. As Kernell notes, we know how the trends in presidential addresses, public appearances, and days of political travel have changed with access to communications technology like radio and television. We know that some contextual factors may dampen the impact of presidential rhetoric, such as the declining prime-time audience for presidential addresses. We know that specific presidents like Ronald Reagan and Harry Truman have found "going public" to be a viable policy strategy.

Kernell's main claim is that this strategy destabilizes traditional institutionalized pluralism, the practice of insular decision making among political elites. That mode of democracy, which is well suited to negotiation and bargaining, is overturned when presidents go public in order to gain policy leverage. This has reduced the power of low-level proto-coalitions of institutional pluralism, made up of combinations of elite actors with mutual needs and complementary resources (legislators, bureaucrats, courts, interest groups, and so on), who were able to negotiate policy with few concerns over public sentiment. Of course, within institutionalized pluralism presidents might still negotiate with proto-coalitions, but time constraints and other considerations weaken their bargaining positions, so proto-coalitions were able to define the president's policy options.

Going public violates a main norm of institutional pluralism ("don't use force") and disrupts the tacit agreement and methods of making and implementing policy. The president is able to transform institutionalized pluralism into individualized pluralism, persuading and coercing by leveraging shifts in public opinion. Certainly, both types of pluralism still exist to a degree. For Kernell, though, presidents increasingly forsake bargaining and take their policy positions to the citizenry. This can backfire on presidents, though, if coercive strategies impair the president's subsequent opportunities for bargaining. This is especially problematic when presidents fail to sway public sentiment on a policy position.

The third claim follows from George Edwards's suggestion in *On Deaf Ears: The Limits of the Bully Pulpit* (2003): that there are limits to the influence of presidential rhetoric. He starts with the axiom that the president can use the bully pulpit to win the support of the masses and gain political leverage for his or her policy preferences. Specifically, he argues that there is little systematic evidence in the vast scholarly literature on executive rhetoric regarding the power of presidential appeals to the public, and the accepted wisdom of politicians is ambiguous at best. Yet this potentially empty maxim has important implications for both how we study the president and the president's strategy. The advent of permanent election campaign is ill-advised if these appeals fall on deaf ears. Moreover, our understanding and assessments of the relative powers of the branches are erroneous if these dynamics are, in fact, not the ones that determine the allocation of political clout among the institutions and sway public sentiment.

Edwards analyzes numerous public opinion polls regarding presidential actions, legislative initiatives, and overall approval, and finds little systematic evidence that presidential rhetoric affects either public support for presidential initiatives or the president's general standing with the public (approval levels). He makes a compelling case and offers intriguing insights. But, it has been argued, he too quickly dismisses relevant counterexamples and contradictory scholarly contributions (Tulis 2004). His position also neglects the rich symbolic aspects of presidential public rhetoric and how symbolism affects policy deliberation (Hoffman 2004). Perhaps more important, a number of relatively recent studies that were not available to Edwards provide additional insight on the question of whether presidential rhetoric can be used to influence other relevant political actors or change public sentiment.

First, can the president use the power of public speech to help form or sway the opinions of the electorate? Coming on the heels of Edwards's indictment of the rhetorical presidency, Druckman and Holmes (2004) examined the question of whether presidents can use the power of public speech to elevate their own standing with the public. Certainly, prior studies have provided ample evidence that a president's public approval level helps explain a wide variety of the executive's political interactions. Druckman and Holmes were specifically interested in whether the president could improve his or her public standing by "priming" citizens' evaluations. They explain that priming is distinct from classic persuasion in that the latter seeks to change others' thinking on a particular dimension whereas the former simply alters the *criteria* on which another bases an overall evaluation. Therefore, while priming is properly characterized as involving a process distinct from traditional persuasion, its results are often observationally equivalent, and it could reasonably be conceived as simply an alternative form of persuasion that is distinguishable from more conventional accounts, which are more rooted in straightforward argumentation.

Through experimental analysis, they showed that President George W. Bush was able to improve people's overall evaluations of him by inordinately focusing on what might reasonably be considered a favorable issue (in this instance, protecting the nation from terrorism) in his State of the Union message. This emphasis shift in rhetoric thus primed viewers' evaluations to turn on this criterion (issue) over other possible concerns (for example, war in Afghanistan, the economy, education). They argue that this dynamic has important implications for executive accountability because if presidents can manipulate the criteria on which they are evaluated, then presidential public approval as a construct or the means of assessing presidential standing may become problematic.

In similar vein, Cohen and Powell (2005) also find that presidents can go public to improve their standing among the populace. In contrast to traditional studies that focused exclusively on national-level public opinion, they assess whether presidents can improve their approval levels with geographical precision (that is, in specific states) by making speeches on the road, outside of the Beltway.

Their findings indicate that such strategically crafted local speechmaking does have a positive impact on state-level presidential approval. The effect, however, does appear to be limited to large states in non-election years. They conclude that presidents are more successful in this endeavor when they present themselves in a presidential fashion, as a national leader and representative, as opposed to a partisan advocate in an electoral context.

So, presidents can evidently raise their approval level among the masses by going public, but can they get people to change the way they think about the current state of affairs? Wood, Owens, and Durham (2005) answer in the affirmative, arguing that the executive can have a substantively meaningful impact on how the public views the economy. They employ vector autoregression analysis to show that the relative optimism of presidents' remarks in their public speeches influences citizens' perceptions of the state (and future) of the nation's economy. They further assert that presidential rhetorical optimism indirectly influences the economy in that it bolsters consumer confidence, which in turn works as an important determinant of U.S. economic growth and employment rates. These findings are important in that they indicate that the president can use the power of rhetoric as a tool to deal with a perennial source of concern that the public has come to expect executives to address: the state of the economy.

The above studies demonstrate that, in different contexts, presidents can persuade the public to view them more favorably or even to have more confidence in the current state of affairs. But does this ability extend to actual policy making? Can rhetoric enable the executive to sway the minds of political elites and get his or her way on Capitol Hill? In a large-scale analysis of 186 pieces of significant legislation (ranging from 1977 to 1992), Barrett (2004) attempts to address this issue. He argues that while the conventional wisdom dictates that going public can yield dividends for the executive in Congress, there is a paucity of literature to support this basic proposition. The findings of his study go some way toward amending that situation. He reports:

> According to the results presented above, there is a strong, statistically signifi-
> cant and positive relationship between the number of times per month a presi-
> dent speaks publicly in support of a particular bill and the president receiving
> his legislative wish regarding that piece of legislation. Plus, this relationship
> remains statistically significant whether examining all bills supported by the
> president, presidential initiatives only, or congressional initiatives supported
> by the president only. These findings clearly indicate that going public is a suc-
> cessful presidential legislative strategy.   (2004, 363)

Barrett cautions that going public is by no means a guarantee of legislative success for the president, and he provides examples of failed attempts to go public from the administrations of Ronald Reagan (Nicaraguan aid), George H. W. Bush (education package), and Bill Clinton (health care plan) to demonstrate this point. Still, his major findings provide strong support for the notion that presidents can use public rhetoric to improve their success in the legislative arena.

Two years later, Brandice Canes-Wrone's book *Who Leads Whom? Presidents, Policy, and the Public* (2006) provided even more support to the proposition that the executive can use public rhetoric to promote his or her cause in Congress. Canes-Wrone examines whether presidential public appeals affect an understudied, yet important legislative outcome: congressional decisions on agency budget appropriations. She does in fact find that presidents' budgetary success is promoted through the use of public appeals. Further, the influence of such appeals does not depend on presidents' approval levels; both popular and unpopular executives can improve their outcomes in congress by going public. Presidents do tend to fare better when their appeals match up with popular public sentiment, but her findings indicate that presidents do not arbitrarily or insidiously pander to public opinion, as they tend to not publicize popular policies that they believe are against the nation's interest or would lead to a bad outcome. This account of executives going public ultimately proposes that the process is one appropriately characterized by context, nuance, and strategic behavior.

One of the most important powers that the president holds is the power of appointment. Perhaps the most high-profile category of presidential appointments is that of U.S. Supreme Court justices. Of course, the president does not have unilateral power to place jurists on the nation's highest court; appointees must ultimately be confirmed by the Senate. In their 2004 study, Johnson and Roberts examine whether presidents can bring the tool of public rhetoric to bear on the Supreme Court confirmation process.

They analyze statements made to promote a nominee during the confirmation process (from the date of the president's appointment of a nominee to the confirmation vote date) for the years 1949 to 1994. They explore two primary questions: (1) Under what conditions do presidents go public with rhetoric promoting a nominee? and (2) Does making such public statements actually help the nominee get confirmed? On the first question, they find that presidents tend to go public when it is most needed. Executives make more public statements to support a nominee when he or she is more ideologically distant from the (filibuster) pivotal senator and when the Supreme Court or the president is ideologically distant from the pivotal senator. Finally, presidential popularity is inversely related to going public for a nominee, the implication being that presidents with high approval do not need to go public to support a nominee; they already have enough political clout. On the second question, Johnson and Roberts find that public appeals by the president have a substantively meaningful and positive effect on senators' voting for confirmation of a nominee.

The studies outlined above prompt us to reconsider the claimed "death" of the rhetorical presidency. Clearly, presidential appeals to the public yield some gains in influencing the public and Congress. Yet Edwards's position still holds some merit and should not be dismissed: scholars have certainly failed to provide overwhelming empirical support for the commanding "bully pulpit" presidency previously advanced by many scholars and political actors. The effect that has been empirically documented is clearly much more nuanced and limited than that.

The evidence of executive rhetorical influence (assembled both before and after Edwards's *On Deaf Ears*) hardly proves that a president comes to the office able to write his or her own policy preferences at will on a clean slate of public opinion. Similarly, the executive cannot brusquely bypass Congress by calling upon the public for policy support.

Moreover, the conventional wisdom within the West Wing—that presidents can categorically make public appeals to control and shape national policymaking—is overstated. Consider for instance, the comment by David Gergen, Ronald Reagan's head of White House Office of Communication, that "everything here is built on the idea that the president's success depends on grassroots support" (quoted in Edwards 2003, 17). In similar fashion, aides of Bill Clinton asserted that the president was unusually confident, even arrogant, about his ability to change public opinion and create political capital by going public (2003, 5). Finally, Kernell recounts an exchange between newly elected president Jimmy Carter and Speaker of the House Tip O'Neill, in which O'Neill warned Carter to be careful not to underestimate Congress or its potential opposition to his policies. Carter confidently replied that he would handle Congress as he had handled the Georgia legislature as governor, by taking his case directly to the citizens of Georgia (Kernell 1997, 45).

While such conventional wisdom suggests that presidents can use rhetoric to obtain public backing and use it as a hammer against other political actors, it is more likely that the impact of rhetoric is limited and depends on context. In other words, public appeals may work for the president if the circumstances are right, but even under ideal conditions it may work only some of the time and with varying impact.

This brings us to an important question: how often must a president successfully employ rhetorical appeals to demonstrate that appeals are in fact an effective executive tool? Consider a brief sports analogy. In many professional sports, meeting a goal one-third of the time will ensure the player a one-way ticket to mediocrity and obscurity. In football, a quarterback who completes one-third of his passes is typically shown the door; a basketball player converting only one-third of his free throws will likely be cut from the squad (unless he leads the league in rebounds). Both players have failed relative to what is typically expected for their task environment. However, in baseball, a player who gets a base hit in one-third of his plate appearances will likely be named an all-star; forty percent of the time and he is a legend. Baseball Hall of Famer Ted Williams famously observed that "baseball is the only field of human endeavor where a man can succeed three times out of ten and be considered a good performer." Context matters, as does the point at which we, as observers, rather subjectively set the bar for success.

If we assume that presidents have limited opportunities to influence public opinion and Congress through other means, then presidents should try to exercise the ability to influence a policy outcome through occasional public appeals. Yet, a low-probability strategy like public appeals is ill-conceived if presidents have many viable strategies for influencing other political actors and the public.

The power of presidential rhetoric probably lies somewhere between an all-powerful hammer for attaining executive policy preferences and an exercise in futility. Employing public appeals may additionally involve political costs in the policymaking process (Kernell 1997); at the same time, it may also yield political gains that scholars have not yet discerned or addressed.

Two Questions about the Rhetorical Presidency

Scholars have focused largely on two potential questions of public rhetoric for presidential leadership: *whether the president's public rhetoric changes the policy positions expressed by other political actors*; and *whether rhetoric influences public opinion or legislative policymaking*. These are important considerations, but we believe we cannot judge the viability of this particular presidential leadership strategy without examining other ways the president's public rhetoric can change the exercise of American policy. The purpose of this section is to describe the limits of how we have answered—and asked—these two questions.

Can the president make people change their policy positions on an issue? This would be a key piece of evidence demonstrating the influence of rhetoric, but it is not the only way presidents gain political power and exercise leadership through public appeals. Much of American politics suggests that political power also lies in the power of shaping how policy questions or concerns are perceived to be important, rather than simply getting people to accept a chosen solution to a policy problem. In other words, presidents can use public rhetoric to help set the policy agenda. In fact, politicians try to set the national political agenda because setting the agenda shapes the boundaries of policy deliberation, distributes power among policy actors, and can even lead to significant social change (see, among others, Kingdon 1984; Riker 1986; Kiewet and McCubbins 1991).

Defining the national agenda allows political actors to gain some control over the questions asked and how they are considered. It is about determining exactly which issue, among the many potential issues that could be addressed, is the one that should be given priority. Government officials recognize the "political stream" of issues that other elites consider important, and they adjust their policy issue attentions accordingly so they can stay relevant (Kingdon 1984, 163). Examining a vast number and type of policy issues on the American political agenda, a rich variety of studies have shown exactly how drawing attention to an issue is central to defining the national agenda and explaining the dynamics of the rise and fall of policy issues (to name just a few, Cobb and Elder 1971; Kingdon 1984; Baumgartner and Jones 1993; Cohen 1995, 1997; Flemming, Bohte, and Wood 1997; Wood and Peake 1998; Edwards and Wood 1999; Yates and Whitford 2005).

In the American political system, the president is in a privileged position for using rhetorical appeals to influence the agendas of the public and other relevant political actors. The president is the only political actor who speaks with a unified voice to a national constituency. His or her access to the media is unrivaled in the political arena. No actor in the American political system is as capable as the president at focusing the policy attention of other political actors (Baumgartner and Jones 1993, 241).

For example, presidents can influence the public agenda (measured as public opinion on the "most important problem") through their statements on the economy, foreign affairs policy, and civil rights (Cohen 1995). Yet, the impact of executive rhetoric decays quickly in all issues but those related to foreign affairs, a point highlighted by those skeptical of the power of presidential rhetoric (for instance, Edwards 2003). Does this limit the viability of rhetoric as an effective executive tool? Certainly the president would prefer that his or her mentioning a policy would change the minds of the public on its place as an important concern for the foreseeable future—or at least until he or she changes his or her own mind. But, more realistically, a president who is truly interested in influencing the public issue agenda will continue to mention an issue over time—or at least as long as he or she finds it useful to promote it. Thus the fast decay of the effect of presidential rhetoric is, in practical terms, perhaps less consequential than some have previously considered it to be.

In addition, there is growing evidence that presidents can use rhetoric to change the issue agendas of other political actors. Presidential public appeals can shape the policy issue agendas of Congress and the media (Edwards and Wood 1999) as well as the issue composition of the Supreme Court's docket (Yates, Whitford, and Gillespie 2005). While a strategic president may seek to change the public's collective mind on solutions to policy issues by rhetorical appeals, presidents also try to define issues that other political actors must engage, and that power is at least as important to advancing our understanding of the viability of public rhetoric as a mechanism for executive policy influence.

While we have focused to this point on debates about how presidential rhetoric can influence the issues that are given attention and deemed important by other policy actors, we also want to emphasize that presidents also use rhetoric to alter the symbolic content of issues. The public nature of the presidency uniquely lends itself to symbolic manipulation, as Edwards and Wayne explain: "One important aspect of political language is the use of symbols, things that are simple or familiar that stand for things complex or unfamiliar. Symbols are frequently used to describe politicians, events, issues, or some other aspect of the political world. Naturally, symbols are not synonyms for what they describe. The choice of symbols inevitably highlights certain aspects of an issue or event and conceals others" (Edwards and Wayne 1994, 121–122). Issue definition is possibly the president's greatest asset in rhetorical persuasion because it limits the range of discourse that surrounds a problem and, consequently, the range of potential solutions (Elwood 1994, 21; Stone 2002). As Elwood states: "Presidents' speeches 'invent' or define the issue, the possible solutions to that issue, and the framework to perceive both the issue and its resolutions. The perspectives presidents present on issues and policy resolutions frequently endure. Those that conflict with the presidential perspective often fall on deaf ears" (Elwood 1994, 20).

While we often think of presidents only in political terms, the manipulation of symbols also plays an important executive role. One way that presidential rhetoric helps define and redefine issues is to construct symbols that make the world simpler, that condense many different meanings and situations that otherwise diverge (Zarefsky 2004). This kind of strategy is important in all large organizations, where having a complicated world means that leaders must help people make sense of the chaotic flow of activities (Weick 1995). In turn, those acts that manipulate symbols change how work in the organization proceeds, which then moves the organization in a different direction (Feldman and March 1981). Just as important, because politicians debate public policy mostly through oblique attacks, the policy arena is ripe for a president to shape the definition of policy through public rhetoric (Majone 1992).

As a result, presidents can use symbols to alter and construct an issue so that policy discourse favors the president and his or her policy proposals. This strategic use of such crafted speech would mean that politicians such as presidents do not "pander" to public opinion (Jacobs and Shapiro 2000) but instead use public opinion to make more effective arguments in favor of their preferred policies. For example, Clinton pollster Dick Morris argued that the White House does not "use a poll to shape a program, but to reshape your argumentation for the program so that the public supports it" (Jacobs and Shapiro 2000, xv).

A second important question about the rhetorical presidency that has received attention has centered on the effect of presidential appeals on public opinion and, consequently, congressional policymaking. Certainly, other paths of influence are relevant for effective presidential leadership, and public appeals have consequences beyond gaining public leverage for use in relations with Congress.

As mentioned, presidential rhetoric may influence the decisions and actions of the media (Edwards and Wood 1999) as well as the Supreme Court (Yates, Whitford, and Gillespie 2005). Other effects are much less studied and understood. Essentially unexamined to date is the possibility that leaders of other countries, when engaged in diplomatic relations, react to the president's domestic rhetoric. Likewise, state government officials may be influenced by the president's policy proclamations; after all, presidents spend much of their calendar barnstorming the states to promote their policy positions (Brace and Hinckley 1992; Edwards 2007).

The way that scholars have answered—and asked—these two questions has important implications for our understanding of the long-term impact of the president's public rhetoric. We depart from these streams of thought by moving to consider the impact of the president's public rhetoric on his or her own administration. Presidents sit at the top of a large and complex hierarchy of agencies and public employees responsible for implementing national policy. Yet they cannot strictly oversee the policymaking of the agents charged with carrying out both the law and the administration's vision for policy.

Does the president change the behavior of the field agents in charge of policy implementation when he or she practices the power of public rhetoric? We argue that this possibility and the others described above can provide a new basis for understanding presidential rhetorical leadership, one that is more than just an exercise in executive-congressional relations. Just as the president could seek to sway the public as a route to gaining leverage for his or her preferred policy solution, so could he or she see policy rhetoric as a means for permeating the layers of bureaucracy that insulate the field agents who actually implement policy. Does the "war of words" that helps define presidential politics also shape the execution of policy?

How Presidential Rhetoric Can Change Agency Behavior

Presidents have built an impressive array of mechanisms that have enhanced their executive oversight of the bureaucracy, in part through the selection of political appointees but also including tools like budget clearance and reorganization (for example, see Moe 1989; Eisner and Meier 1990; Durant 1992; Wood and Waterman 1994; Hammond and Knott 1996). While many studies show evidence of presidents changing the behavior of public agencies, there are no guarantees here. Even Reagan's acclaimed attempts to centralize and politicize oversight of the bureaucracy met with only limited success (Durant 1992). For presidents, then, there is a premium on ways of influencing the behavior of the bureaucracy's employees that can be implemented without difficulty.

Presidents who want to gain some control over the agents of policy implementation and leave an ideological imprint on the direction of American governance must exploit all potential means by which to guide and control policy decisions. Just as presidential rhetoric can influence public opinion or legislative agendas, we argue that rhetoric can change the behavior of public agents in the direction of his or her policy vision. In a telling insight, one of Ronald Reagan's chief speechwriters, Tony Dolan, made the case that executive rhetoric is central to presidential administrative leadership, arguing that:

> They think that what governing is about is meetings, conferences, phone calls, rules, and decisions. That's wrong. I would argue that ideas are the stuff of politics. Ideas are the great moving forces of history. If you acknowledge that, then not only do you make speechwriting important, you make it your most important management tool you have. Ronald Reagan knows how important his speeches are. Not only do they provide a statement of purpose for the government, it is through his speeches that managers understand where they're going.   (MUIR 1992, 41)

Presidents may consider policy rhetoric as helping provide guidance for the implementation of policy by the agents of government. Of course, public appeals can serve as important signals of policy direction and priority for cabinet agency officials, but rhetoric can also provide useful policy signals for mid- and lower-level implementation agents. A central reason is that agents receive these signals both directly (observing the president's statements in the media) and indirectly through higher-level administrators. Indeed, agency reports sometimes begin with a quote from one of the president's speeches.

There are many demands on the president's time, and there exists only limited ability to monitor how agencies implement policy personally. As Dolan's quote indicates, administration officials may see public statements as a valuable source of policy direction guidance.

Former secretary of the Treasury Donald Regan recounted in his memoir his early days in Washington, when he observed government officials trying to figure out the policy vision of the administration. He specifically points out that as treasury secretary, he never once had a one-on-one meeting with Ronald Reagan regarding economic policy and that he had to figure out the president's policy preferences "like any other American, by studying his speeches and reading the newspapers" (Regan 1988, 142). As he elaborates:

> My basic position was simple. Ronald Reagan had been elected by the American people to carry out the ideas and programs he had discussed in his campaign. My job was to identify these promises and do my best to translate them into policy and programs. Resorting to an old habit, I went in search of the basic data. If the President would not come to Treasury, then Treasury would go to the President. I called for all of Reagan's speeches and interviews in which he referred to economic matters. I read the economic portions of the Republican platform with great care. I reviewed the economic theories on which the President's remarks were said to have been based and discussed them with my staff.   (1988, 157)

There is good evidence that this approach to discerning and disseminating the president's policy agenda is typical for cabinet officials. In the Reagan administration, agency officials in both high- and mid-level positions based their own policy speeches for subordinates, special clientele, and other political actors on presidential speeches (Muir 1992, 178, 180–182). The contrast is stark: presidential policy preferences filter down through layers of bureaucratic actors, each with his or her own set of preferences, competing influences, and opportunities for deviation from what the executive wants; in contrast, presidents may (wisely) prefer to communicate by making unfiltered policy pronouncements. In addition, this approach fits with the position established above that presidents use rhetoric to enhance the implicit power of the presidency as an institution, change the dimensions of debate between the competing branches, and tilt policy toward their own preferences—all by using a ready media. As Edwards and Wayne note:

> The press also may serve as a means of presidential communicating in more straightforward ways. Those in the White House often believe that since most high-level bureaucrats read the *New York Times* and the *Washington Post*, they can communicate with these officials about policy matters more rapidly through news stories than through normal channels. The White House also uses other media outlets such as television, newsmagazines, and specialized publications to send messages to government officials.   (1994, 263)

This reasoning supports the basic proposition that both presidents and agency officials communicate by way of executive public appeals; presidents anticipate (or at least hope) that those who make policy real in our large, complex democracy earnestly consider the president's policy statements and that those statements serve as a valid and important guideline of the administration's policy direction. How would a president benefit from such an approach to policy guidance? Why would a public employee respond? Why would this phenomenon persist and make a difference?

First, in practical terms, the regional nature of most federal agencies (through the use of field agencies for carrying out the implementation of policy) makes a single, cohesive communication process (especially one that is unilaterally controlled, like presidential public statements) a more effective way of disseminating information about the executive's core policy goals and priorities than one requiring restatement and construction by regional agency supervisors. Communication is valued if it emanates from a single source, provides a consistent message, and leaves less room for a field office to construe the construction differently. This leaves fewer opportunities for misinterpreting presidential preferences and for substituting one's personal preferences for those espoused by the president. If a bureaucrat tries to reinterpret the president's message or substitute his or her policy druthers in implementation, then he or she could easily be "called out" by other bureaucrats or agency opponents, who possess, in the president's public remarks, ready and tangible evidence of the administration's policy goals. This simple idea echoes the sentiment of one of Pressman and Wildavsky's classic lessons on policy implementation: "Experience with the innumerable steps involved in program implementation suggests that simplicity in policies is much to be desired. The fewer the steps involved in carrying out the program, the fewer the opportunities for a disaster to overtake it. The more directly the policy aims at its target, the fewer decisions involved in its ultimate realization and the greater the likelihood it will be implemented" (Pressman and Wildavsky 1984, 147). In a phrase, the basic wisdom imparted is "keep it simple and direct"—this general precept is perhaps nowhere more appropriate than in presidential communication with the bureaucracy.

Second, when the president speaks, the president speaks. The president's public rhetoric takes place in an institutional context and is personalized in specific ways—aspects that give presidential public appeals and pronouncements more impact than edicts passed down by a memorandum through layers and layers of bureaucracy. In public appeals, presidents bring the majesty and stateliness of the executive office to bear on the process of government officials weighing policy initiatives. Further, the same presidents who relied on their personal appeal and ability to communicate effectively when trying to gain office can, through public oratory, rely on these same virtues when trying to get bureaucrats to hew to the policy vision they and their staff have developed for the country.

One criticism of a claim that the executive is able to practice "rhetorical control of the bureaucracy" is that the president is simply "preaching to the choir," that his or her words fall on ears that are already inclined to follow his or her policy vision. Such appeals indeed may have the effect of galvanizing the "members of the choir" that are actually "fence sitters" (those experiencing criticism for that policy position, and thus holding doubts) or "backsliders" who are complacent in how they reveal effort. This perspective of bureaucrats is rooted in concepts of "types" seen in Downs (1967) and also the literature on principal-agency theory (Miller and Whitford 2007).

Likewise, public pronouncements by the president of his or her policy vision can give agency officials ready proof that the agency is acting in a consistent manner with administrative goals and priorities as well as ammunition for countering criticism, because they can claim that such rhetoric shows the president to be behind their decisions. Finally, the president's policy declarations give him or her opportunities to settle disputes within the inner circle. Going public can settle internal debates among public officials.

We also emphasize that this strategy works both for the president as a politician and the president as an executor of the law. The logic of the bully pulpit is in part a recognition that presidents are navigating a political system under the constraint of a constitution that limits their powers and forces them to work in concert with other, sometimes antagonistic public officials. Over time, the president has moved outside those constraints to use public rhetoric for manipulating the symbols and content of policy debates, and so served to define and redefine the American public policy agenda.

As an executive, the president is faced with navigating a large and complex implementation infrastructure that emphasizes the "separation of politics and administration" but recognizes the inherently political nature of policy implementation. In this world, presidents can use public rhetoric to traverse bureaucratic hierarchies and make sense of the difficult policy environment for public officials (Weick 1995). They can condense varieties of experience by constructing an executive vision of what public officials "ought to do" in carrying out the law. These acts, while partly strategic and partly symbolic, have real consequences for the operations of large, complex organizations (Feldman and March 1981). As presidents construct a rhetorical vision of policy that has political intentions, it can also be a vision of policy that has executive consequences.

Discussion

Do presidents intend for their public remarks to change the behavior of those public officials who implement policy? Is it sensible for those agents to pay attention to presidential pronouncements and to use them for discerning the administration's policy priorities? Our position here is that there is a logic underpinning both how the president constructs a public agenda using rhetoric and how public officials use such constructions to make sense of a complex policymaking environment. In the chapter that follows, we show how recent presidents sought to construct a public agenda in the war on drugs and how that agenda can focus and shape the behavior of the public bureaucrats who actually carry out the policy initiative.

Before turning to that narrative, we offer two considerations that underscore the problem of policy implementation in large, complex democracies and are particularly relevant for understanding the war on drugs as part of the president's portfolio. The first is that the vast majority of the bureaucrats who implement the national policies that are decided in Washington, D.C., do not work in that city. Like all large, spatially distributed nation-states, American national government relies on field service systems for extending national power into local areas (Truman 1940). As Fesler showed in *Area and Administration* in 1949, how governments use these systems to extend power and govern large, dispersed nation-states is fundamental to a conception of governance. And as Kaufman showed in *The Forest Ranger* in 1960, being "in the field" is a continuing threat to the consistent application of national laws because of the usual variance in local circumstances, preferences, and political values. While the language used to describe this implementation problem is now seen in terms of "principal-agency" (Brehm and Gates 1997; Miller and Whitford 2007), the problem remains the same; it is eternal.

The second aspect to consider is the fundamental power wielded by police investigators and prosecutors. In his 1969 book *Discretionary Justice,* Kenneth Culp Davis highlighted the mismatch in our understanding of the content of the legal system, that we know more about statutes and judges than we do the police and prosecutors. James Eisenstein focused on this lack of attention to the U.S.

Attorneys in his 1978 book *Counsel for the United States.* But political science continues to ignore, for the most part, the prospects for police and prosecutorial power in the service of a state run by politicians. Yet a government strong enough to protect individual rights is also strong enough to confiscate (see, for example, Olson 1993), so the problem of democratic control of police power is inherent. The war on drugs, in its many incarnations, continues to be as much about power as it is about the protection of the public's health.

These themes are part of the president's problem in shaping his of her own and the political system's policy agenda, as well as the policy outputs democracies presume flow from those agendas. Accordingly, we will return to these themes throughout the book.

CHAPTER THREE

A Presidential History
of the War on Drugs

The war on drugs is a presidential construct. By this we mean that some presidents have made it central to their issue agenda while others have deemphasized narcotics control and turned to other domestic and foreign policy issues. Presidents have used the war on drugs for political gain—electorally, at the polls, and as part of a broader issue strategy—and in doing so have helped construct the meaning and content of American narcotics control policy. This political construction has facilitated a social construction and driven the scale and scope of enforcement efforts. Presidential involvement in narcotics control has coevolved with the presence of narcotics in society. Understanding these paths of presidential involvement with the issue of the presence of narcotics in society provides a framework for assessing the effects of presidential agenda-setting on federal and state enforcement effort.

In this chapter we offer a history of the origins and development of narcotics control in the United States, describe the ways that American presidents have engaged this policy area as political actors, and provide an interpretation of how the war on drugs and narcotics control have changed over the last three decades. Our purpose is to illuminate the implications of this coevolution for presidential leadership, rather than to provide an exhaustive history of drug use in America.

. We start by discussing the path of development of narcotics control policy from the time of Roosevelt to the 1960s, an era largely defined by early reactions to drugs like opium and followed by a period of enforcement but not widespread societal acceptance of the use of narcotics. The second period, which we characterize by referring to the administrations of Lyndon B. Johnson and Richard M. Nixon, was marked by attempts by presidents to gain control of the implementation of drug control policy, partly in reaction to growing use among the population and partly in response to perceptions that narcotics use contributed to a growing crime problem. This period also marks the most intense discussions about substance abuse treatment as a preferred solution to the social problem of narcotics, but it also includes the first use of the phrase "war on drugs." Following that, the Ford and Carter administrations struggled with institutional innovations that solidified presidential control of the bureaucracy in this area; President Jimmy Carter's administration also represents a change point: consideration of reducing the role of enforcement for the control of certain substances followed by a pro-regulatory stance that emphasized policing and prosecution.

These changes were fully embodied in the Reagan administration with its emphasis on "just say no," military-style tactics for narcotics control and interdiction, and its struggles with national trends like crack use. The George H. W. Bush era is a central point in the war on drugs. As we show in chapter 4, rhetoric is at an all-time high, and the Bush administration engaged in the war on a number of fronts. The last two eras—the Clinton and George W. Bush administrations—were marked first by a lack of change (continuity, really) from previous time periods and then by a shift in priorities following the events of September 11, 2001. In some ways, "the song remained the same" in that narcotics received some attention—largely as part of concerns about narcoterrorism—although presidential attention was mostly engaged with other, more pressing issues.

This extended narrative helps show the context within which the president struggled to set a national agenda on drugs in some periods, and in other periods chose to deemphasize his role in the debate. It also provides a glimpse into the "big picture" of the institutional environment that defines how bureaucrats—both police and prosecutors—worked to identify what it is that they should be doing when they tried to implement the law.

These events and the stories they convey about presidents and the agendas they set are understandably complex, for if we know anything about the American experience with narcotics control, it is that the debate has no natural boundaries. This history shows that narcotics and other drugs tap into problem definitions or stories that relate to public health, crime and punishment (or law and order), freedom and liberty, and (not surprisingly) power and control.

The War on Drugs: From Roosevelt to the 1960s

The war on drugs has a long and convoluted history. The role of the federal, state, and local governments has increased over time, in part due to changing public perceptions of the health and safety issues associated with drug use and what is needed to help limit those problems. Government's role has broadened and deepened, extending from interdiction to enforcement to treatment and social marketing. What has remained constant are the roles of government in defining the problem of drug use, establishing policies and agencies to govern that use, and helping construct the public's understanding of narcotics as central concern for government.

During the first half of the twentieth century, government first regulated and then banned the use of broad categories of drugs, including opiates, narcotics, and marijuana. Of course, public recognition of what we now think of as "drugs" has been ever-present in the American experience (Schlosser 2003, 19). The first anti-morphine law was enacted in 1860 in Pennsylvania, and a law prohibiting cocaine was passed in 1897 in Ohio (Belenko 2000, xxxiii). Domestic production increased and expanded, with marijuana eventually becoming an ingredient in patent medicines. The first federal attempt to regulate such uses was the Pure Food and Drug Act of 1906 (the "Wiley Act," after Harvey Washington Wiley, a government chemist). This act gave the Department of Agriculture's Bureau of Chemistry the power to prohibit the interstate transport of unlawful food and drugs, centered on product labeling and notification about ingredients like alcohol, heroin, and cocaine (Anderson 1958). It passed with support from the pharmacy trade and the Bureau of Chemistry (Musto 1999, 10). The Wiley Act exposed the ineffectiveness of existing state laws governing the distribution and possession of narcotics. Just as with the prohibition attempts of the early twentieth century, other attempts sought to reduce the use of drugs by outright banning, such as the 1875 San Francisco Opium Den Ordinance (Segal 1986; Manderson 1999). In 1914 El Paso banned the sale or possession of marijuana; by 1931 it had been outlawed in twenty-nine states (Schlosser 2003, 20); other states also tried to prohibit the use of cocaine in the early twentieth century (Spillane 2002).

The Harrison Act of 1914 was the first national law to regulate the sale of narcotics like opium, heroin, and cocaine. However, its framers relied on the government's revenue powers (rather than prohibition) to police morals by taxation. Specifically, the Harrison Act set taxes on the transfer of cocaine and opiates at exceptionally high levels and restricted transfers to medical channels. The Act's passage, however, was not widely noted, mostly because of the high-profile efforts to prohibit alcohol (Musto 1999, 66). Agents in the Treasury Department began to enforce the Act's revenue provisions in 1915 (Wisotsky 1986). Several court cases addressed the Act, but it survived in an era of increasing public support for the use of revenue and police powers against problems associated with the availability of drugs (King 1953).[1] The Narcotic Division was established in the Bureau of Internal Revenue in 1921 and assumed enforcement responsibilities under the Harrison Act.[2] The Division prosecuted over twenty-five thousand doctors for Harrison Act violations from 1919 to 1924, and its 170 agents closed many addiction maintenance clinics (Wisotsky 1986; Musto 1999, 183). The 1922 the Narcotic Drugs Import and Export Act (the "Jones-Miller Act") formed the Federal Narcotics Control Board (FNCB, composed of the secretaries of the Treasury, state, and commerce) for regulating the import and export of specified narcotics.

Use dropped with the restriction of opiates by taxation. In contrast, initial reductions in alcohol consumption were accompanied first by increased involvement of organized crime in production and distribution and later by consumption beyond pre-prohibition levels and increased potency (Lee 1963). It also appears that many switched to narcotics like those regulated under the Harrison Act, including opium, marijuana, patent medicines, and cocaine (Thornton 1991). While the Prohibition Unit was relatively ineffective at enforcement (and was filled by patronage), the Narcotic Division, placed under the civil service, was effective (Musto 1999, 183).

In 1930, the Federal Bureau of Narcotics (FBN) was set up within Treasury, consolidating the functions of the FNCB and the Narcotic Division. President Herbert Hoover appointed Harry J. Anslinger as first commissioner. Anslinger's personality, policies, and appointments defined both the FBN and the war on drugs until his retirement in 1962; over his service through six presidential administrations, Anslinger had as much of an impact on narcotics control as J. Edgar Hoover had on the Federal Bureau of Investigation (FBI), the FBN's occasional rival. FBN agents were trained to "make arrests, gather evidence for presentation in court, test and handle seized narcotics, tail suspects without being seen, and

rule their informants with an iron fist" (Valentine 2004). The event that led
to this reorganization was the investigation by Treasury of drug trafficking by
Arnold Rothstein, a onetime labor racketeer with rumored connections to Tam-
many Hall. This revealed the growing size of the drug trade—and the possibility
of using the agency as a mechanism of power.[3]

After the end of Prohibition in 1933, efforts moved from alcohol to narcotics.
Anslinger's FBN enforced the Harrison Act, and international anti-narcotic activities expanded when the Geneva Convention on the Limitation of the Manufacture of Narcotic Drugs was ratified in 1933.[4] The United States increased its
involvement in the League of Nations and attended the 1936 Conference for the
Suppression of the Illicit Traffic in Dangerous Drugs. One motivation was a new
concern: marijuana.

Marijuana was covered in the Wiley Act but was conspicuously missing from
the Harrison Act; it did not make the final version in part due to pharmaceutical
industry opposition (Musto 1972). The 1937 Marihuana Tax Act did not specifically criminalize the possession or use of marijuana, instead using revenue powers to reduce demand (a transfer tax of $1 per ounce if registered and $100 per
ounce if not registered. It made production and distribution difficult, expensive,
and risky. By 1937 all 48 states had restricted the manufacture and sale of marijuana (Bonnie and Whitbread 1970, 1034). Most enforcement was by local police,
with occasional FBN involvement (Musto 1999, 228).

Enforcement took a stronger, more rigid turn with the passage of the Boggs
Act of 1951. The Act specified similar penalties for offenses related to marijuana
and heroin (two to five years for first offenses; five to ten years for second offenses). It was motivated by an observed increase in narcotics use between 1947
and 1951, especially among teenagers. Anslinger argued that marijuana and heroin should be grouped together because the former was a "stepping stone" that
led to the use of harder drugs like heroin. By 1956, twenty-eight states had passed
"little Boggs Acts." Use appeared to decrease with the Boggs Act, so Congress
responded with the most stringent legislation yet: the 1956 Narcotic Control Act,
which greatly expanded the federal role in reducing drug use, production, and
trafficking, including mandatory sentences, harsher penalties, the authorization
for agents to carry weapons and make arrests without a warrant, and the option
of deportation (Bonnie and Whitbread 1970).

Narcotics were not a pressing concern of the Kennedy administration.[5] In late
1962, Kennedy convened a White House Conference on Narcotic and Drug Abuse
for assessing the nature and magnitude of addiction in the United States (with

emphasis on California and New York). In early 1963, Kennedy established the Advisory Commission on Narcotic and Drug Abuse (E.O. 11076).[6] The Commission heard testimony and eventually offered a broad range of recommendations, but the report was received shortly before the assassination. One recommendation that did make it into law was the Narcotic Addict Rehabilitation Act (NARA) of 1966, which offered the alternative of self-commitment for users seeking to avoid prison time (although a national system of drug treatment would have to wait until the Nixon administration).

The path of development of narcotics control policy from the time of Roosevelt to the 1960s was first defined by early reactions to drugs like opium. Following that, there were periods of enforcement, with the major role played by Anslinger's FBN in part because the FBI saw no benefits in taking on the messy area of narcotics (Wilson 1989, 108). Another defining aspect of this was the lack of widespread societal acceptance of the use of narcotics, although society started to shift toward the end of this era. The problems came next, though the foundation for their social construction was already laid.

The Modern Era: Johnson and Nixon

Recreational drug use rose in the 1960s, permeated the middle class, and in some sense became fashionable among young, white, and educated Americans. Increased use of illegal drugs was one of the most dramatic of the social changes of the 1960s: "The use of marijuana in colleges in 1960 was almost unknown; in 1970, it is commonplace" (Goode 1970). This era represents a point of change in the societal presence of drugs in the United States. There was a dramatic decline during the 1930s to 1950s in the number of people who had personal knowledge of the widespread use of drugs (Musto 1999, 245). By 1968, drug use had increased, although social impressions of the effects of narcotics were probably out of step with actual use. Of course, society also changed a great deal during this era in other respects—with increased economic well-being, the Vietnam War, anti-poverty initiatives, and the struggle for civil rights.

In this history, we concentrate on presidential leadership in narcotics control. Johnson and Nixon were most troubled by statistics from the FBI Uniform Crime Reports showing increased crime rates during the 1960s; the crime rate increased five times faster than the increase in population from 1958 to 1965. Their strategic responses to the problems of crime and drugs were framed by a shift in public opinion: the percentage of respondents saying that crime-related problems are the most important national problem moved from 5.6 percent in 1957 to 37.9 percent in 1972 (Stinchcombe et al. 1980).[7]

With the increased use of drugs came a greater variety of drugs. In 1965 Congress passed the Drug Abuse Control Amendments to increase the control of the Food and Drug Administration (FDA) over hypnotics and stimulants (for instance, amphetamines, barbiturates, hallucinogens); the Act also created the Bureau of Drug Abuse Control (BDAC) within the FDA. Efforts had been made since the 1940s to address the abuse of barbiturates and amphetamines sold without prescription. In the 1960s, the evolving use of LSD, which had been discovered in 1943, only reinforced the impression that this area was important work. The BDAC built on its already established capacity, including over 300 trained agents with undercover experience; FDA Commissioner George Larrick, expecting that the BDAC might be merged with the FBN, established it as a separate organization (FDA 1981).

Johnson's main attempt to consolidate power in the area of narcotics control came in 1968 when Reorganization Plan Number 1 merged the FBN and the BDAC, forming the Bureau of Narcotics and Dangerous Drugs (BNDD) in the Department of Justice (DOJ) with six hundred agents (Wisotsky 1986). The FBN had responsibility for the control of marijuana and other narcotics (mainly heroin); the BDAC was responsible for the control of depressants, stimulants, and hallucinogens (LSD, for instance). This merger also gave control of narcotics and other dangerous drugs to the main agency for federal law enforcement. Attorney General Ramsey Clark appointed John E. Ingersoll as BNDD director and made him responsible for working with local governments, administering international operations, and conducting research and public education on drug abuse. Between 1968 and 1973, the BNDD expanded its international and interstate operations to include foreign offices, task forces involving federal, state, and local officers, and enhanced regional enforcement. The number of agents grew to 1,361 in 1972, and the budget quadrupled. Figure 3.1 shows the development of the drug enforcement infrastructure from the FBN to the current Drug Enforcement Administration. During this time, agencies like the BNDD had main responsibility for narcotics investigation; while there may have been conflicts with other agencies, like the U.S. Customs Service, the FBI largely shied away from involvement (Wilson 1989, 108).

In 1969 Richard M. Nixon became president, winning election on a moderately conservative platform that stressed law and order as a central theme. There were many reasons for this strategy, but mainly it was a response to shifting public

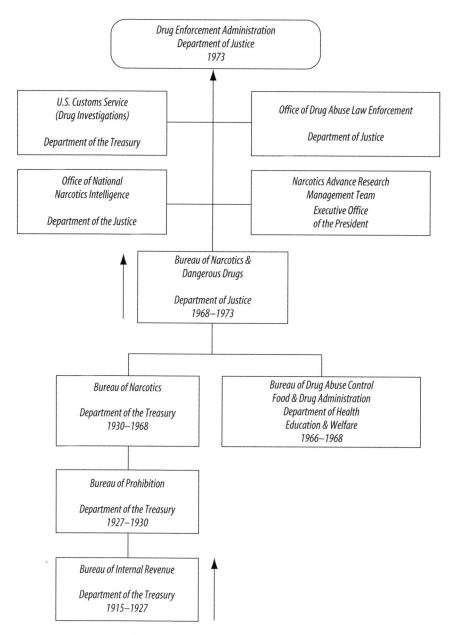

Figure 3.1. A Timeline of Administrative Developments in the War on Drugs

opinion about the war on poverty. In 1967, Nixon asked, "Why is it that in a few short years a nation which enjoys the freedom and material abundance of America has become among the most lawless and violent in the history of the free peoples?" (Nixon 1967, 49); he found his answer in the growing permissiveness toward law violations and disorder and in the indulgence of crime due to sympathy for those who had become criminals. Crime was a mounting concern, but the use of drugs was a criminal activity that "could be framed as purely escapist and pleasure driven" (Baum 1996, 6). Nixon cited the mounting traffic in drugs as an indication of what was wrong with America: "As I look over the problems in this country, I see one that stands out particularly. The problem of drugs" (quoted in Baum 1996, 12).

On July 14, 1969, Nixon announced his intention to tackle the problems of drugs and crime in his "Special Message to the Congress on Control of Narcotics and Dangerous Drugs," calling narcotics a "serious national threat to the personal health and safety of millions of Americans."[8] The first public use of the term "war on drugs" by a president occurred in a speech delivered by Nixon in Laredo, Texas, on September 22, 1972.[9] He argued for more legislation, international cooperation, measures to curb trafficking, education and research initiatives, some coordination of existing rehabilitation efforts, and the involvement of local enforcement officials. That year he charged the Special Presidential Task Force Relating to Narcotics, Marijuana, and Dangerous Drugs and its leaders (the attorney general and the Treasury secretary) with developing a strategy for controlling drug smuggling and marijuana cultivation. One result was Operation Intercept, which basically closed the Mexican border in September 1969 and is considered the most extensive attempt to curb the importation of illegal drugs (Gooberman 1974). Customs officials called it an "unprecedented . . . historic effort" that "proved for the first time we could effectively interdict the flow of marijuana into the U.S."[10] Operation Intercept followed a blow to the marijuana tax when the Supreme Court sided with Timothy Leary, finding that the tax requirement constituted double jeopardy, meaning the government could not pursue interdiction for marijuana within the United States.[11] Operation Intercept increased the aerial smuggling of marijuana, but it did reduce the overall supply of marijuana, while perhaps shifting demand to other, harder drugs (Baum 1996, 24).

Nixon sought to respond to public perceptions that blended different kinds of drug use. The greatest incidence of use was for marijuana. Yet evidence pointed to heroin use as a cause of burglary and other crimes in the cities; for example, an August 1969 study of people coming into the Washington, D.C., jail system found that 44 percent tested positive for heroin (DuPont 1971; Kozel et al. 1972). Nixon may have benefited in 1968 from blurring these perceptions, but they also framed the responses that Nixon called for in his war.

One result was the reorganization of enforcement for narcotics control. The Comprehensive Drug Abuse Prevention and Control Act of 1970 consolidated over fifty drug laws and established a uniform system for controlling narcotic and psychotropic drugs. It increased funding for prevention and treatment, established penalties for trafficking, and reduced the penalties for marijuana possession. Moreover, Title II (also called the "Controlled Substances Act") established "schedules" for narcotic substances; meanwhile, the power to "schedule" drugs moved from the Department of Health, Education, and Welfare (HEW) to the DOJ. Control varied by schedule: some substances were prohibited; others limited use to medical purposes (marijuana). Federal enforcement also expanded at the intrastate level.

Some see this as the beginning of the modern war on drugs. Musto argues that it was a transition point between law enforcement for reducing drug use and consideration of a therapeutic approach (Musto 1999, 255). It did not rely on mandatory minimum sentences (even allowing for probation for the first conviction of possession of marijuana) but did provide for "no-knock" searches. It gave the BNDD and the Law Enforcement Assistance Administration (LEAA) significantly more resources, expanding local grants for narcotics control and demand management (Goldberg and DeLong 1972). The Act also called for a National Commission on Marihuana and Drug Abuse, a move that would have unexpected consequences.[12]

Two events show how narcotics control had entered the American political lexicon. In 1970, Keith Stroup, who had worked with Ralph Nader at the Consumer Product Safety Commission, formed the National Organization for the Reform of Marijuana Laws (NORML) to pursue marijuana decriminalization (Anderson 1981). Its board of directors was notable, including prominent insiders like former attorney general Ramsey Clark, and Senators Phil Hart and Jacob Javits (Carlson 2005). Having a formal opposition gave the Nixon administration one more worry; for example, while the administration resisted it, NORML testified before the National Commission on Marihuana and Drug Abuse.

The second event allowed Nixon to consider the broader implications of its strategy. On December 21, 1970, Elvis Presley delivered a letter to Nixon expressing his desire to be named a secret "Federal Agent at Large" in the drug war as a way of influencing young people's decisions about drugs. He claimed special abilities and opportunities: "I have done an in-depth study of drug abuse and Communist brainwashing techniques and I am right in the middle of the whole thing where I can and will do the most good." Nixon staffer Dwight Chapin wrote to H. R. Haldeman that if Nixon was interested in meeting "bright young people," Presley might be just the person (Haldeman's response: "You must be kidding"). During a visit to the Oval Office the same day, Elvis brought a present for Nixon (a loaded, nickel-plated .45 automatic), indicted the Beatles as "a real force for anti-American spirit," and received in turn a badge identifying him as a "Special Assistant" in the BNDD.[13] Unfortunately, Nixon could not use the event to demonstrate his commitment to the cause of controlling crime and narcotics, since Elvis asked that the ceremony be kept secret (to make him a more effective agent).

The Nixon administration continued to face pressure to deliver on its law-and-order promises: for example, *Washington Post* editor Katherine Graham strongly urged John Ehrlichman to find a way to reduce the crime rate in Washington, D.C. (Baum 1996, 15). Much has been made of the administration's solution—enhanced treatment efforts, including the use of methadone—and that current drug control efforts do not rely largely on treatment (see, for example, Massing 1998). Essentially, the White House identified treatment as a way of reducing street-level crime, so it pursued treatment programs and expanded access. Based on the D.C. jail study, Robert DuPont was brought in to found the D.C. Narcotics Treatment Administration and provide methadone to heroin addicts. The Nixon administration expanded the program, calling it "one of the keystones of the District's success in crime reduction, and a national leader in the fight against hard drug abuse," because data appeared to show that the program had reduced burglaries and other crimes in D.C. (Musto 1998, 41).[14]

Nixon's 1971 Special Message to the Congress on Drug Abuse Prevention and Control called for increased funding for treatment but also paired it with increased support for federal enforcement efforts.[15] He created the Special Action Office of Drug Abuse Prevention (SAODAP) for coordinating federal efforts; its director, Dr. Jerome Jaffe, was the first American "drug czar" (Musto 1999, 252).[16] Jaffe, an expert on methadone treatment, was skeptical of the link between drugs and crime (Baum 1996, 42).[17] SAODAP was to break NIMH's hold over treatment efforts and gain centralized control before the 1972 election (Epstein 1977). Nixon hoped that treatment would reduce the crime rate. But the 1967 report of the President's Commission on Law Enforcement and the Administration of Justice noted "only minimal comprehensive data are available relative to the issue of the drugs/crime relationship" (Katzenbach 1967, 229); in 1976 the Panel on Drug

Use and Criminal Behavior argued that "convincing empirical data on drug abuse and crime . . . are generally unavailable" (Shellow 1976, 5). In any event, Domestic Policy Advisor Egil Krogh warned Nixon that the strategy might not work in time to make a difference in the election: "Even if all drug abuse were eradicated, there might not be a dramatic drop in crime statistics on a national level, since much crime is not related to drug abuse" (Epstein 1977).

In 1972, the National Commission on Marihuana and Drug Abuse called for decriminalization and other methods for demand management. It also called for a single agency to oversee enforcement, research, and treatment. Nixon refused to recognize the report because of his opposition to decriminalization, but soon revisited the topic of reorganization (Musto 1999, 256).

Up to this point, most enforcement was local, although federal agents were sometimes involved when and if it supplemented local efforts. Nixon realized early on that "law and order" meant enforcement and that federal agents could produce results on narcotics in a "responsive" way—with statistics to back it up (Epstein 1977). But Krogh found it difficult to direct federal enforcement. In 1970 the main method was to use block grants through the LEAA, but block grant funding is difficult to shift quickly (Epstein 1977). In the short run the options were limited: international efforts, some BNDD operations, and support for treatment. International operations probably reduced the supply of narcotics, at least temporarily: Operation Intercept, opium production in Turkey, and breaking up the "French Connection," a Marseilles-based heroin consortium involving the Mafia. As a result, supply was short for narcotics in a number of markets.

Domestic enforcement was hampered by limited capacity and a lack of authority for wide operations. The Harrison Act made enforcement the domain of Treasury agents. Ingersoll found that the FBN lacked intelligence-gathering ability for operating against major suppliers; the BDAC's experience was with pharmaceutical companies. The agency also suffered from corruption scandals going back to when Anslinger was director; Ingersoll even questioned the agency's performance metrics (see Epstein 1977).[18] For example, Ingersoll asked Attorney General John N. Mitchell for the authority to change the BNDD metric from total arrests to the value of heroin shipments seized, content to leave smaller busts and other narcotics to local officials (Epstein 1977). As most BNDD busts did not take place in the United States, though, dollar street value in America was suspect; other metrics were similarly debated within BNDD. Overall data show increases in the amount of narcotics seized but falling arrest rates per agent, much as Ingersoll would have expected (Goldberg and DeLong 1972).

But Ingersoll's strategies did not help Nixon's reelection effort. Nixon chose to elevate drugs as a key campaign issue, framing McGovern and the Democrats as the candidate and party of "acid, abortion, and amnesty." On one hand, the BNDD claimed fewer arrests during the first term, and BNDD statistics showed an increase in the number of heroin users during that time. Krogh countered by requiring pre-clearance on all BNDD press statements and then calling for more arrests to direct attention to the war on drugs. Ingersoll agreed to pre-clearance but balked at increased arrests. Ingersoll, fearing the implications of increasing arrests for political purposes, obtained support from Attorney General Mitchell to resist Krogh's overtures. Nixon needed more arrests, but a running war between BNDD and the Customs Service made interdiction difficult; Krogh recalls saying, "You know, gentlemen, the president has declared war on drugs, but shooting each other isn't part of it."[19] Having BNDD as the main enforcer came at the expense of other agencies (for example, Treasury) in the area of narcotics control.[20]

Ehrlichman and Krogh feared repercussions at the polls for low performance on narcotics control. SAODAP and its emphasis on treatment was one solution; SAODAP also helped consolidate federal efforts. The administration saw an opportunity for greater consolidation. It first created a Cabinet Committee for International Narcotics Control to coordinate at the highest levels. Just before Christmas 1971 the administration then announced on national television the naming of a special consultant to the president for drug abuse law enforcement to head the new Office for Drug Abuse Law Enforcement (ODALE) created by Executive Order 11641 and placed at the Department of Justice; among the ODALE assets were all BNDD agents (around three hundred) and new tools made available by recent legislation—RICO, no-knock, and so forth (Baum 1996, 68). The head of ODALE was Ambrose; Liddy was its architect, although by that time he was overseeing the White House "plumbers" (Epstein 1977).

ODALE was to shift the war on drugs from the operation of a small force of agents for interdicting drugs outside the United States (supplemented by a treatment network) to a series of BNDD strike forces located around the United States. ODALE also had the authority to assign LEAA grants to state and local governments without regard to traditional funding rules. ODALE was weaker than its designers envisioned: the CIA rejected the plan to involve CIA agents directly (Epstein 1977). But ODALE was just one more step in the politicization of enforcement. Johnson's creation of BNDD also was politically motivated: "Drugs have always been a political football. . . . Johnson's main reason for moving the

Bureau [of Narcotics] from Treasury was to strengthen the crime-busting image of Ramsey Clark" (Epstein 1977).[21]

Although it only existed for eighteen months, ODALE carried out intensive operations throughout the country, using both federal and local resources, with an eye toward disrupting heroin trafficking on the street level.[22] As Krogh notes, the key for such organizations is their performance measures: "If you're in a law enforcement organization, the operational indices are that we've seized more narcotics. We've arrested more people. We've convicted more people. We have a larger population of people [in jail] that were involved in drug crimes than before" (Krogh interview). Ambrose agreed. When he met Nixon to discuss the problem of lack of enforcement, he argued, "Well, basically, the weakness, Mr. President, has been on the impact on street sellers." Nixon agreed. On a campaign trip to New York, he told Ambrose why enforcement mattered, according to Ambrose: "We were talking about it, and the question came up of treatment. And Nixon was sitting there, as usual, in his kind of reflective, quiet way. And he looked out the window of the helicopter, and he turned to Bud and me and whoever else was there, and he pointed—we were flying over Brooklyn, I guess—and he said—you know, he said, 'You and I care about treatment. But those people down there, they want those criminals off the street.' And that was the way he said it. And it was probably 99.9 percent right."[23] ODALE responded by using the tools at its disposal, including operations in thirty-three target cities within a month. Total arrests rose quickly (six thousand arrests in eighteen months), with publicity to match.[24] Though short-lived, ODALE was notably prominent in Nixon's "war on drugs" (Goldberg 1980).

The 1972 Drug Abuse Office and Treatment Act funded SAODAP but included a sunset provision of 1975, just as ODALE also had a sunset provision. In 1973 Nixon declared "an all-out global war on the drug menace" when he sent Reorganization Plan Number 2 to Congress.[25] The problem was that "the federal government is fighting the war on drug abuse under a distinct handicap, for its efforts are those of a loosely confederated alliance facing a resourceful, elusive, worldwide enemy. Certainly, the cold-blooded underworld networks that funnel narcotics from suppliers all over the world are no respecters of the bureaucratic dividing lines that now complicate our anti-drug efforts." The proposal created a single federal agency, the Drug Enforcement Administration (DEA), to coordinate all drug control activities, that is, from the BNDD, Customs, ODALE, and the Office of National Narcotics Intelligence.[26] The first administrator was John R. Bartels, formerly of ODALE.

The plan for DEA was to replace merit-system employees with appointees, including, according to speculation, Ambrose, Liddy, and E. Howard Hunt (Epstein 1977). Ingersoll's position as head of BNDD was abolished. Yet some of the possible appointees became entangled in Watergate (including Krogh, Hunt, and Liddy), so Bartels inherited many from the agencies that preceded it.[27] It had resources: five hundred Customs Service agents were transferred to the DEA, which now employed more than four thousand agents and analysts (including fifty or so CIA agents). But it inherited many of the tensions that existed before its creation. Bartels failed to manage the unification and eventually was replaced by Peter Bensinger. Enforcement increased, but the DEA was criticized for "papering the record" of its arrest rates (of inflating its arrest statistics).

The last major drug issue event of the Nixon administration was the 1973 creation of the National Institute on Drug Abuse (NIDA), its mission being to "lead the Nation in bringing the power of science to bear on drug abuse and addiction." NIDA, established by the Drug Abuse Office and Treatment Act of 1972, became a component of NIMH. NIDA was the next incarnation of SAODAP, whose director became the head of NIDA.[28] The strategy shifted slightly, moving from direct oversight of treatment capacity to the development of a decentralized system of treatment run by the states themselves (Musto 1999, 257). During the Carter administration, centralized planning was taken over by a new office, the Office of Drug Abuse Policy (ODAP).

Some date the turning of the tide—the change from a strong emphasis on treatment—in the Nixon administration to the president's statement of September 11, 1973: "We have turned the corner on drug addiction in the United States—haven't solved the problem, because we have a long way to go. There is a long road after turning that corner before we get to our goal of getting it really under control, but we have turned the corner. The numbers, the statistics, are beginning to be better."[29] Reasons for this shift may have been Nixon surviving the 1972 election, the lack of observable street-level effects from the Vietnam heroin debacle, falling public interest, and the lack of clear avenues for new action on the issue of narcotics control (Goldberg 1980, 43).

On August 9, 1974, President Nixon resigned. The war on drugs now had to compete with other issues for resources, including resurrecting the image of the presidency as an institution. The war on drugs had evolved from a way to reduce crime to the mass provision of treatment to street-level enforcement by federal agents wielding new and powerful tools against drug traffickers and users. Structurally, the war on drugs was now the business of a new and consolidated DEA.

In sum, this second period in the evolution of the modern war on drugs was the time of real presidential attempts to gain control over drug policy. This redoubling of efforts was partly in response to the growing use of narcotics in the population, even though its use was mostly restricted to certain age groups. For Nixon, the focus came largely in response to the national perception (fed, in part, by him) that narcotics were a main cause of the growing crime problem. This narrative helped define the problem of drugs as the 1970s began. As Stone suggests, the problem of problem definition is "solved" by actors wielding stories, with support from the policy languages of symbols, numbers, causes, interests, and decisions (Stone 2002). We see each of those operating to support a social construction during this time period. Nixon set the stage for the enforcement regimes to follow.

It did not have to be so. As the events make clear, this was the time of the most intense high-level discussions about substance abuse treatment as a preferred way to solve the social problem of narcotics. It was, as Michael Massing puts it in his 1998 book, the time when we got closest to *The Fix*. Indeed, historians of the drug war like David Musto see this as a time of lost opportunities, a time when some simple choices led us down a path that forever changed the face of American public health policy (Musto 1999).

Of course policy is path-dependent, and it is difficult to unravel the choices made once a nation is several years into a new regime. But we want to be clear that this era was also a time of strategy and choice—and that Nixon did not inadvertently shift the debate from treatment to enforcement, that his choices and policy leadership were fundamental in setting the stage for the next twenty years. Indeed, this is when we see the first use of the phrase "war on drugs." This is when the DEA is born. And it is the start of a long period in which drugs became a means to political ends.

Change and Continuity: Ford and Carter

One problem Gerald Ford as president faced was to put himself in a position to run for election as president for the first time. On September 12, 1974, he followed up on his address to a Joint Session of Congress by restating his main priorities: reduced spending, a solution to the budgetary impasse, and key energy and economic development bills; neither crime nor narcotics were mentioned.[30] On November 18, 1974, he repeated his call for these issues but again mentioned neither drugs nor crime.[31] The first major statement by Ford on drugs occurred more than a year into office, when he noted the release of the Domestic Council

Drug Abuse Task Force's White Paper on Drug Abuse. This slender paper recommended that "priority in Federal efforts in both supply and demand reduction be directed toward those drugs which inherently pose a greater risk to the individual and to society." Namely, the White Paper downgraded marijuana and cocaine to the status of low-priority drugs but elevated heroin, amphetamines, and mixed barbiturates. It targeted enforcement at the highest levels of trafficking and encouraged expansion of methadone programs (Domestic Council Drug Abuse Task Force 1975). The early Ford program of action toned down the street-level enforcement talk of Nixon. By the late 1970s, though, the implications of not addressing the cocaine trade were being felt throughout the nation.

Interestingly, Ford opposed the creation of an executive-level office on drug abuse. SAODAP had moved to NIDA; ODALE had become the DEA; Congress created ODAP in early 1976.[32] Ford signed the bill, but stated "I have consistently held, however, that such coordination can best be carried out by existing departments and agencies, without an additional agency for that purpose."[33] Ford requested that Congress rescind the funds provided for ODAP. But Congress wanted ODAP because it thought that without executive-level representation, enforcement would overshadow funding for drug abuse prevention (President's Commission on Organized Crime 1986). Ford's solution was to not staff it, and it was on hiatus until Jimmy Carter took office.

Ford revisited narcotics control in 1976 by emphasizing the need to control high-level trafficking. Some accounts argue that Ford showed only limited interest in enforcement (for example, see Baum 1996); however, in April of that year Ford requested increased authority over high-level interdiction efforts—specifically, mandatory minimum sentences for trafficking in heroin and other narcotics and a major expansion of seizure powers (then limited to property less than $2,500).[34] He reemphasized tax enforcement against traffickers but also sought to strengthen treatment and rehabilitation options.[35] More important, he announced new collaborative efforts with Latin American countries to reduce production. The program would become Operation Trizo, a poppy eradication program that involved the use of herbicides similar to those used in Agent Orange.[36] Carter would experience the full impact of these efforts.

Ford faced an electoral opponent who chose to make something of the war on drugs. Carter advocated marijuana decriminalization at an early stage of the campaign. Knowing that marijuana still resonated with many voters (especially those in his base), Ford did not directly endorse decriminalization. Both treated decriminalization lightly, though, because they each had family members who had used the drug (Anderson 1981). State marijuana laws were trending toward partial decriminalization anyway: Oregon in 1973; Alaska, California, Colorado, Maine, and Ohio in 1975; Minnesota in 1976; Mississippi, New York, and North Carolina in 1977; and Nebraska in 1978 (DiChiara and Galliher 1994, 42).[37]

But public sentiment was shifting. Notably, the Nosy Parents Association, started by neighbors Marsha Keith Schuchard and Sue Rusche of Atlanta in 1976, was the beginning of the anti-drug parent movement. This confluence of events had implications not only for the Carter administration but also for Ronald Reagan's resurrection of the war on drugs.

The Carter administration started down a different path for narcotics control, one that marked a departure from almost all of the approaches that had been tried since the FBN. Nixon spoke of a war on drugs, while Ford spoke of finding an appropriate federal role. The White Paper even called for an end to "unrealistic expectations of total elimination of drug abuse from our society" (Domestic Council Drug Abuse Task Force 1975, 5). Ford did not stand down from the war on drugs, but he did not expand it either. In contrast, Carter sought to roll back a number of important elements of the war on drugs, starting with its strong (and growing) emphasis on domestic enforcement (Bertram et al. 1996, 109). This shift in focus did not start with his embracing of decriminalization during the campaign, for during his tenure as governor of Georgia, Carter established a drug-abuse program that had almost all of the state's six thousand addicts in treatment by 1972 (Baum 1996, 92). At the same time, Carter advocated the expansion of other elements of the war on drugs, including international interdiction of supply and the use of forfeiture rules against traffickers.

Carter's main weapon in this restructuring of the war was Peter Bourne, a psychiatrist who ran Georgia's treatment programs. Bourne became his special assistant for health issues to the president and was charged with reorganizing drug control. As such, he also became the most influential and highest-ranking drug authority in American history (Musto 1999, 260).[38]

The first step taken was to argue in March 1977 for the decriminalization of marijuana; among those testifying were Bourne and officials from the DEA, NIDA, NIMH, Customs, and the DOJ (Musto 1999, 260). The specific compromise was to advocate replacing the criminal penalties for possession of less than an ounce with a civil fine. Carter made the issue of decriminalization a central issue of the first year of his presidency.[39] Early versions of the drug message were even written with the help of Keith Stroup of NORML (Baum 1996, 94). In his 1977 "Drug Abuse Message to the Congress," Carter called for enhanced international cooperation and enforcement, including using forfeiture for penalizing drug violators.[40] With regard to marijuana, Carter argued as follows: "Penalties against possession of a drug should not be more damaging to an individual than the use of the drug itself; and where they are, they should be changed. Nowhere is this clearer than in the laws against possession of marijuana in private for personal use. We can, and should, continue to discourage the use of marijuana, but this can be done without defining the smoker as a criminal." To that end, Carter advocated "legislation amending Federal law to eliminate all Federal criminal penalties for the possession of up to one ounce of marijuana. This decriminalization is not legalization. It means only that the Federal penalty for possession would be reduced and a person would receive a fine rather than a criminal penalty. Federal penalties for trafficking would remain in force and the states would remain free to adopt whatever laws they wish concerning the marijuana smoker." This is the closest the federal policy agenda ever moved toward marijuana decriminalization.

Of course, just as the political agenda moves, so do markets, including those for illicit substances like narcotics. Efforts during the Nixon administration to reduce the flow of heroin from areas like Turkey did reduce availability of the drug in the United States. But those successes also created opportunities for other areas to flourish, and in the case of heroin it was Mexico. The "heroin highway" from Durango to Chicago became a major trafficking route, and by 1974 traffickers from Mexico owned about 75 percent of the U.S. heroin market.[41] By 1977, cocaine use also expanded into high-level markets throughout the United States, but its profile was limited by lack of access. Bourne himself considered it a low-priority policy concern, although at that point smokeable cocaine was beginning to emerge in Latin America (Baum 1996, 98). So the administration concentrated on heroin and barbiturates as the main narcotics causing the public harm. Bourne reported at the 1978 meeting of the United Nations Commission on Narcotic Drugs that heroin deaths and retail purity had both fallen, evidence that heroin interdiction efforts were having success. He thought the main payoff, though, was from efforts like Operation Trizo, in which herbicides were used on opium poppies (Musto 1999, 261).

But Mexico was also using herbicides for other interdiction efforts, namely against marijuana plantations, which were seen as a significant domestic problem. They used paraquat, which soon led to the issue of paraquat-contaminated marijuana making its way onto the U.S. market.[42] NORML made this a front-page issue, emphasizing that the drug war was actually endangering the health of users of narcotics (Anderson 1981, 190). In fact, Mexico was spraying the fields with paraquat from the United Kingdom, not the United States. But the United States had provided the helicopters Mexico used for spraying so that Mexico could treat poppy fields with a different herbicide (Musto 1999, 262). In any case, it was not clear whether paraquat was endangering the health of users.[43] Carter staffers like Bourne were troubled by the hostility NORML showed over paraquat, given the ongoing commitment to decriminalize possession of small amounts of marijuana. But it became clear that Stroup used the issue to rally the NORML base; Bourne noted later, "Many of them were concerned with finding an issue that would regenerate their revenues and their membership."[44]

Bourne resigned on July 20, 1978, after a media firestorm over his decision as a licensed doctor to prescribe methaqualone to a member of his staff. Bourne had also prescribed drugs for other members of the Carter team, including diet pills for Hamilton Jordan, but in this case the name on the prescription was fictitious.[45] Afterward, investigative journalist Jack Anderson broke a second story that Bourne had snorted cocaine at NORML's Christmas party the previous year. Bourne argued that the first charge was innocuous and that the second was false; he was at the party and had handled a vial, but he had not used drugs (Anderson 1981). But as the national director for drug policy, these charges made it impossible for him to carry out his duties. Bourne resigned, the last mental health professional to guide American drug policy.[46]

Four months later Carter signed the Psychotropic Substances Act of 1978, legislation Bourne had pursued during his last days that changed enforcement against major traffickers. Carter saw opportunities to clarify American narcotics control policy, especially with regard to international interdiction, the expanded use of forfeiture, and decriminalization. The initiative for decriminalization ended with Bourne; after him, forfeiture and international interdiction efforts would expand.[47] The Act expanded forfeiture to up to $10,000 in money or items of value held by persons in exchange for a controlled substance as well as proceeds that could be traced to such exchanges.

In many ways, the Carter administration represents a clear change point in the long-term evolution of the war on drugs. The administration vetted and then abandoned plans to decriminalize the possession of marijuana. Carter named a health care professional to the most prominent position in the war on drugs—and then lost that person to a media firestorm about alleged drug use. The administration supported expansions in the international interdiction of narcotics, including the use of strategies that led to a counter-mobilization against people like Bourne. Carter supported and gained the ability to use forfeiture as a tool against trafficking in narcotics.

Another way in which the administration represents a point of change is shown in the backlash against marijuana, initiated largely by the Nosy Parents Association. Schuchard and a group of parents in Atlanta, seeking to understand the effects of marijuana on their children, contacted DuPont (then NIDA head) based on an interview he had given with *Science*.[48] DuPont visited the group and their children in June 1977 and came away troubled about decriminalization, that marijuana was permeating the fabric of society, increasing among younger students, and affecting many families (Massing 1998, 145). Afterward he limited his statements on decriminalization and encouraged Schuchard to write a handbook for preventing drug use.[49]

Bourne's successor, Lee Dogoloff, held meetings with Schuchard and her group and, based on survey data showing an increase among high school seniors using marijuana on a daily basis, began pushing a message that marijuana was a problem for parents of teenagers (Baum 1996, 124). Likewise, the DEA's Peter Bensinger advocated increasing, not eliminating, federal penalties for possession. In May 1979, with the elections now on the horizon, the White House Strategy Council prepared a list of policy solutions calling for a "war on marijuana," including a crackdown on trafficking but also limiting criminal penalties for users.[50] Yet Carter (through Dogoloff) quickly distanced himself from decriminalization (Baum 1996, 129).[51] With the help of Dick Williams, a player in narcotics policy for three administrations (Nixon, Carter, and Reagan), Dogoloff shifted policy attention away from the "hard drugs" / "soft drugs" distinction, away from the concern for treatment solutions for heroin users, and toward a concern about marijuana. In Baum's view, "Lee Dogoloff and Dick Williams together effected the biggest change in drug policy since Nixon launched the Drug War" (1996, 135).

One can see the dimensions of the implementation problems faced during this era. Political executives found themselves not only with an actual social problem, but also with public perceptions, theories of cause, and tools they were being urged to wield to just "make things work." So both the Ford and Carter administrations struggled with those institutional innovations that enhanced the president's control of the implementation of this policy arena and its bureaucracy.

This is why President Jimmy Carter's administration also represents a change point—first consideration of whether and how to reduce enforcement, and then increased emphasis on policing and prosecution. Faced with this kind of choice,

Carter was able to bring change to the policy process, mostly because of the power that had been assembled in the position of the drug czar and bureaucracy in the DEA. In effect, Bourne showed how presidents could try to effect change through institutional levers. The DEA gave the president field agents over which he could assert control.

But this era also shows that Carter tried to act as a leader by working to reshape the narrative that permeated the drugs story. Despite this, Carter may have underestimated the power of the narrative itself, especially for other politicians who saw an opportunity in the stories being woven into that narrative by groups like the Nosy Parents Association. The Reagan administration saw a role for the president in that narrative.

The Next War: Reagan

Ronald Reagan entered office with a mandate for change largely driven by public concern about inflation and international events like the confinement of hostages in Iran during the latter part of the Carter administration. Most of his legislative agenda centered on policy solutions perceived as stimulating economic growth (such as tax cuts), curbing inflation (reductions in government spending), and building national defense capacity. For a number of important reasons, though, Reagan embraced the war on drugs as a political and rhetorical device for most of his eight years in office. Of course, Reagan's use of rhetoric for furthering his agenda is legendary among modern presidents.

Reagan gained office at the time when the parent movement was reaching its height. Schuchard and others had succeeded in making marijuana a concern of many parents, perhaps especially those already in the Reagan base of conservatives (both religious and economic). But the larger trend was that marijuana use was declining in the population as a whole at the same time that cocaine was building toward a critical point. Cocaine use increased from two million users in 1972 to a high of around nine million users in 1982, falling to seven million users in 1992, with one to two million of those being heavy users (Rydell and Everingham 1994, 1). Estimates of cocaine use, though, suggest that consumption rose from 50 metric tons in 1972 to almost 300 tons in 1985, a level that did not decrease from then until 1992. Expenditures on cocaine peaked around $115 billion around 1982; the estimated street price of cocaine has fallen steadily since 1977. Moreover, by 1985 crack cocaine had appeared as the main alternative to the use of powder cocaine: the first "crack house" was found in 1982 in Miami, and the drug appeared in New York in 1983. The "crack epidemic" lasted at least until 1990.

Reagan's war on drugs centered on giving police and prosecutors additional tools for enforcement and then encouraging the use of those tools against users, producers, and traffickers. However, a central rhetorical theme throughout his presidency was to reduce demand by targeting parents and children with public education efforts. For example, in his news conference of March 6, 1981, Reagan noted, "With borders like ours, that, as the main method of halting the drug problem in America, is virtually impossible. It's like carrying water in a sieve. It is my belief, firm belief, that the answer to the drug problem comes through winning over the users to the point that we take the customers away from the drugs, not take the drugs, necessarily—try that, of course—you don't let up on that. But it's far more effective if you take the customers away than if you try to take the drugs away from those who want to be customers."[52]

A key carrier of that message was First Lady Nancy Reagan. Her well-known "Just Say No" drive has been documented in a number of places (Meier 1994, 49; Baum 1996, 141; Bertram et al. 1996, 111), but its timing warrants a little description. When Ronald Reagan was governor of California, Nancy Reagan had made efforts to increase children's awareness of the hazards of drug use; after he won the presidential race, she saw in the changed attitudes (evidenced by the new parent movement) an opportunity to revisit that policy issue (Radcliffe 1980). She directed her staff before the inauguration to prepare for a new focus on drug abuse, starting with a long series of meetings with experts on narcotics control and education (Gamarekian 1980; Radcliffe 1981). She concentrated more on these efforts following perceptions that negatively identified her with spending money for redecorating the White House (Rosellini 1981). Her education efforts increased in 1983 with a new advertising attack on drug abuse through the Advertising Council with the theme "Just Say No," the group's first anti-drug campaign since 1973; major television events followed (Carmody 1983; Dougherty 1983).[53]

Reagan's first-year initiatives included consideration of a merger for the DEA and the FBI, a boost in federal cooperation with local agencies, and a decision to draft the Department of Defense (DOD) and the CIA into the war on drugs. First, Attorney General William French Smith and Associate Attorney General Rudolph W. Giuliani indicated that DOJ would make narcotics a priority. In turn, Peter Bensinger, a Republican who had served in the Carter administration, stepped down as DEA administrator after budget cuts were threatened for the

DEA; his place was taken by Francis Mullen, who at first served as both interim DEA administrator and assistant director of the FBI (Babcock 1981a). DEA officials saw the appointment of Mullen, the first FBI special agent to head the DEA, as evidence of a forthcoming FBI takeover, yet some at DOJ saw an FBI takeover as removing the DEA from the realm of politics (Babcock 1981b; Pear 1981; Wilson 1989, 267).[54] Mid-year Smith and Giuliani stepped up pressure by ordering the U.S. Attorneys to confer with state and local authorities in fighting street crime (Pear 1981). Then in late 1981 Reagan obtained amendments to the Posse Comitatus Act, passed in 1878, which prohibited the use of troops in domestic law enforcement (Inciardi 1986, 208; Baum 1996, 167; Hammond 1997).[55] What Reagan wanted was coordination to make available military training, intelligence, equipment, and detection capabilities for narcotics interdiction.[56]

In early 1982, DOJ announced a reorganization under which the DEA would report to the FBI, which expanded the FBI's power to investigate drug cases beyond those connected to organized crime (Thornton 1982a). With the change, the DEA then reported to the FBI director rather than the attorney general, a change that also brought different resources, promotion opportunities, and a clash of cultures (Wilson 1989, 267). One reason for not having a full merger was that it would have required congressional approval (Pound 1982).[57]

Reagan's agenda embraced both enforcement and demand reduction. For example, in an October 1982 radio address, he first had Nancy Reagan address the country on the problem of drugs. He then referred to a recently implemented strategy for the prevention of drug abuse and drug trafficking, a task force in south Florida led by Vice President George H. W. Bush. He then called for an expansion of this new approach to law enforcement: "Well, for the first time, the actions of the different Government agencies and departments dealing with narcotics are being coordinated. There are 9 departments and 33 agencies of Government that have some responsibility in the drug area, but until now, the activities of these agencies were not being coordinated. Each was fighting its own separate battle against drugs. Now, for the very first time, the Federal Government is waging a planned, concerted campaign."[58]

The campaign was in response to substantial reorganization in the international trafficking of narcotics. The rising tide of cocaine entering the United States was mostly a result of the development of coordinated action by traffickers such as the Medellín cartel.[59] Production, refining, and trafficking centralized in Colombia in the 1970s using Mexico and Florida as the main entry routes to the U.S. markets; by 1980, according to DEA estimates, trafficking in Florida was a

$7 billion industry (Davenport-Hines 2002, 433). In 1981, Pablo Escobar (along with the Ochoa family and Carlos Lehder Rivas) launched a coordinated trafficking effort based in Colombia, using Norman's Cay in the Bahamas (later, Panama) as a transit route; Miami became the center of the cartel's U.S. operations.[60]

Reagan named Carlton Turner to be his drug adviser in 1981, at the behest of the parent movement (Massing 1998, 158). On one hand, Turner helped orchestrate the First Lady's rhetorical agenda on demand reduction. On the other hand, he also saw an important role for strong enforcement. In late 1981 he investigated the growing perception that Miami was a transit point for narcotics, concluding that a federal task force to intercept shipments into the United States was needed, although at that point he saw it largely as a marijuana problem (Massing 1998, 164). He advised Reagan to create the Vice President's Task Force on South Florida, a cabinet-level body headed by George H. W. Bush; it came into being in January 1982.[61] The task force drew on hundreds of agents from the DEA and FBI (along with resources from Customs, ATF, IRS, and the Army and Navy). The task force also targeted bankers and businessmen working with drug traffickers and offshore banks to launder money. This was the prototype for the later Organized Crime Drug Enforcement Task Force Program announced in October 1982 (three weeks before the midterm elections); by 1984 there were thirteen task forces relating to drugs. This expanded the approach fostered in the south Florida task force nationwide.[62]

Reagan then centralized control over drug policy in 1982 by naming Turner director of the Drug Abuse Policy Office (created by Executive Order 12368). At that event, the audience—which included the heads of eighteen agencies, the vice president, military leaders, and the IRS commissioner—was told, "We're rejecting the helpless attitude that drug use is so rampant that we're defenseless to do anything about it. We're taking down the surrender flag that has flown over so many drug efforts; we're running up a battle flag. We can fight the drug problem, and we can win. And that is exactly what we intend to do."[63] One of Turner's key initiatives was to require all agencies to report how much of their budgets were devoted to the war on drugs (Baum 1996, 166).

Two changes at the DEA in 1982 altered its operations. First, the imposition of FBI control required a reorganization of DEA headquarters. Specifically, in 1975 DEA had adopted central tactical units for managing efforts against major suppliers. In 1982 these units were replaced with drug-specific operations, and the headquarters was organized along the lines of "drug desks"; each desk directed and coordinated investigations for that drug. This replaced the domestic/foreign geographic organization. At the same time, the DEA structure was centralized with upper-level management positions moved from the regions to headquarters; field operations used FBI procedures for reporting to headquarters. New training procedures were instituted, mainly at the behest of the FBI (Wilson 1989, 267). Notably, regional quotas (arrest goals) were scrapped in favor of an agency-wide goal. Mullen said, "In the past, we concentrated on arrests. Now we're concentrating on convictions at the highest levels" (DEA 2003a, 48).[64]

In May 1982, Reagan strongly advocated anticrime legislation to expand forfeiture to all property used in drug trafficking or racketeering activities.[65] In September he pushed for revisions of the exclusionary rule and limits on the ability of federal courts to intervene in state criminal proceedings.[66] The broad implications of this legislative offensive were that federal agents needed for it to be easier to convict dealers and impose longer mandatory minimum sentences (Bertram et al. 1996, 113).[67] Reagan's proposed reforms (the Violent Crime and Drug Enforcement Improvements Act of 1982) survived the Senate virtually intact (passing 95–1) but did not make it out of the House. Instead, the House passed a "mini-crime" bill that included a provision for a drug czar (appointed by the president, with the advice and consent of the Senate) in the waning days of the 97th Congress. Reagan vetoed the bill.[68]

In the 1983 State of the Union address Reagan declared "an all-out war on big-time organized crime and the drug racketeers who are poisoning our young people."[69] He followed up his veto by introducing the Comprehensive Crime Control Act of 1983, which packaged together many of the original proposed reforms and again called for reform of the bail process, the exclusionary rule, and the forfeiture laws.[70] The Senate quickly passed the Reagan bill largely intact (91–1); Reagan went public in early and mid-1984 urging House action.[71] In July 1984 the Supreme Court established the "good faith" exception to the exclusionary rule in *United States v. Leon*.[72] The House passed the Comprehensive Crime Control Act of 1984 in September.[73] The president signed it into law in October, thus creating a new National Drug Policy Board and giving prosecutors substantial new powers to enforce drug laws, including mandatory minimums, alterations to bail, and strong forfeiture rules.[74] Of course, forfeiture was already in place: as Reagan noted in March 1984, "But we're the owner now of a fleet of cabin cruisers and yachts and airplanes and helicopters and trucks and cars. And down there, the last time I was in Florida I remember being taken into a big building there at the airport and shown what we had intercepted, but also on a table that was about the size of that desk, the first time in my life I saw $20 million in cash stacked up there in bills that had been taken away from the drug dealers. That had to hurt."[75]

While the federal authorities had been using both civil and criminal forfeiture to combat the drug trade since the early 1970s, the 1984 legislation greatly strengthened government capabilities in this regard. The 1984 legislative amendments expanded the scope of property that could be confiscated under civil forfeiture to include real estate with a connection to drug trading or manufacturing. The legislation also contained provisions that helped to keep drug traffickers from hiding or moving their assets after arrest. This was accomplished through extension of the "relation back" rule to criminal forfeiture cases. This rule basically gives the government title to the property (and the ability to seize it) at the time of the crime, which prevents drug traffickers from shifting assets to third parties while awaiting conviction. While this rule was already available in civil forfeitures, the 1984 amendments extended it to criminal forfeitures (Levy 1996). This enabled enforcement agencies to expand their forfeiture opportunities (since the court system was getting clogged with civil forfeiture cases) and also had the effect of hampering the ability of defendants to retain expensive legal counsel, since their assets were no longer available to pay fees. Perhaps the most momentous aspect of the 1984 amendments was the change from requiring that funds obtained by enforcement agencies through forfeiture go to the Treasury's General Fund to allowing such funds to be retained by the enforcement agencies themselves or shared with cooperating state and local enforcement entities (Blumenson and Nilsen 1998).

Of course, the market for drugs was shifting throughout the 1980s, as were the main arrangements for shipping narcotics to the United States. In March 1984, Colombian officials raided the Tranquilandia cocaine production facility and destroyed drugs and materials estimated at $1.2 billion. After the Medellín cartel carried out high-profile assassinations, the government called for extradition of the perpetrators to the United States, including the cartel's co-founder Carlos Lehder. The cartel began to splinter, with its leaders fleeing to Panama for safe haven. Pablo Escobar eventually testified against the others. In mid-1984 the war on drugs collided with the Cold War when DEA operations were exposed to show Nicaraguan involvement in the drug trade, leading to mass federal indictments of the cartel's leadership. Colombia was not well-equipped to deal with the Medellín cartel, and it would be some time before the cartel would suffer permanent damage. Cocaine transport routes moved from south Florida to Mexico following the successes of the South Florida Drug Task Force. Following the February 1985 murder of DEA agent Enrique Camarena in Mexico, the Customs Service held a six-day crackdown on the Mexican border modeled after Nixon's Operation Intercept, in part due to concerns about complicity by Mexican officials (Russell 1985). The growing concern on American streets was crack and "cocaine babies" (Baum 1996, 219).

In 1985, Edwin Meese became the new attorney general, and Jack Lawn, the new DEA administrator. The death of Camarena had an enormous impact on DEA operations and on perceptions of how committed neighboring countries were to stopping the flow of narcotics. Meese sought to use media messages and other methods to shift the tenor of the war toward stronger pressure on users and defense attorneys (Baum 1996, 214).

But it was the death of basketball player Len Bias in June 1986 by a cocaine overdose that had broader impact on legislative efforts on narcotics control. In July, in order to show the prevalence and ease of access of drugs, the DEA helped Senator Alfonse D'Amato and Rudolph Giuliani, now U.S. Attorney for Manhattan, buy crack in New York City in an intelligence-gathering exercise (Anderson and Dunlap 1986). After a second athlete, football player Don Rogers, died of a cocaine overdose the same month, President Reagan sought to reassure people that he was working to gain control over narcotics, advocating drug testing for federal employees and the allocation of additional funds. It was clear that momentum had shifted, that both the president and Congress were racing toward legislative responses that would in part change perceptions about the state of the narcotics problem.[76] There followed notable appearances at the National Conference on Alcohol and Drug Abuse Prevention, radio addresses, and a national campaign (including E.O. 12564 on drug testing in the federal workforce and a proposed Drug-Free America Act). Specifically, in September 1986 Reagan proposed federal workforce testing, testing in schools, changes to block grants for substance abuse treatment, expanded international efforts for interdiction, and new tools for prosecution of traffickers (including mandatory minimums and tools against money laundering).[77]

Reagan had legislation on his desk by October, one week before the mid-term elections. The Anti-Drug Abuse Act of 1986 appropriated $1.7 billion for enforcement, with $97 million for prisons, $200 million for education, and $241 million for treatment. It created many mandatory minimum penalties for drug offenses, even first offenses.[78] Differential mandatory minimums were imposed for crack and powder cocaine, an unintended result of which was that African-American defendants became more likely to face mandatory penalties than white offenders were (United States Sentencing Commission 1997, 8).[79] It established the Office for Substance Abuse Prevention (OSAP) and the White House Conference for a Drug-Free America. It also required that the president certify the performance of various countries with regard to cooperation on drug interdiction efforts in order to receive foreign assistance (DEA 2003a, 66). The president would later cut almost $1 billion from the $4 billion bill (all for treatment and grants to the states).[80] But Reagan benefited: "Easily the most prominent beneficiary of the drug furor is Ronald Reagan. Just weeks ago, the President seemed trapped in a thicket of thorny problems, not the least of which were budget and trade deficits and sanctions against South Africa. On the horizon were equally unpleasant questions about tax reform. Drugs, by contrast, were far down the list of priorities" (Duffy 1986, 28).

Yet things were not completely positive. In February 1987 a federal grand jury indicted Panama's military dictator Manuel Noriega on charges of racketeering and drug trafficking; Noriega had formed close ties with the Medellín cartel and allowed it to launder money and build cocaine laboratories in Panama. It was soon learned that Noriega had also formed ties with Oliver North, who had arranged arms sales to Iran and funding of the Contra rebels in Nicaragua; in 1989 the Kerry Committee Report concluded that those implementing this plan had received financial and material assistance from drug traffickers (Cockburn and St. Clair 1998).

The tail end of the Reagan administration saw a return to an earlier initiative: the creation of a national drug czar. Congress passed the Anti-Drug Abuse and Control Act of 1988 in the waning days of the administration. It established the Office of National Drug Control Policy (ONDCP), whose director would be the nation's drug czar. The purpose of ONDCP was to set national priorities and implement a national strategy for narcotics control, a research-based collection of long-range goals and measurable objectives.

The Act was an election-year thrust to push drugs to the forefront of the political agenda (Musto 1999, 277). Vice President George H. W. Bush, leader of the South Florida Task Force, was facing Massachusetts Governor Michael Dukakis in the race to succeed Reagan. The Act helped bridge the gap between Congress and the president, but it did so by again increasing criminal penalties for offenses related to trafficking, creating new federal offenses and drug control requirements, funding state and local drug enforcement, changing the certification process established in 1986, and calling for negotiations with governments whose banks could help identify money laundering and drug transaction funds. The Act also created the organization that would later become the Center for Substance Abuse Prevention. A side effect of the legislation was to create an official vocabulary for discussing drugs and alcohol, moving away from "hard and soft drugs" to just "drugs" and from "recreational use" to "use" (Musto 1999, 278).

The changes that began in the Nixon administration were strengthened during Carter, although Carter's commitment to an enforcement strategy was less than total. The changes became fully embodied in the Reagan administration with its emphasis on "just say no," the advent of military-style tactics for narcotics control and interdiction, and heightened perceptions about national trends like cocaine and its cousin crack. We can speculate about what drove Reagan's desire to situate the nation's focus on drugs. Was it Mrs. Reagan's need to draw attention away from other concerns? Did it evolve from family experiences? How much was it entangled with his anti-Communism efforts in Latin America? These debates drive much of the modern literature on the drug war.

Our focus is different. Reagan's narrative reflected his administration's recognition that drugs were defined by constituencies that valued interdiction over treatment options—indeed, by heroes and villains, almost—and that admonition to greater action would help reconcile the diverse views about the best way to implement the law, which were still being sorted out in a fairly young federal bureaucracy. The power of the president now could be exercised through a bureaucracy wielding more tools to solve the perceived problem of drugs. And the president and his staff understood full well the power of messages as a mechanism for traversing distances to influence people. While analysts of Reagan's war on drugs worry about why he chose to push the agenda, we are just as interested in the impact of those choices and his means for carrying them out.

We describe in chapter 4 how the president's attention to narcotics, as reflected in his rhetoric, varies a great deal even within a single administration. Like Nixon, Reagan moved midway through his administration to emphasize narcotics in his policy agenda. What he did not do is move back to the treatment regime. Instead, his trajectory was further into enforcement, to emphasize criminals and their just rewards.

Expanding the Threat Narrative: George H. W. Bush

George H. W. Bush intensified the drug war in part because he understood its political value. The purpose of his first televised address was to present to the nation his national drug control strategy for dealing with the "threat" of narcotics.[81]

He first showed a bag of crack, bought near the White House in a DEA sting just a few days before.[82] He voiced the view that "the gravest domestic threat facing our nation today is drugs." The war effort was redoubled—and just: "If we fight this war as a divided nation, then the war is lost. But if we face this evil as a nation united, this will be nothing but a handful of useless chemicals. Victory—victory over drugs—is our cause, a just cause. And with your help, we are going to win."

In 1989 he appointed William Bennett as the first head of ONDCP and drug czar. As secretary of education and head of the National Endowment for the Humanities, Bennett called for "personal responsibility," a call that carried over well to narcotics control policy; he lobbied Bush for the position starting as soon as the election concluded (Bennett 1992). One of the first products of ONDCP was the new National Drug Control Strategy required by the Anti-Drug Abuse and Control Act.[83] The resultant document coincided with President Bush's speech in September 1989. Along with the required plans, targets, and strategies, Bennett's document called for a new goal: "zero tolerance" of drug use. Specifically, drugs were not a "health problem," they were a "morals problem" (Baum 1996, 264). The theory relied on James Q. Wilson's "contagion model" of crime (Wilson and Kelling 1982; see also Baum 1996, 273). This model argues that individual behavior depends on attributes of the neighborhood, including both sociodemographics and law enforcement leniency toward less serious offenses in a given neighborhood.

Bennett embraced enforcement as a primary means for fighting the war on drugs. Meese's successor at DOJ, Dick Thornburgh, saw the same value in an enforcement orientation. Baum summarizes Thornburgh views on treatment thus: "The attorney general is not the secretary of HHS" (Baum 1996, 292). In that regard, the DOJ directed the U.S. Attorneys to ignore the ethics rule of the American Bar Association barring prosecutors from contacting individuals without their lawyers present. The DOJ argued that U.S. Attorneys like those in New York City are "charged with the enforcement of federal law and nobody—emphasize nobody—can interfere with that duty" (Finkelman 1993).[84]

A number of initiatives paved the way for greater enforcement. In the National Defense Authorization Act for Fiscal Years 1990 and 1991 Congress authorized the U.S. military to aid drug interdiction efforts at the border as the "single lead agency"; since that time, the military has spent over $7 billion on interdiction efforts (Hammond 1997). In February 1989 U.S. military forces arrested Manuel Noriega and brought him to the United States to be tried for laundering drug money (he was convicted in 1992). In December 1989, DEA Administrator Jack

Lawn overruled an administrative law judge's decision to move marijuana from Schedule I to Schedule II of the Controlled Substances Act, an act that would have allowed physicians to prescribe marijuana for medical purposes (DEA 2003a, 68). Bush signed the Crime Control Act of 1990, classifying many types of anabolic steroids under Schedule III of the Controlled Substances Act of 1970. There were plenty of prosecutors to pursue those convictions, too; during his time at DOJ, Attorney General Thornburgh doubled the number of federal prosecutors (Baum 1996, 327).

But in August 1990 the agenda shifted when Iraq invaded Kuwait. The Republican Party lost ten seats in the House and did not gain in the Senate in the 1990 midterm election. Along with these changes, press coverage of the war on drugs fell dramatically: according to the *Readers' Guide to Periodical Literature*, coverage fell from 244 stories in 1989 to 138 in 1991 (Baum 1996, 304). Shortly afterward, Bennett resigned as director of ONDCP to become head of the Republican National Committee (RNC), to be succeeded at ONDCP by Robert Martinez four months later. On his way out, Bennett made sure to declare victory in the war on drugs, a judgment with which many in Congress disagreed (Baum 1996, 309). (Bennett quit as head of the RNC two weeks later.) Bennett's departure was preceded by that of DEA Administrator Jack Lawn in August 1990, who was replaced by Robert Bonner. Bonner would be the first federal prosecutor and federal judge to serve as DEA head (DEA 2003a, 76).[85]

For the next two years the war on drugs went essentially as it had the previous two years. One major initiative of the latter half of the Bush administration was Operation Weed and Seed, an attempt to limit crime and drug dealing by linking enforcement activities and community-based human services programs; the evidence for its effectiveness has been decidedly mixed (Dunworth and Mills 1999; Bridendall and Jesilow 2005).[86] Yet Weed and Seed signaled a shift in the tenor of drug control efforts. Rather than the strong enforcement orientation of the first two years, the second two years of the Bush administration focused on bridging enforcement and social service provision, or at least trying to show the American public that it saw a need for a balanced approach.

The George H. W. Bush era is a central point in the war on drugs. We show in chapter 4 that the role of rhetoric reached an all-time high during this period. What makes the Bush administration different is how it engaged in the war on a number of fronts, and how it saw the fight (at least at the beginning) in starkly moralistic terms. By the time Bush claimed office, the country was almost sixteen years into the "war on drugs" (thinking back to Nixon's 1972 speech) and eight years into an enforcement regime. Reagan had tested the political waters by using the rhetoric and found it useful.

But the change brought on by Iraq's invasion of Kuwait shows how presidential attention moves with the times. The Bush initiative was replaced with attention to more pressing matters in the Middle East. Even so, the bureaucracy remained. The enforcement focus was in place, and the tools were still in the hands of agents around the world charged with implementing the law. One purpose of this book, shown below in models presented in chapters 5 through 7, is to see whether that shift in attention translated into less focus on drugs in arrests and prosecutions by the DEA, the U.S. Attorneys, and at the state and local levels.

Failure to Change: Clinton

William Jefferson Clinton ran for president as a moderate and New Democrat. Led primarily by the Democratic Leadership Council, the policy agenda of the New Democrats centered on smaller government and greater effectiveness (Hale 1995). Lee Brown, Clinton's nominee for director of ONDCP, was the former police chief of Houston and police commissioner of New York City. Bonner would continue to serve as DEA administrator until October 1993, being replaced then by Thomas Constantine, former superintendent of the New York State Police. But Clinton also promised a balanced approach to the war on drugs. As a politician of a new generation, one that had grown up with increasing use of drugs like marijuana, many saw Clinton as uniquely positioned to change the focus from enforcement toward other options, perhaps even expanded treatment (Baum 1996, 331). His nominee for surgeon general, Jocelyn Elders, signaled the likelihood of change because of her long-term interest in public health matters, especially for children.

One of Clinton's first moves was to reduce the staff of ONDCP from 146 to 25, a reduction of 83 percent; this represented one-third of all cuts at the White House, which Clinton had promised would be 25 percent smaller (Hart 1995).[87] He did not name Brown drug czar until April 1993 but promised that the drug czar would have cabinet status, which continued the symbolic importance of ONDCP in the war on drugs. While some see this restructuring of ONDCP as an attempt to improve policy advice and move implementation back to other agencies and the states (Hart 1995), others see it as an intentional shifting of emphasis from active engagement with narcotics control to a policy of benign neglect (Musto 1999, 282).[88] Yet, Clinton later used three executive orders (E.O. 12880 in

1993, and E.O. 12992 and E.O. 13023 in 1996) to extend the power of the ONDCP and to create the President's Drug Policy Council. His proposal (part of the "Reinventing Government" movement) to merge the DEA and the FBI in full failed, a move that would have completed the changes in 1982 that gave the two agencies combined jurisdiction over narcotics (Lewis 1993). The powers of the ONDCP expanded again in 1994 with the passage of the Violent Crime Control and Law Enforcement Act; the Act also imposed the death penalty for crimes associated with drug dealing.

In December 1993, Elders offered her view on narcotics policy to the National Press Club: "I do feel that we would markedly reduce our crime rate if drugs were legalized" (Labaton 1993). The comment reverberated because of Republican and Democratic attention to early Clinton moves to deemphasize narcotics control, or at least to emphasize rehabilitation over prosecution. The White House quickly squashed any ideas that a study of decriminalization was forthcoming; Clinton reiterated his campaign position that his brother Roger (a former addict) would likely have died if drugs had been more widely available. Eight days later Elders's son was picked up for dealing cocaine in Arkansas (he was later sentenced to ten years in prison). A year later she left after a flap over school sex-education courses (just after the massive Republican gains in the 1994 midterms). In the interim, though, she chose not to restart federal medical marijuana studies the Bush administration had closed (Baum 1996, 335). Lee Brown would leave a year later after Congress threatened budget cuts for ONDCP (Abrams 1994).

Clinton's replacement for Lee Brown, former general Barry McCaffrey, was confirmed and took office in March 1996, just as the president approached reelection. Up to this time the DEA had continued to carry out operations at a number of levels, although the primary concern remained interdiction from international sources. A main example of these efforts was the arrests of the Cali Cartel in Colombia, although an unintended consequence was strong growth in Mexico-sourced heroin, cocaine, and marijuana (DEA 2003b, 20). By 1995 a new threat, methamphetamine (also known as "speed" or "crank"), had also emerged as a concern, especially in California. The emergence of meth could be seen in the sharp increase in use as well as the increasing numbers of domestic labs for its production.[89] This would signal a coming long-term shift in the relative efficacy of an interdiction strategy that focused on international trafficking.

McCaffrey faced a number of challenges, including the Republican perception that the Clinton White House had sought to deemphasize the war on drugs and the ONDCP. More important, states were seeking to challenge the ban on the medical use of marijuana through ballot initiatives like those in California and Arizona. In 1996 many of these passed; as drug czar, McCaffrey was faced with the problem of states authorizing physicians to violate federal law; rather than threaten patients, McCaffrey instead sought to use the DEA to revoke the licenses of prescribing doctors (Pacula et al. 2002).[90] McCaffrey saw the initiatives as ushering in a legalization regime (Clark 2000).

Almost as a counterpoint, drug enforcement efforts hit several milestones in 1997. For example, the DEA budget crossed the $1 billion threshold for the first time (DEA 2003b, 24).[91] One attribute of this raised effort was McCaffrey's new budget for advertisements intended to suppress demand. The five-year, $1 billion advertising buy included two innovations: in many cases, the ads were not identified as coming from ONDCP; in some cases, rather than ads ONDCP procured agreements to incorporate anti-drug messages into prime-time shows (Forbes 2000).[92] The advertising was designed to respond to rapidly rising rates of drug use among teenagers; half of the funds came from the private sector.

The Clinton administration had argued that the answer was enhanced treatment—indeed, treatment on demand (Bertram et al. 1996, 117). This position appeared to have support in data: RAND Corporation studies argued that drug treatment and education are more cost-effective than interdiction by a factor of seven (Rydell and Everingham 1994). In the first two years of the Clinton administration, the anti-drug budget shifted so that about forty percent was spent on programs to reduce demand, an increase from thirty percent in the previous Bush administration (Abrams 1994). That changed with succeeding budgets. Enforcement continued to play an important role. DEA Operations Reciprocity and Limelight in 1996 targeted the Mexican border. In 2000, Clinton named Donnie Marshall as DEA administrator, the first DEA special agent ever to fill that position. During the Clinton years, there were significant changes in the nature of drug use patterns, changes that brought new challenges for enforcement and treatment. The rise of methamphetamines was accompanied by a gradual shift toward a wide range of synthetic drugs (including ecstasy). Marijuana, cocaine, and heroin continued to be used, but the administration faced a wider range of concerns than at any other time in the history of the modern war on drugs.[93]

Despite this, the Clinton era was mostly marked by a lack of change from the strong enforcement regimes put in place during the Reagan and Bush administrations. There were murmurs about too little staffing or sky-high budgets, but few perceived a wholesale change in approach. Clinton's engagement with the issue of narcotics varied from that of previous presidents, so the president's definition of drugs as a public problem also changed. Some were surprised how much Clinton emphasized enforcement over treatment.

Clinton had come of age at a time when drug use was greater than ever before; indeed, it was precisely the time when Nixon and others were building a social construction of drugs that identified clear heroes and villains. His knowledge of drugs in society (whether one inhaled or not) probably made it more important for him to engage narcotics as a presidential initiative than otherwise might have been the case. As noted above, this was probably reinforced by unique events for his appointees, but the single most important constraint he faced was the vast changes in the complexion of Congress with the 1994 Republican Revolution. The legislation he signed throughout the term, some of which included harsh new penalties for drug use and trafficking, largely indicates the context in which he acted. The clearest evidence of little movement away from the construction as it had developed at that time was the low profile that treatment continued to receive; enforcement continued to dominate national policy.

The New Threat: George W. Bush

George W. Bush narrowly won the presidency in a contest against Vice President Albert Gore, who carried with him the legacy of eight years of Democratic control of the reins of government. Drugs played a role in the election. For Bush, the administration's record on drugs was "one of the worst public policy failures of the 1990s," which he proposed to reverse by offering $2.7 billion in increased spending (Ratcliffe and Roth 2000). Like much of the campaign, the positions often came down to competing numbers. Bush claimed that from 1992 to 1997, teen drug abuse had increased, with heroin use doubling and the average age of initiation dropping from 27 in 1988 to 18 in 1997. Gore responded with a call for $5.3 billion in new spending to include local prevention and treatment grants, a national media campaign, and tougher penalties for dealing to children. While Clinton argued that he had not inhaled, Gore admitted he had occasionally used marijuana while in college. Allegations that Bush had used cocaine in the 1970s surfaced during the campaign but were not established to be factual; Bush refused to answer all questions about drug use while younger.

Even so, in contrast to previous elections, narcotics policy played a small role in framing the interaction between the candidates. Gore focused on treatment and diversion, Bush on faith-based treatment as a part of his "compassionate conservatism" view of social services provision (Schmidt 2000). Bush had shown some orientation toward enforcement while Texas governor. In the election year, the Clinton administration had backed a $1.6 billion aid package to Colombia to strengthen interdiction efforts. One reason for the lack of attention (compared to previous years) was that the problem was getting harder to solve even as professionals in the field were beginning to understand what approaches did not work. Specifically, the question of treatment versus prison was given limited coverage because it was difficult to point to clear successes. Joseph Califano, former secretary of health and human services, noted, "It's the stealth issue, boy. . . . They're unsure about what to do about it" (Schmidt 2000).

The closeness of the election result made it exceptionally difficult for Bush to offer a strong initiative on narcotics control. Slight shifts were apparent. In his confirmation hearing, Secretary of Defense Donald Rumsfeld, asked about Clinton's Colombia initiative, characterized the war on drugs as "overwhelmingly a demand problem. . . . If demand persists, it's going to get what it wants. And if it isn't from Colombia, it's going to be from someplace else" (Will 2001). Bush delayed naming his drug czar until May 2001, when he nominated John Walters as director of ONDCP. Walters had been William Bennett's chief of staff and then a staffer on supply reduction at ONDCP during the previous Bush administration. Bush reiterated that "the most effective way to reduce the supply of drugs in America is to reduce the demand for drugs in America. Therefore, this administration will focus unprecedented attention on the demand side of this problem."[94] The new effort would be with regard to treatment: first a state-by-state inventory of needs and capacity and then efforts to close the treatment gap. This slight shift was seen in conversations between Bush and Mexican President Vicente Fox in which Bush noted that the long-term solution was demand reduction, even though the trend is toward greater collaboration on enforcement (Weiner and Thompson 2001). He reinforced these efforts by naming former congressman and former U.S. Attorney Asa Hutchinson DEA administrator in July 2001; Hutchinson left in 2003 when the Department of Homeland Security was created, and his replacement was Karen Tandy, a long-term DOJ prosecutor.

The attack on the World Trade Center on September 11, 2001, changed much of the plans to forge a moderate attack on the drugs trade, both in the United States and in supplier countries. The focus shifted broadly to narcoterrorism: the use of the drug trade by terrorist organizations to assemble funds for arming, equipping, and training members. The DEA sees narcoterrorism as a subset of terrorism and reports that a third of the international terrorist organizations identified by the State Department are linked to narcotics trafficking (DEA

2003b, 53). Of course, the DEA and others have long recognized this connection, given the involvement of groups like FARC and the ELN in Colombia and the Shining Path in Peru in the cocaine trade, and many find the IRA-FARC connection particularly troubling (Murphy 2005).[95] In practical terms, 9/11 shifted attention to Afghanistan, where heroin trafficking was long connected to the Taliban; identified connections between the Taliban and al Qaeda would help justify the later Operation Enduring Freedom in that country. DEA operations included Operation Containment, which sought to break connections between the heroin trade and support for remaining Taliban forces in Afghanistan (DEA 2003b, 54). At the same time, the DEA increased operations against other narcoterrorist groups, like FARC and others in Colombia. At home, a number of legalization/decriminalization initiatives made ballots around the country in the 2002 election cycle, but most failed.

The general strategy of the Bush administration was to rely on three mechanisms for reducing overall drug use: prevention, treatment, and interdiction (ONDCP 2007, 8). Interdiction takes place in the context of domestic production and distribution (largely now synthetics and marijuana, as well as the abuse of prescription drugs like pain relievers) and international efforts to reduce the flow of drugs from Mexico, Colombia, and South Asia. Prevention centers on education and community action, largely through partnerships with state and local public and nonprofit organizations. For the Bush administration, treatment included screening and intervention as well as traditional referral and treatment programs; drug courts increasingly play a role in diversion.

Generally speaking, the eight years of the Bush administration started with the prospect of increased attention to the war on drugs, but just as in his father's case, the president's attention was pulled elsewhere. Treatment continued to play a small role in the overall debate about how to win the war. Following the events of September 11, 2001, narcotics received some attention because of the shift in priorities toward border protection and concerns about narcoterrorism. Tools for the bureaucracy were strengthened, and funds increased for interdiction efforts at home and abroad. The use of narcotics continued to evolve with changes in the internal and external markets for drugs, including the continual growth in methamphetamine production and sales (Owen 2008).

What changed for the president was the construction of the war, although there were really two types of change. First, the lens of narcoterrorism fed into the continuing evolution of the identities of those involved in the "contest between good, but weak, interests and bad, but strong, interests" (Stone 2002, 134).

But the language of conflict surrounding the war on drugs also changed to the now-familiar "war on terror." On one hand, aligning the types of villains helped accentuate the causes and solutions that had now become part and parcel of narcotics policy narratives. On the other hand, the identification process may have weakened the connection to drugs per se by exposing recipients of messages to different targets. It may have taken time to become clear to DEA officials (or the U.S. Attorneys, or the states) that by prosecuting drugs cases they were part of frontline of the war on terror (see Dolan 2005). This helps show how the drug war as a rhetorical device has changed over time.

Discussion

We began this chapter with the claim that the war on drugs is a presidential construct. Over time, presidents have varied in the degree to which they have emphasized it as part of their issue agenda, depending in part on how other domestic and foreign policy issues staked claims on their attention. Our view is that the war on drugs resonates at the polls, or in negotiations with Congress, or in claims for public attention. Presidents have worked the topic, and in doing so they have politically constructed the meaning and content of American narcotics control policy.

In the end, our focus is on how this political construction has facilitated a social construction: that in the end, after a brief time during the Nixon administration, national efforts at defining the problem of drugs have moved almost entirely away from treatment as a preferred option; in doing so, those efforts have driven the scale and scope of enforcement efforts.

This chapter centers on the history of the origins and development of narcotics control in the United States because it provides a foundation for understanding how American presidents have changed narcotics control over the last seven decades, and the last three decades more specifically. These changes offer a lens on the rise of narcotics as a problem for presidential leadership. An exhaustive history of drug use in America is outside the scope of this chapter, but the paths of presidential involvement with the issue of the presence of narcotics in society help us visualize the effects of presidential agenda-setting on federal and state enforcement effort.

The eras detailed here—from Roosevelt to the 1960s, the administrations of Lyndon B. Johnson and Richard M. Nixon, the Ford and Carter administrations, the advent of the war with Reagan and its evolution during the George H. W.

Bush era, and finally the Clinton and George W. Bush administrations—show how perspectives have changed over time and how non-enforcement solutions have become displaced from the larger debate. Cause and consequence, evidence and reason: all mostly center on the use of police and prosecutor as instruments of power in a struggle among the forces of society.

The jury is out on President Obama's plans for the war on drugs. Narcotics did not play a large role in debates during the presidential campaign. Details on his use of narcotics in younger years were scarce—although not as scarce as in the case of George W. Bush; perhaps the most pointed discussion has been about his use of cigarettes. The first several years of his administration are likely to be dominated by the economy and concerns about American involvement in Iraq and Afghanistan. While the policy needs in the area of narcotics may be acute, the president's ability and willingness to take on drugs as a way of controlling the debate are limited by other issues on the public agenda.

We are tempted, as most commentators are in this policy arena, to refer to standards drawn from the study of public health, social welfare, or human development for measuring the impact of these policy shifts and, accordingly, to make judgments about the value of presidential strategies. The simpler approach is to take those strategies and consider their consequences in a political and social context, to acknowledge that the bureaucrats who implement the law may be responding to many different influences, that presidential strategies for influencing the debate may shape what they do to make the law real. To that end, we turn in chapter 4 to data-based descriptions of the political and social context, including how the president talks about the war on drugs.

CHAPTER FOUR

The Words of War

Political Rhetoric and the War on Drugs

Our focus is on how the president can move the political agenda and change the implementation of policy. The president does so when he or she uses the bully pulpit to define narcotics control policy, constructs a view of what the government ought to do about drugs, and establishes symbols that condense a complex array of activities into a clear view of where policy should move. The presidential strategy of public rhetoric has many facets, is driven by multiple motivations, and has a wide range of effects and consequences. In this chapter we move from the broad landscape of presidential involvement in the war on drugs to focus on the public statements made by the presidents, both while in office and when they campaign as candidates. We do so through a quantitative and qualitative analysis of political rhetoric on narcotics policy, which we place in its political and social context. We close this chapter by returning to our central theme: how presidents can employ public rhetoric as a viable tool for policy leadership.

A Context for Construction

Presidents allocate: they allocate their time, energy, and attention across the many issues that compete for space on their agenda. The president's position in government means that he or she must at least address (if not solve) the kinds of important social and economic concerns that regular Americans face on a day-to-day basis, and then there are the unusual events like wars that also claim his or her attention. The president cannot attend to—let alone solve—most of these problems. Yet all presidents face the critical decisions of how to spend their time and energy as well as their political capital.

How the president (or Congress or the courts) allocates time and attention to one issue over another is the essence of agenda setting. We know that agenda setting is central to both politics and public policy processes (see, for example, Cobb and Elder 1971; Kingdon 1984; Edwards and Wood 1999; Jones and Baumgartner 2005). Even a cursory glance at the evolution of the war on drugs shows that recent presidential administrations have made it a focus of their attention. But in order to see fully the long-term transformation of the president's issue attention—of the waxing and waning of their focus—we need to understand the context within which they make those choices (Cohen 1997; Hill 1998; Light 1999; Yates and Whitford 2005). How extensive is the actual problem of drug abuse? Do people care about narcotics?

We start by looking at how estimated narcotics use evolved over the time when the war on drugs came to the forefront of politics and public policy. Chapter 3 shows how presidents interpreted the evolution of drug use in the nation, both before and during the modern war on drugs; here we offer a graphical account. Figure 4.1 shows the estimated number (in thousands) of new initiates (first-time users) for marijuana from 1965 to 1999, cocaine, hallucinogens, and heroin from 1962 to 1989. Marijuana initiates reached a high point in the early 1970s and were trending downward by the time Ronald Reagan took office. Hallucinogens and heroin initiates had plateaued by this time as well. Only first-time cocaine use was on the rise at the beginning of the modern war on drugs in the early 1980s, and even this trend tapered off by 1982. Together these trends suggest that politics lags context and that policy postdates the reduction in demand from new initiates that largely dominated politics in the 1980s.

Of course, context is contextual: what is "objective" depends on the beholder, and population-level indicators of drug use are diverse and can lead to different

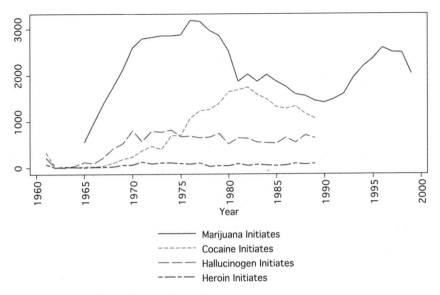

Figure 4.1. Initiates (in thousands) of Illegal Drugs, 1962–1999

conclusions. Consider the drug use trends shown in figure 4.2. The data show the incidence of daily marijuana use among twelfth-grade high school students. We see the unmistakable spike in heavy marijuana use just prior to Reagan's first term, and a drop in use until beginning of the Clinton administration. Since then there has been an upswing in usage at the twelfth-grade level. These data fueled the concern over narcotics use (at least marijuana) at the beginning of the Reagan administration.

Federal officials also observed changes in the number of annual deaths due to drug use. Figures 4.3 and 4.4 show national trends in drug-related mortality rates; the first is the national annual number of deaths per 100,000 population due to drug use, and the second shows the cross-sectional distribution of mortality rates across the states.[1]

We see competing interpretations of the incidence of drug-use in the United States. Figure 4.3 shows a significant upswing in drug deaths. In contrast, figure 4.4 shows only a mild increase across the states, with the typical state's mortality rate being roughly flat over time. Figure 4.4 shows side-by-side box-and-whisker plots. Box plots help us visualize both the movement of a typical case (here, a state) and variation across the states. The bottom and top lines in each box show the first and third quartiles (respectively) for each year's distribution of drug

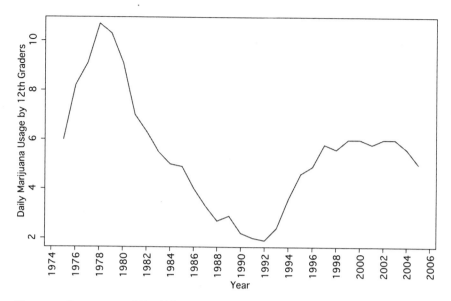

Figure 4.2. Percentage of Twelfth Graders Who Use Marijuana on a Daily Basis, 1975–2005

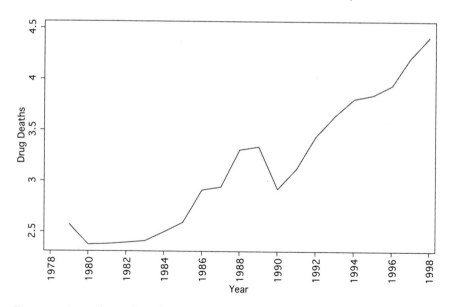

Figure 4.3. Annual Number of Drug Deaths in the Nation per 100,000 Citizens, 1979–1998

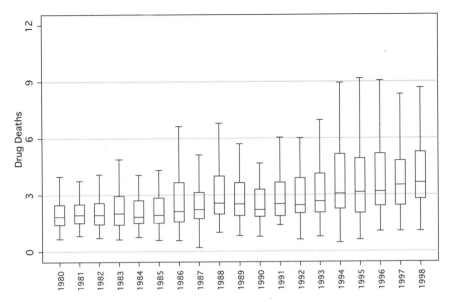

Figure 4.4. Distribution of State Drug Deaths per 100,000 State Citizens, 1980–1998

deaths, so the box represents the inter-quartile range; the middle line is the median (second quartile). The whiskers range downward and upward to the "inner fences."[2]

This suggests that many of the drug deaths in figure 4.3 were likely in large-population states like California and New York. Yet the presidents had reasons to attend to narcotics, reasons to make the drug problem a national priority.

Another way of assessing "the times" in which presidents make agenda-setting decisions is to consider how important other relevant actors considered the drug problem. Accordingly, we turn our focus to how the public saw the problem of narcotics. Certainly, public opinion is key to understanding the political and social context in which the president makes allocative decisions about his or her policy agenda. His or her role as the only elected official with a national constituency makes the president cognizant of how the public sees social problems (Cohen 1997). Figure 4.5 shows how the public has viewed the relative importance of the drug problem and government's response, tracking the percentage of people who think that government is spending "too much," "too little," or "about right" money on the issue. The responses are aggregated by region to reflect any local differences in sentiment. Across all regions, most respondents believe that too little money is

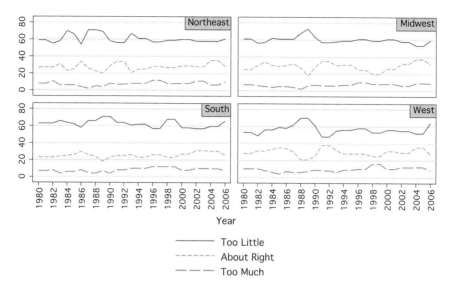

Figure 4.5. Public Opinion on Whether Enough Money Is Spent to Deal with Drug Addiction, by Region, 1980–2006

committed to the problem of narcotics. The responses vary (both across regions and across time), yet most have believed and continue to believe that not enough is being done to solve the problem.

Figure 4.6 shows how the proportion of people who perceive that too little money is being spent to deal with drug addiction varies both across time and geography. While the amount is regularly in the range of 50 percent, it spikes in 1989 at over 70 percent, and some regions record results lower than 50 percent at times since 1980. In our study, we use these two types of variation in the data on regional public opinion to identify change over time and cross-sectional variation, both of which can change how frontline field agents implement the war on drugs. Temporal changes show how "the times" shape the presidential and agency incentives to act on narcotics policy. Yet field agents face different demands for action that reflect local concerns.

Presidents also care about how much attention Congress and the media give to a problem (see Edwards and Wood 1999). Figure 4.7 shows congressional attention, reflected as the percentage of all congressional hearings devoted to narcotics policy in a given year. Figure 4.8 shows media attention as the percentage of all stories in the *New York Times* related to the drug problem.[3]

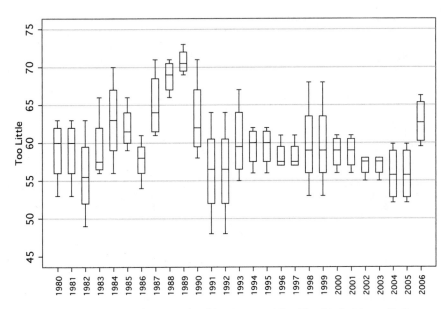

Figure 4.6. Distribution of Regional Public Opinion That Too Little Money Is Spent to Deal with Drug Addiction, 1980–2006

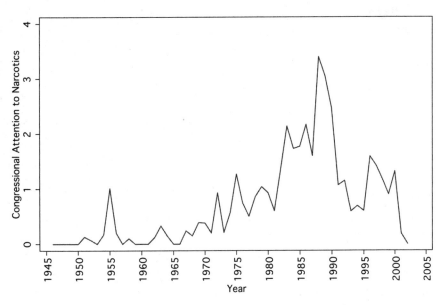

Figure 4.7. Congressional Hearings on Narcotics as a Percentage of All Congressional Hearings, 1946–2002

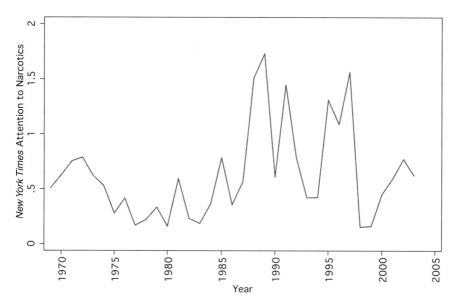

Figure 4.8. Percentage of Stories in the *New York Times* Related to the Drug Problem, 1969–2003

Both Congress and media attention peaked in the late 1980s; congressional attention has since trended downward, but media attention surged upward in the mid-1990s. Both show substantial variance from year to year. While an upswing in either congressional or media attention could depend on a unique event like the drug-related death of basketball star Len Bias in 1986, it is more likely that attention is driven by a complex set of factors (see Baumgartner and Jones 1993; Wood and Peake 1998).[4]

The Presidential Construction of the War on Drugs

Politicians and policymakers make construction choices in a political and social context. "Objective" conditions and "the times" shape the environment in which the person occupying the White House emphasizes some issues in their rhetoric over others. Yet the president develops some issue priorities well in advance of taking up residence in the White House, namely, on the road to the presidency. Presidents as politicians often bind themselves to issues that they as executives focus on: the issues they campaigned on and that they perceive won them the office. Party platforms are a central point in the process for building a national policy agenda (Walters 1990). More important, these platforms are often an accurate guide to the agenda the winner will pursue once in office if administrations try to keep promises made during the campaign (Pomper 1980). Of course, party platforms are the products of many actors, but the nominee is often influential, especially when an incumbent runs for reelection (Fine 1994). Platforms let a candidate define his or her own and his or her party's vision and persona (Walters 1990, 438).

Figure 4.9 shows how the attention paid to narcotics by party platforms has changed across presidential campaigns from 1972 through 2008. We measure attention by the words pertaining to the drug problem as a percentage of the platform's total word count. The drug problem received little attention during Carter's run in 1976 and during Reagan's campaigns. Both platforms showed sharp increases in their focus on narcotics in 1988, and while attention dipped soon after, it remained relatively high for platforms until 2004. More important, the platforms of both parties are almost in lockstep in their attention to narcotics.

A signature moment of the campaign is the nomination acceptance speech, when candidates get their first chance to speak as party leader and competitor in the general election, to "go public" on chosen issues. Of course, the war on drugs

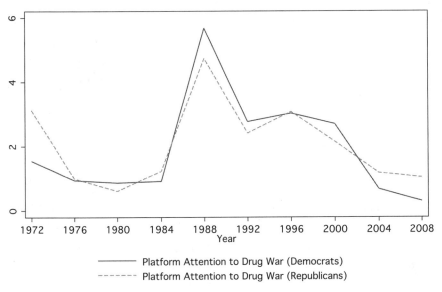

Figure 4.9. Percentage of Party Platforms Devoted to the War on Drugs, 1972–2008

has never dominated acceptance speeches, but it is a recurring topic that has produced some memorable moments. Neither candidate's speech in 1976 or 1980 mentioned the drug problem. In 1984 Walter Mondale did not address narcotics, but Reagan alluded to the drug problem in a sardonic commentary on Democratic Party priorities, quipping, "If our opponents were as vigorous in supporting our voluntary prayer amendment as they are in raising taxes, maybe we could get the Lord back in the classrooms and drugs and violence out."[5] Both candidates in 1988 made limited, caustic reference to the drug problem. George H. W. Bush framed the war on drugs with his now famous reference to Willie Horton, stating, "I'm the one who believes it is a scandal to give a weekend furlough to a hardened first degree killer who hasn't even served enough time to be eligible for parole. I'm the one who says a drug dealer who is responsible for the death of a policeman should be subject to capital punishment."[6] Dukakis tried to attack Bush's commitment to the drug war by highlighting the vice president's dealings with Manuel Noriega: "We're going to have a real war and not a phony war on drugs; and, my friends, we won't be doing business with drug-running Panamanian dictators anymore."[7] Bill Clinton engaged the drug problem in both campaigns, even though Republicans focused on his overseas drug use and turned "didn't inhale" into an election punchline. In 1992 he questioned Bush's support for the war on drugs and enforcement, asserting, "He's talked a lot about drugs, but he hasn't helped people on the front line to wage that war on drugs and crime. But I will."[8] In 1996, both Clinton and Bob Dole spent significant time on the war on drugs, but in 2000 both candidates made only sparing comments on the drug problem; in 2004 neither candidate mentioned the drug problem at all. The only "drug problem" the candidates referenced in that race was the need to make pharmaceutical drugs more affordable.

Similarly, presidential debates have incorporated rhetoric on the drug problem, at least since these debates resumed in 1976. For example, in the 1992 debates, the journalist Sander Vanocur asked the candidates (Bush, Clinton, and Ross Perot) about the viability of alternatives to enforcement-based solutions to the drug problem (for example, legalization) that had been advocated by thinkers like Milton Friedman and William F. Buckley. In response, the candidates tried their best to distance themselves from the idea and to establish themselves as the candidate most concerned about the drug problem:

BUSH: No, I don't think that's the right answer. I don't believe that legalizing narcotics is the answer. I do believe that there's some fairly good news out there. The use of cocaine, for example, by teenagers is dramatically down. But we've got to keep fighting on this war on drugs.

PEROT: Anytime you think you want to legalize drugs, go to a neonatal unit—if you can get in. They're between 100 and 200% capacity up and down the East Coast. And the reason is crack babies being born, babies in the hospital 42 days. Typical cost to you and me is $125,000. . . . Just look at those little children, and if anybody can even think about legalizing drugs, they've lost me.

CLINTON: Like Mr. Perot, I have held crack babies in my arms. But I know more about this, I think, than anybody else up here because I have a brother who's a recovering drug addict. I'm very proud of him. But I can tell you this. If drugs were legal, I don't think that he'd be alive today. I am adamantly opposed to legalizing drugs. He is alive today because of the criminal justice system.[9]

President Bush followed the exchange with a reply that vigorously stressed his support for DEA agents and state and local authorities in the fight against drugs. This exchange among the candidates shows the "ratcheting up" phenomenon that can pervade narcotics policy. It is rare that a politician, regardless of partisanship, would ever want to be considered soft on drug control.

Issues debated during a presidential campaign typically find their way into the administrative policy agenda. While the war on drugs has become a mainstay of presidents' public rhetoric and agenda in recent decades, how presidents emphasize the drug problem varies over time. Figure 4.10 shows the degree to which the drug problem has been prioritized in presidents' public statements over time. This series shows our measure of presidential attention to narcotics as measured by his rhetorical emphasis on the war on drugs. This is the primary independent variable we employ in our statistical analysis in chapters 5 through 7. The variable is constructed from presidential statements made in public settings in which he directly referenced the drug problem; this approach is consistent with measures used in other studies (Cohen 1995; Edwards and Wood 1999). We constructed this measure by first searching the index of the *Public Papers of the President* for executive mentions of drug policy topics, reading the paragraphs to ensure their substantive relevance, and then counting the number of paragraphs for each year. We accounted for variation in the amount of presidential communications in a year and standardized this score by dividing it by the number of pages in the

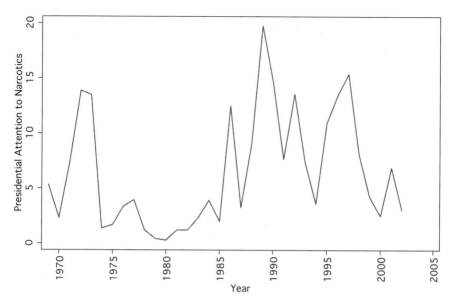

Figure 4.10. Presidential Attention to Narcotics, 1969–2002

year's public papers and multiplying it by one hundred (in other words, drug paragraphs per 100 pages of text).

The Office of the Federal Register publishes the *Public Papers of the President,* which is the official publication of federal government that contains the public writings, addresses, and remarks by the U.S. presidents. Historically, it was published on a regular basis in physical format. Those volumes contain the president's papers and speeches during a specified time period if they were distributed by the Office of the Press Secretary. For our purposes, the material is coded by date, so we use those dates to construct our measures of presidential attention. These data are not regularly made available in electronic format.

The data indicate that Reagan, in the early years of his administration, made more use of drug rhetoric than did Carter. The serious upswing in rhetoric on narcotics began in 1984. The variation in the series after that point is remarkable. Drug rhetoric ebbs and flows throughout the time period, with the highest points of drug rhetoric coming between 1986 and 1997—even the lows after 1984 were higher than any total from the late 1970s and early 1980s. Presidential rhetoric peaks in 1989, the first year of the George H. W. Bush administration, but the second-highest peak is in the Clinton administration. The highest point during the Reagan administration was 1986.[10]

Just what did presidents say about the war on drugs? We characterize the character and tone of presidential rhetoric on the drug problem as "eclectic" (recognizing that some might call it "erratic"). We see the presidents' public statements on the drug problem as a mixture of thematic approaches, ranging from hope, courage and patriotism, to grave concern, approbation, and even fear. While the identity of the originator of the term "war on drugs" might be debated, Richard Nixon was the first president to use the phrase or some variant thereof (for example, "war on drug abuse" or "war against drugs") in public speeches. He began incorporating these war-themed phrases as early as 1971 and continued to use them for the rest of his administration. In a 1973 radio address he used stories, statistics, and passionate language to help make his case.

> Drug abuse is still public enemy number one in America. Let me tell you about some of the tragic letters I have received at the White House from victims of drugs.
>
> One tells about a 5-year-old boy hospitalized in Missouri. Someone gave him LSD.
>
> One is from a boy 18 years old who had spent 11 months in a mental hospital trying to get rid of his drug addiction. He started with marijuana. He is asking me for help because his 14-year-old brother has begun to use drugs.
>
> Another is from a mother in California. Her son committed suicide. He could not end his drug habit, so he ended his life.
>
> One of the things that comes through so forcefully in these letters is the sense of despair of people who feel they have no place to turn for help, and so they write to the White House. I intend to help them.
>
> We have already made encouraging progress in the war against drug abuse. Now we must consolidate that progress and strike even harder.
>
> One area in which I am convinced of the need for more immediate action is that of putting heroin pushers in prison and keeping them there. A recent study by the Bureau of Narcotics and Dangerous Drugs revealed that more than 70 percent of those accused of being narcotics violators are freed on bail for a period of 3 months to 1 year between the time of arrest and the time of trial. They are thus given the opportunity to go out and create more misery, generate more violence, commit more crimes while they are waiting to be tried for these same activities.

The same study showed that over 25 percent of the federally convicted narcotics violators were not even sentenced to jail. When permissive judges are more considerate of the pusher than they are of his victims, there is little incentive for heroin pushers to obey the law, and great incentive for them to violate it. This is an outrage. It is a danger to every law-abiding citizen, and I am confident that the vast majority of Americans will support immediate passage of the heroin trafficking legislation I will propose to the Congress next week.

This legislation will require Federal judges to consider the danger to the community before freeing on bail a suspect for heroin trafficking. That is something they cannot legally do now. It will require a minimum sentence of 5 years in prison for anyone convicted of selling heroin. It will require a minimum sentence of 10 years to life imprisonment for major traffickers in drugs. And for offenders with a prior conviction for a drug felony, those who persist in living off the suffering of others, it will require life imprisonment without parole.

This is tough legislation, but we must settle for nothing less. The time has come for soft-headed judges and probation officers to show as much concern for the rights of innocent victims of crime as they do for the rights of convicted criminals.

In recent days, there have been proposals to legalize the possession and the use of marijuana. I oppose the legalization of the sale, possession, or use of marijuana. The line against the use of dangerous drugs is now drawn on this side of marijuana. If we move the line to the other side and accept the use of this drug, how can we draw the line against other illegal drugs? Or will we slide into an acceptance of their use as well?[11]

While Gerald Ford was distracted from the drug war in the early days of his administration as he tried to increase confidence in the government following the Watergate scandal, he picked up the theme as his election drew near. In a September 1976 speech, he commented:

We all know, tragic as it is, as much as one-half of all street crime today is committed by drug addicts to support their habit. Since taking office, I have reorganized our programs and priorities to make maximum use of our anti-drug resources at the Federal level. I met with the heads of state of Mexico, Colombia, and Turkey to secure their cooperation in the international war on drugs. I proposed legislation which would close the loopholes that permit drug traffickers to prey on the young. I directed the Internal Revenue Service to reinstitute and emphasize a tax enforcement program aimed at high-level drug traffickers. Since then, the IRS, aided by the Drug Enforcement Administration, has identified over 375 suspected big-time pushers for intensive investigation and action. And I called for more than three-quarters of a billion dollars in a year, a single 12-month period, to finance the fight against drug abuse.

For every young person who dies of drug overuse—and there were almost 5,000 of them last year—there are thousands more who did not die but can only go through the motions of living. We are making progress. Total Federal seizures of drugs and arrests of drug traffickers are up sharply over previous years. Cooperation among Federal agencies is far, far better.

But our ability to deal with drugs depends, to a large extent, on the cooperation of other governments to work with us. Because Mexico today is the major source of heroin entering the United States, the first foreign head of state with whom I discussed narcotic-control cooperation was the President of Mexico. And last Friday, I met with the new President-elect of Mexico. He has assured me that during his 6-year term as President of that country, he will give the United States full cooperation in this problem. And the record shows that with the continuing and growing support of the Government of Mexico, we can drastically curtail this source of drugs in the next year, and in the next year.

I call upon States and local governments to move forward with us until we bring the drug traffic under control. And I believe as I see the response of this wonderful organization here, representing not only local but State and international chiefs of police, we have a great opportunity to work together to do the job for the people throughout this world, and let's do it.[12]

Although Jimmy Carter's administration is remembered for his advocacy of rehabilitation, treatment, and prevention programs and his suggestion that decriminalization of marijuana might be advisable, he certainly did not ignore the place of enforcement in his public rhetoric on the drug problem. In a set of remarks given to a group of reporters assembled in the White House briefing room, he commented:

This afternoon I have a statement to make about the drug abuse problem following which, Dr. Peter Bourne will be available to answer specific questions.

Today I'm sending Congress a message which expresses my strong concern about the crime and sickness and death caused by the abuse of drugs, including barbiturates and alcohol.

The estimated cost of drug abuse in this country is more than $15 billion per year. I'm ordering the Attorney General to concentrate on breaking the links between organized crime and drug traffic, to enhance cooperation among all law enforcement agencies, and to ensure more certain conviction and quick punishment for those who traffic in drugs.[13]

Known as "the Great Communicator," Ronald Reagan was often able to mix quite a number of themes (fear, concern, patriotism, idealism, and so on) in a single speech. For instance, in 1986, Reagan, joined by his wife Nancy in the West Hall of the White House, gave an address to the nation on their campaign against drug abuse. He began the speech in a hopeful, but cautionary tone:

America has accomplished so much in these last few years, whether it's been rebuilding our economy or serving the cause of freedom in the world. What we've been able to achieve has been done with your help—with us working together as a nation united. Now, we need your support again. Drugs are menacing our society. They're threatening our values and undercutting our institutions. They're killing our children.

From the beginning of our administration, we've taken strong steps to do something about this horror. Tonight I can report to you that we've made much progress. Thirty-seven Federal agencies are working together in a vigorous national effort, and by next year our spending for drug law enforcement will have more than tripled from its 1981 levels. We have increased seizures of illegal drugs. Shortages of marijuana are now being reported. Last year alone over 10,000 drug criminals were convicted and nearly $250 million of their assets were seized by the DEA, the Drug Enforcement Administration.

The president followed up by outlining some of the administration's recent accomplishments in the war on drugs, but then outlined new fears and concerns:

Despite our best efforts, illegal cocaine is coming into our country at alarming levels, and 4 to 5 million people regularly use it. Five hundred thousand Americans are hooked on heroin. One in twelve persons smokes marijuana regularly. Regular drug use is even higher among the age group 18 to 25—most likely just entering the workforce. Today there's a new epidemic: smokable cocaine, otherwise known as crack. It is an explosively destructive and often lethal substance which is crushing its users. It is an uncontrolled fire.

And drug abuse is not a so-called victimless crime. Everyone's safety is at stake when drugs and excessive alcohol are used by people on the highways or by those transporting our citizens or operating industrial equipment. Drug abuse costs you and your fellow Americans at least $60 billion a year.

After Nancy discussed her "just say no" campaign, the president outlined his recent plans for the war on drugs, including government employee drug testing, tougher laws for offenders, and increased funding. He then ended the speech on an uplifting, patriotic note:

In this crusade, let us not forget who we are. Drug abuse is a repudiation of everything America is. The destructiveness and human wreckage mock our heritage. Think for a moment how special it is to be an American. Can we doubt that only a divine providence placed this land, this island of freedom, here as a refuge for all those people on the world who yearn to breathe free? . . . As we mobilize for this national crusade, I'm mindful that drugs are a constant temptation for millions. Please remember this when your courage is tested: You are Americans. You're the product of the freest society mankind has ever known. No one, ever, has the right to destroy your dreams and shatter your life.[14]

Though hardly known as a great communicator, George H. W. Bush took up the mantle of the war on drugs rhetoric with gusto when he assumed office. At a 1990 anti-drug rally in Billings, Montana, the president framed the drug crusade as an urgent, unifying cause and emphasized the need for concerted action in the war on drug abuse:

But like all wars, we must be united in our efforts as a country and as a community. Parents, teachers, children, law enforcement officials must join as one. Business, labor, the professions—all must be a part of this crusade for a drug-free America. Each of you here today, by your presence, is sending the dealers of death a strong Montana message: We will not surrender our children. We will not surrender our community. Billings, Montana, is in this fight to win— and win it you will, win it we will. . . .

To win the war on drugs, we must have a united effort. This isn't Republican or Democrat or liberal or conservative: it's got to be bipartisan. But now, it's time for Congress to act. Our children, our communities, and our cops have waited long enough.[15]

While such dramatic speech on drug policy helped to define the Reagan and Bush administrations, Bill Clinton was not prepared to cede Republicans a monopoly on such themes. In a 1997 radio address, President Bill Clinton's appeal to government officials and the nation was reminiscent of Reagan's statements a decade earlier: "We must fight drugs on every front, on our streets and in our schools, at our borders and in our homes. Every American must accept this responsibility. There is no more insidious threat to a good future than illegal drugs. I'm counting on all of you to help us win the fight against them."[16] Two years later, he voiced a similar message of zero tolerance for drugs:

> At the end of this century, we've made great progress in our efforts to free our children and our communities from drugs and crime. As we begin a new century and a new millennium, we have an enormous opportunity to finish the job, to harness all the resources of the criminal justice system—our courts, our prosecutors, our prisons, our probation officers, our police—to break the drug habits of prisoners and people on parole and probation. We have to break this cycle. We have to give all these people a chance to be drug-free and to be productive citizens again. It is the only way we can ever, in the end, assure our children the future they deserve.[17]

While George W. Bush's presidency soon came to be dominated by other wars—the war on terrorism and the more traditional wars in Afghanistan and Iraq—he found time to address the drug problem and, in fact, was able to tie the drug problem and terrorism together on occasion. In a 2005 speech in McLean, Virginia, he incorporated both into speech defending the Patriot Act:

> Let me give you some examples of how Federal prosecutors and law enforcement agents have used the PATRIOT Act to get results. Mike Battle, the former U.S. Attorney for the Western District of New York, is with us. Mike helped prosecute the Lackawanna Six terror cell. See, there was a terror cell existing in the United States of America. And Mike and law enforcement officials there in the summer of 2001 started investigating the Lackawanna Six. But they had to set up two separate investigations, a criminal investigation for drug crimes and a separate intelligence investigation for terror activity. And agents from the two investigations did not discuss their findings with each other.

Then Congress passed the PATRIOT Act, and the two sides started sharing information. See, prior to the PATRIOT Act, parts of the same FBI office couldn't discuss a case with each other. And as a result of information sharing, the agents discovered that the suspects had attended an Al Qaida training camp in Afghanistan. The prosecutor used the information to build a convincing case, and today, all six of the Lackawanna folks are in Federal prison. In other words, the PATRIOT Act worked. We've got hard-working people in the field, and so we gave the people tools—simple tools—that said, "Here, this will enable you to better do your job." You can't ask people on the frontline of the war on terror to protect the American people and then not give them the tools necessary to do so.

Carol Lam is with us. She's the U.S. Attorney from the Southern District of California. The information-sharing provisions in the PATRIOT Act helped Carol and her team connect the dots in an Al Qaida drugs-for-weapons plot. They put together such a strong case that two defendants admitted their plans to sell drugs for Stinger missiles and then sell those missiles to the Taliban. They're now in prison, thanks to Carol's good work and thanks to the ability for prosecutors and law enforcement to use the tools of the PATRIOT Act to better protect the American people.[18]

Discussion

Presidents make public pronouncements on the drug problem that blend messages of eternal vigilance, cooperation against a common enemy, and threat to self, family, and community. These are all images and themes associated with wartime rhetoric. The war on drugs metaphor is itself part of a series of war metaphors employed by presidents, from Lyndon Johnson's "war on poverty" to Gerald Ford's "war on inflation" and the current "war on terrorism." Metaphors like these often embed tenets usually reserved for traditional wars: the idea that the policy campaigns can be unequivocally won or lost; the conception of a threatening entity or "Other" (although its identity is not as straightforward as in traditional warfare). The war metaphor excludes alternative ideas and polarizes groups who question the crusade (Elwood 1994, 23). Presidents employ the symbolism of war to gain leverage in promoting their policies and raise the stakes for other policy actors.

Indeed, the war metaphor permeates many areas of political and social life but resonates especially in the case of crime. It forms a basis for arguments about governance (Simon 2007). Criminologists see the war metaphor as tapping into a latent populism (Steinert 2003). In practical terms, this is because bureaucrats figure out how to apply a rule ("arrest") to a situation ("that guy") they encounter by figuring out how similar the two are, and they do so by "reasoning by analogy and metaphor" (March and Olsen 1989, 25). Functionally, at the level of the bureaucrat, this is how the war metaphor resonates.

Likewise, what the president achieves by using rhetoric in the case of the war on drugs is probably not very different than what they would achieve in the case of other issues were they to decide to "go public" in the same way. Essentially, the president attempts to win the hearts and minds of the American people and other political actors. One difference in our approach is that, whereas most see presidents as often going public to move the public and Congress, we push the debate over presidential power in another direction by arguing that presidential rhetoric can change how field agents implement policies, how they enforce drug laws. But we also emphasize a second difference: in the war on drugs, presidents have sought to define the terms of debate over policy, and in doing so they have reinforced (and probably extended) existing social constructions about drug use and drug users that go back to the country's founding. Of course, this second difference strengthens the likelihood that presidents will be successful in shaping the behavior of public agencies seeking both to serve the president and to enforce the law: to do what they "ought to do." In these ways, then, such public appeals have important consequences for presidential leadership and American social policy.

Recall that our purpose here is to examine how presidents reach across time and space to change the behavior of agents in the field. The data shown in this chapter help paint a picture of three aspects of that problem. The first is that presidents allocate different amounts of their rhetoric, of their attention to different policies on the agenda, and that those allocations change over time. The second is that the content of that allocation (what presidents actually say) largely refers to an enforcement-based approach to the drugs problem. It taps into a social construction that emphasizes the "dangerous other"; it helps build that construction, too. Finally, these messages are part of a complicated policy arena, a political context, that presents implementing agents with a range of possible influences.

Those agents wield the power of the state. We now turn to three vignettes, each built on data exercises that ask how and when field agents respond to the widely varying levels of attention presidents have paid to the war on drugs in the public rhetoric. Our first vignette comes from the case of the primary investigatory agency for drugs crimes, the DEA. Does the president, through his or her use of the bully pulpit, affect the discretionary pursuit of targets in the war on drugs?

CHAPTER FIVE

Presidential Policy Leadership and Federal Enforcement

The Drug Enforcement Administration

O ur claim is that presidents lead through public rhetoric, which means that we can view the modern war on drugs through the lens of presidential attempts to use rhetoric to shape politics, policy, and the administration of the law. This is the first of three chapters in which we consider this theory of how presidents can shape governance and the implementation of policy by examining the enforcement of the modern war on drugs. The purpose of these chapters is to test this claim empirically, in three distinct settings where policy is implemented to observe the dynamics of presidential rhetorical leadership across a variety of political and administrative contexts.

We begin with the president's influence on the direction of the front line in the federal government's drug war: the Drug Enforcement Administration (DEA). Our focus is on the president's ability to overcome significant management hurdles when he or she uses the bully pulpit to set the agenda and guide the enforcement efforts of the DEA. Of course, the president's public rhetoric and efforts at setting the policy agenda compete with other factors for influencing DEA narcotics enforcement. We show evidence, though, that the DEA does respond to the president's public rhetoric—in other words, that enforcement rises when the president shifts attention to narcotics and falls when the president addresses other issues—and that the effects of presidential rhetoric are robust to the inclusion of other external and internal causes of narcotics enforcement. The DEA responds to executive policy priorities, despite the significant geographic and social distances that separate the chief executive and the field agents who both serve him or her and carry out the law.

The DEA: The President's Agency for Fighting Drugs and Enforcing the Law

As part of a larger reorganization plan, President Richard Nixon sought in 1973 to streamline and strengthen the various federal agencies involved in narcotics enforcement. Executive Order 11727 brought about a new "superagency" to lead the way: the Drug Enforcement Administration. The main purpose of the new agency was to organize a more efficient effort against narcotics that also would heighten the profile of the federal policy initiatives Nixon believed would "turn the corner" on the drug problem. The administration also hoped that reorganization and the development of a new agency would put aside problems perceived to stem from rampant competition between the agencies involved in narcotics enforcement, thus helping move federal efforts toward cooperation. The new agency was formed under the Department of Justice, but it was anything but novel. As described in chapter 3, the new DEA's regulatory ancestors dated back to the Bureau of Prohibition; creating a new agency meant pulling together agents and other personnel from the Bureau of Narcotics and Dangerous Drugs, the Narcotics Advance Research Management Team, the U.S. Customs Service, the Central Intelligence Agency, the Office of National Narcotics Intelligence, and the Office of Drug Abuse Law Enforcement. Moreover, some of those agencies remained active players in enforcement efforts against the use of narcotics in the United States. The DEA, though, was designed to be the premier drug control "superagency" of the executive branch.

The DEA is an enforcer. Its chief mission is to investigate and bring to justice those selling or using drugs. It also facilitates and coordinates the efforts of other agencies ranging from state and local authorities to officials in foreign countries. Over the years, though, its role has grown to encompass a wide range of activities, some of which fall well outside the traditional enforcement efforts like investigation and apprehension. Some of these include the diversion control of pharmaceuticals and chemicals, crop eradication and suppression, and educational and preventive programs like the Teens In Prevention program. We want to be clear that the DEA's activities go well beyond enforcement through arrests; even the DEA designates as important other forms of control that are consistent with its core mission of combating narcotics.

More important, the DEA investigates and apprehends drug dealers and users by proactively seeking them out. Their enforcement activities are not based on a formal baseline of demand for enforcement; unlike the traditional enforcement entities of state and local police, where agents react primarily to client reports and complaints, the DEA targets narcotics trafficking. Local police organizations worry about their "clearance rate": the proportion of citizen reports or complaints they clear or solve by arrest. In contrast, the DEA neither investigates and clears reports from citizens, nor is there a defined referral mechanism. Arrests come from undercover and surveillance work ("sting" operations). The DEA largely defines its own caseload, which makes its actions and effort levels fungible. In practical terms, this ability to define a caseload means that the DEA experiences significant organizational slack, that is, the amount of resources the organization holds compared to what it must do in order to maintain its existence (Cyert and March 1963; Cohen, March, and Olsen 1972). Arrests are measurable, but the question of how many arrests "ought to be made" remains.

There is good reason to believe that many at the DEA disagree over the efficacy of arrest and prosecution for combating drug use. As discussed in chapter 3, at the time Nixon formed the DEA, demand reduction was more central to the national anti-drug strategy than it was in later administrations (Nixon's Special Action Office for Drug Abuse Prevention was located within the executive office of the president). The DEA, like others in the war on drugs, does not uniformly support enforcement as the only solution compared to a balanced approach to fighting drugs. For instance, Robert Stutman, special agent for the DEA during the Reagan and Bush administrations, argued: "The RAND Corporation has done two or three studies showing that dollars we spend on treatment and prevention give us a far greater return than dollars we spend on enforcement. The general point is that we have never adopted the strategy that a lot of people think is truly a winning strategy. No one has yet demonstrated that enforcement will ever win the war on drugs."[1] DEA Administrator Jack Lawn, who served under both Reagan and Bush, recalled an exchange during the 1980s with Senator Joseph Biden:

> He asked me if I was satisfied with the budget because I had been nominated
> by a Republican president, and he of course was on the other side of the aisle,
> he said, "Do you have enough?" I said, "Well I have enough for this year, but

we will have to build more jails, because we're going to arrest more people, we're going to convict more people, we're going to seize more drugs, we're going to seize more assets. But until someone gets serious about education, prevention and treatment, we're the last line of resistance." And Joe Biden said, "Jack, that's heresy coming from a law enforcement officer." I said, "No, ask law enforcement people. The other components are indeed missing."   .

Such statements do not mean that DEA agents or administrators advocate abdicating their legal responsibility to investigate, arrest, or seize operations; these have remained the agency's core functions. The problem has more to do with the age-old debate over how drug enforcement agencies ought to do their jobs. The DEA's enforcement mechanism is highly fungible; it is proactive in its caseload. Just as the BNDD faced the question of how to measure its performance—indeed, what was the best way to reduce the sale of and demand for drugs on the street—so has the DEA struggled with the proper balance between prevention and enforcement in the nation's drug war. Those perceptions color what drug agents consider to be the appropriate intensity of investigation and apprehension, which historically has been reflected in agency enforcement outputs.

The effect of ambivalence about the intensity of enforcement is compounded by the way responsibility has historically been divided across a broad variety of police departments. Narcotics policy has seen long-running battles between the FBI and the DEA and between the DEA and Customs. Federal agencies work cases that happen in cities and towns all over the country but that also cross state and national borders. Drug cases require both broad and deep enforcement effort: they require working across borders (both political and organizational) and intensive effort to breach the defenses of large, complex drug trafficking organizations. When there is no natural "baseline" for enforcement performance, agents face a range of competing alternatives. It is in this kind of environment that we believe president rhetoric can serve an important clarifying role. Presidential rhetoric can explain what DEA agents "ought to do" about drugs by constructing the natural targets of their enforcement efforts.

Breaking Down Agency Barriers by Public Appeals

How can the president govern this kind of agency? His or her main direct link to the frontline agents in the war on drugs is the DEA administrator, whom he or she nominates with the advice and consent of the Senate. The administrator relies on his or her own deputy administrator and a core group of high-level administrative officers (a chief of operations, chief inspector, chief of intelligence, and so on)—all located in Washington, D.C. However, virtually all enforcement flows out of the many field offices. The problem, then, is to lead a decentralized, independent group of field agents spread throughout the states (as well as agents in international offices). Having field offices brings the presence of the federal agency to the far reaches of the country, but it also proscribes meaningful executive oversight: the president and his or her staff simply cannot closely monitor how policy is implemented around the world (see Wilson 1978). Indeed, in 1989 DEA headquarters was almost moved out of Washington to Arkansas or Mississippi; in the end, Attorney General Edwin Meese chose to keep headquarters close to his offices. This suggests a tension: the president can enhance his or her direct control over DEA headquarters only at the expense of weakening the control of headquarters over its own field agents; conversely, enhancing the control of headquarters over its field agents will weaken the president's direct control over the DEA. This situation causes us to expect a net loss of oversight of policy by the Oval Office (Whitford 2002).

Moreover, the president appoints the top DEA officials (and can remove them), and he or she can do this on the basis of ideological congruence or political loyalty if he or she pleases. On the other hand, none of the field agents and few Washington-based policy officers are appointed. They are career civil servants who obtain their positions through a competitive, nonpartisan process and can only be removed for cause on specific legal grounds after a full hearing (Nelson 1989). This makes direct executive oversight and control rather tenuous. Unlike other government field agents like forest rangers, whose discretion is limited by soft incentives or cultural binding, drug agents have always been notoriously independent (Kaufman 1960; Valentine 2004). On one hand, the comments of DEA's Stutman and Lawn indicate that not all in the agency believe in the efficacy of enforcement and the overall anti-narcotics initiative; on the other hand, narcotics agents spend a lot of time with actual drug traffickers. None of these features of the DEA cause great certainty that the DEA sees clearly what it "ought to do."

Given these features, how can presidents affect how these dispersed and autonomous agents implement policy? Presidents already use rhetoric for political and agenda-setting reasons, and we argue that the president can use public rhetoric for executive reasons as well. Does the president's public rhetoric provide guidance for agencies about the administration's policy vision? Does the DEA's behavior reflect the president's attention to the war on drugs?

We recognize that agencies such as the DEA are the target of many sources of policy guidance or influence beyond any motivations held by DEA field agents. Agencies must balance many competing sources of policy advice when deciding how to implement policy. Moreover, any one source may provide competing guidance. For example, an agency reacting to congressional guidance will likely encounter many signals about what the agency should do, since legislatures are composed of many factions. In contrast, the president speaks with (comparatively) one voice and is elected by a single national constituency, which facilitates a more consistent, harmonious, and discernable policy message; that message may even have the support of the nation.

Our position is that the direct and personalized nature of the president's public appeals can reinforce executive governance of the bureaucracy if his or her message reaches agents with the help of the media (Edwards and Wayne 1994). The president's public statements are directed to many but leave less room for reinterpretation. Of course, agency officials might try to reinterpret those statements, but the public nature of the statements makes it easier for others to challenge them when they stray too far from the publicly stated positions of the president. Public statements also bring the cachet of the Oval Office. They emphasize the skills and attributes that brought him or her to the White House through political campaigning. It is safe to assume that presidential statements carry more weight than internal memoranda or agency directives.

At the level of the field agent, policy campaigns provide guidance and reinforce beliefs about what they ought to do when they implement policy on a day-to-day basis. We suspect this is especially true for those agents who have mixed feelings about the efficacy of the agency's policy direction or who have become complacent in their efforts when faced with competing views (from the public or other actors like the media). As an example, consider Ronald Reagan's statements at a 1988 White House ceremony honoring law enforcement officers slain in the war on drugs. He first paid tribute to the deceased agents and recounted the circumstances of their deaths in graphic detail. Then the president shifted his comments to his administration's achievements in enforcement, noting that drug convictions had doubled since 1979. He followed that with a historical and political perspective on the drug war:

> You see, we too often forget how the level of drug abuse reached the proportions that it did. Back in the 1960's and 1970's, America crossed a deadly line.

The use of illegal drugs became not just condoned but even celebrated by a permissive cultural establishment whose slogan was "Just Say Yes." It was a time when all the restrictions on personal behavior were under attack. Some liberal politicians decried our prohibitions on drugs as conservative, moralistic, reactionary, and old-fashioned—or simply remained silent that there even was a drug problem. . . . And tragically, countless thousands of young lives were needlessly destroyed. The truth was that drugs are killers, but for nearly a generation that vital message was ignored by a whole group of people who should have known better. The leaders of that destructive generation remain the forgotten accomplices in the epidemic of illegal drug use; they cannot escape blame when a law enforcement officer dies in the battle.[2]

He followed this with an impassioned argument for the administration's proposed Criminal Justice Reform Act, which (among other things) provided for capital punishment in the case of death resulting from drug dealing or the murder of a DEA officer. He noted, "When drug syndicates commit murder, our sympathy should be with the victims, not the killers. It's time for the Congress to pass this bill and make it law. It's time for us to send our own message to people who kill cops."

Reagan's public message did not involve a point-by-point elaboration of what he wanted in terms of enforcement levels in the following year, yet the substance of the signal was clear: his administration supports strong enforcement actions and seeks to promote an approach to fighting drug use based on law and order. His message provided policy direction and showed that the executive office encouraged and supported enforcement agents. An enforcement agent would not interpret that message as indicating that investigation and prosecution levels were too high or that the administration wanted to pursue other strategies for combating drug use. The president makes such statements in public forums for largely political and agenda-setting reasons, but doing so also works to galvanize agencies and prove to them that their actions are consistent with the administration's goals and priorities.

Our primary hypothesis is that the DEA's field agents adjust their enforcement activities in reaction to the policy signals the president sends about the war on drugs. Specifically, we test the hypothesis that enforcement levels (arrests) move with presidential attention to the war on drugs in his public statements. In the next section we describe our research design for assessing this claim and also review some alternative causes that may drive DEA enforcement.

Research Design

Introduction

The nineteen DEA field divisions are scattered across the fifty states; each state has at least one field office.[3] Since reconciliation of the DEA with the FBI in the 1980s, a special agent in charge (SAC), a career civil service employee, heads each division. The SACs report to the DEA administrator and Deputy administrator, who are located in Washington, D.C. The DEA administrator can transfer SACs and other DEA field agents but cannot demote or fire them without cause.

We treat the states as our units of analysis rather than the field divisions. We use states rather than the boundaries of the DEA field divisions since those boundaries have changed over time, and the DEA has not made the historical boundaries of the divisions available; this is similar to approaches used to study enforcement behavior at the Internal Revenue Service (Scholz and Wood 1998). We revisit this issue below in our description of DEA staffing data, which are also not available at the division level for national security reasons.[4]

DEA Enforcement

Our measure of DEA enforcement is the number of annual DEA drug arrests per 100,000 state citizens, which we then transform as a natural logarithm. Figure 5.1 shows the cross-sectional distribution of the aggregated level of DEA arrests in the United States from 1980 to 1998.[5] We see that the annual arrest rates trend upward during the first term of the Reagan administration and then rise abruptly in Reagan's second term. We describe below how the shift in 1985 is due to the forfeiture provisions that were part of Reagan's 1984 omnibus crime legislation initiative.

More important, DEA arrest rates vary substantially across the states. We might expect that most of the fifty states would have low arrest rates with a few having high rates (for example, Florida due to the interdiction efforts we noted in chapter 3). In fact the opposite seems true: most states have higher arrest rates.

Our key explanatory variable reflects the degree to which a president makes the war on drugs a policy priority in his or her public speeches. Our variable, described in chapter 4, is the portion of presidential public statements that refer to narcotics. Presidents work within finite schedules, so decisions about the allocation of valuable time on speeches and appearances on a specific policy initiative such as the war on drugs provide insight into how central that issue is to their overall policy agenda. For the DEA, it serves as a key signal available to employees

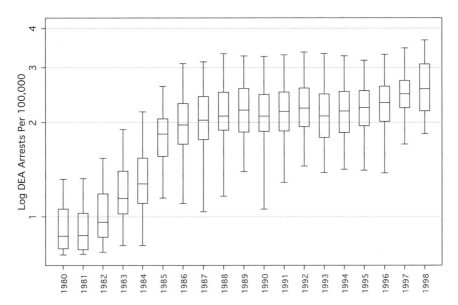

Figure 5.1. DEA Arrests per 100,000 State Citizens

about the extent to which the president values their enforcement efforts vis-à-vis other strategies for solving the narcotics problem.

Competing Causes

Of course, presidential policy signals are only one potential cause of DEA enforcement efforts. Agencies may respond to a broad array of governmental and private actors, each with its own priorities for how the agency makes policy (Waterman, Rouse, and Wright 1998; Whitford 2002). These competing causes also influence implementation, either by structuring the agencies internal dynamics or by shaping the agency's policymaking environment (Noll 1985). We offer several factors that may also affect DEA enforcement efforts. We present detailed descriptions of how we conceptualize and measure all variables in appendix A.

Enforcement Demand

The DEA does not work through referrals or reports from citizens or other governmental actors in the same way that other enforcement agencies do. In a typical situation, DEA operations do not clear or solve reported crimes through arrest but rather engage in covert investigations (for instance, undercover work or surveillance) in the search for finding infractions and making arrests. We start by asking whether DEA field agents perceive a caseload within their jurisdiction. Field agents live and work in local areas; they try to understand the nature and intensity of the drug problem, the circumstances in which they live and work, and the extent of drug use. We estimate this perceived caseload (or implicit task environment) by constructing a proxy measure for the extent and intensity of drug use within a given state. Of course, determining the degree of actual drug use in a state (as distinct from arrests for drug use) is a challenge. Clearly, field agents build impressions and take information from their interactions with users and traffickers. We prefer a measure that has face validity, is quantifiable, and, importantly, is limited in its dependence on enforcement activities. In contrast, state enforcement efforts obviously reflect not only actual use but local enforcement discretion as well. Our measure reflects the scale of drug markets in the most unfortunate but also objectively observable consequence of such activity: deaths attributable to drug abuse. The indicator is the annual number of citizen drug-related deaths in a state per 100,000 state citizens as reflected in the CDC's mortality database (described in chapter 4).[6] We expect DEA enforcement to be greater when there is a greater incidence of deaths from drug abuse.

Competing National Signals

While the president has unparalleled access to the public and has the advantage of speaking with a single voice, it is a mistake to think that the president is the only national actor whose signals field agents might respond to. We reconsider the traditional position that field agents will respond to the other major actor in our system of separated powers, the agenda signals coming from Congress (see Moe 1987). Members of Congress also have finite time and opportunities to spend on issues, so time spent on one issue means less time spent on another. We estimate the policy priorities of Congress by focusing on their relative attention to drug policy issues in their hearings. Our measure of Congressional drug policy attention is drawn from the Congressional Hearings Data Set compiled by Baumgartner and Jones, part of their larger Policy Agendas Project (Jones and Baumgartner 2005). This measure is the annual percentage of congressional hearings devoted to the drug problem. We expect that as Congress signals its interest in the drug problem by paying more attention to it in its deliberations, the DEA will intensify its enforcement efforts.

We also want to take into account the entity some have come to regard as the "fourth branch" of government: the national media (Cater 1959; Cook 1993). Media outlets exercise extraordinary discretion in determining what news is deemed important enough to report in its finite journalistic space, and they also provide a conceptual "frame" that helps define and interpret the meaning and construction of phenomena and events (such as drug use) as important social problems (Beckett 1994, 428–430). We expect that as media outlets come to pay more attention to drug use as a social concern, DEA field agents respond by stepping up their enforcement efforts. We measure media emphasis on the drug problem as the percentage of stories appearing in the *New York Times* that deal with the issue in a given year. This measure is also drawn from the Baumgartner and Jones Policy Agendas Project.

Local Policy Influences

As noted, DEA agents do not live and work within a policy vacuum. They perform their jobs and live their lives like other citizens: within the social context of their community. As a result, they may be affected by and take into account the proclivities of the people they encounter, and that changes how they see the nature and direction of their mission. Furthermore, convictions, which are the ultimate outputs of their work, are part of a long sequence of policy decision points, some of which will be influenced by other local and regional actors (local federal judges and juries, for example). We address two local influences: public sentiment and elite ideology. We first consider regional public sentiment on the importance of the drug problem. This measure reflects the annual proportion of a region's respondents who think that not enough resources are being spent to combat the drug problem. We also take into account the policy preferences of state elites. Our measure here is an ideology index of primary state political institutions (Berry et al. 1998); this is a general "liberal-conservative" approximation of elite ideology of the state in which the DEA field agents work. While the drug war enjoys support from both Democrats and Republicans, many consider the Republican Party and conservatives more inclined to pursue approaches to the drug problem predicated on law and order (Meier 1992, 43). We expect that more people saying that the government is not doing enough on drugs, or working in a state with generally conservative political elites, will increase DEA enforcement.

Internal Dynamics

Finally, we account for internal features and characteristics of the DEA that may change over time or locale. Of course, the presidential branch might try to change enforcement activities of the DEA by adjusting staffing or appointing like-minded leaders.

As we discussed in chapter 3, agency budgets may not accurately reflect the availability of resources to the agency on a year-to-year basis. Instead, we examine the impact of a more direct measure of the agency's enforcement resources: staff levels. Cases require people to make them. The substantial personnel hours required for the investigation and apprehension of suspects make the agency sensitive to adjustments in staffing (whether up or down), which may have ramifications for enforcement levels. As noted, state-level measures are unavailable due to national security restrictions. The models we present below include the national total of DEA staff, including field agents; this time series is correlated with DEA budgets at $\rho=0.97$.

Presidents may also seek to change enforcement through their power of appointment. DEA field agents and field-level managers (SACs) are career bureaucrats; however, the president appoints the DEA administrator, who controls the tenor and tone of how the agency implements the law. Presidents would prefer administrators who closely match their own preferences on the agency's mission. This is complicated by incomplete information on the part of the executive as to the policy preferences of the appointee. We capture the impact of individual administrator characteristics by including fixed effects for the tenures of the DEA administrators in our study: from Peter Bensinger (appointed by Jimmy Carter) through Thomas Constantine (appointed by Bill Clinton).[7]

Finally, we account for the potential effects of the federal forfeiture amendments, outlined in chapter 3, which were designed to enhance federal and state enforcement capabilities in the war on drugs. We include an intercept shift for the years following the passage of the first of the forfeiture amendments to the federal criminal code proposed by the Reagan administration and passed by Congress in 1984.

Estimation

Our data analysis includes the variables described here to assess the independent effect of presidential rhetoric on the war on drugs on DEA enforcement efforts. We model the causal relationship by using a version of generalized linear models, specifically generalized estimating equations (GEE), which are appropriate for panel data (Zeger, Liang, and Albert 1988).[8] The main advantages of the GEE approach are the availability of flexible error correlation structures, robust standard errors, and alternative distributional assumptions. This procedure is appropriate for either cross-section–dominant or time series–dominant data.

Most importantly, this procedure yields parameter estimates that are uncontaminated by the effects of heteroskedastic and autocorrelated errors. We discuss this estimation approach in more detail in appendix D.[9]

Results

Tables 5.1, 5.2, and 5.3 show three different models of DEA arrest rates. They represent three different specifications: one includes fixed effects for the DEA administrators, one includes an intercept shift for the adoption of enhanced federal forfeiture rules, and the third table shows a specification that includes both.

Table 5.1 shows the GEE estimates of the coefficients for the competing causes of DEA enforcement described above. These results provide credible evidence of presidential administrative leadership through public rhetoric. First, we find no evidence of an accounting relationship between our measure of the baseline demand for enforcement, state per capita drug deaths, and DEA arrest rates.

Table 5.1.   GEE Estimates for DEA Arrests per 100,000 State Citizens
(Including Fixed Effects for Administrators)

Variables	Coefficient	SE
Drug Deaths	−0.0019	0.0159
Presidential Rhetoric	0.0046	0.0016***
Congressional Hearings	0.0831	0.0151***
Local Priority Opinion	−0.0001	0.0016
Local Institutional Ideology	0.0010	0.0007
Press Coverage	−0.0138	0.0116
Ln DEA Staff Capacity	22.8919	2.0727***
Bensinger	−0.1223	0.0255***
Lawn	0.3303	0.0413***
Bonner	0.2334	0.0564***
Constantine	0.3503	0.0592***
Constant	−260.8157	23.6884***
Observations		854
Link Function		Identity
Family		Gaussian
Working Correlation Matrix		AR (1)
ρ		0.89
Wald χ^2 (11)		813.79***
Scale Parameter		0.1957

*p < 0.10 (two-tailed tests)   **p < 0.05   ***p < 0.01

Table 5.2.   GEE Estimates for DEA Arrests per 100,000 State Citizens
(Including Intercept Shift for Forfeiture)

Variables	Coefficient	SE
Drug Deaths	0.0088	0.0155
Presidential Rhetoric	0.0032	0.0015**
Congressional Hearings	0.1024	0.0143***
Local Priority Opinion	−0.0009	0.0016
Local Institutional Ideology	0.0008	0.0007
Press Coverage	−0.0023	0.0107
Ln DEA Staff Capacity	21.9777	1.5318***
Post-Forfeiture Period	0.3398	0.0413***
Constant	−250.4201	17.5183***
Observations		854
Link Function		Identity
Family		Gaussian
Working Correlation Matrix		AR (1)
ρ		0.89
Wald χ^2 (11)		573.46***
Scale Parameter		0.1922

*$p < 0.10$ (two-tailed tests)   **$p < 0.05$ ***$p < 0.01$

Instead, DEA agents react to presidential attention to the drug war. Enforcement is higher when the president speaks about the war on drugs; it falls when the president turns to other policy topics.[10]

Our focus is on how the president can use rhetoric to shift the behavior of the field agents who implement narcotics policy. We offer a hypothetical to describe the magnitude of that effect. Suppose that the president had to choose between making no statements and maximizing his or her attention to the war on drugs. To assess the predicted effects of this choice on DEA arrests, we calculated the expected arrest rate (log arrests per 100,000 population) at the state level when presidential rhetoric was at its minimum in the data (zero) and when it was at its maximum (twenty; all other variables were held at their means).[11] We then calculated the number of expected arrests for each state in each year of our data given its population. Recall that our dependent variable is the arrest rate for each state, yet for impact we want the expected number of arrests for each state. We predict the arrest rate, adjust it for the population, and then estimate the number of arrests at the state level. The total impact across our sample for a president who chooses to maximize his or her public rhetoric on the war on drugs was an

Table 5.3.   GEE Estimates for DEA Arrests per 100,000 State Citizens
(Including Fixed Effects and Intercept Shift)

Variables	Coefficient	SE
Drug Deaths	−0.0019	0.0159
Presidential Rhetoric	0.0046	0.0016***
Congressional Hearings	0.0832	0.0151***
Local Priority Opinion	−0.0009	0.0016
Local Institutional Ideology	0.0010	0.0007
Press Coverage	−0.0138	0.0117
Ln DEA Staff Capacity	22.8919	2.0727***
Post-Forfeiture Period	0.3503	0.0597***
Bensinger	−0.1223	0.0255***
Lawn	−0.0199	0.0441
Bonner	−0.1169	0.0235***
Constant	−260.8157	23.6884***
Observations		854
Link Function		Identity
Family		Gaussian
Working Correlation Matrix		AR (1)
ρ		0.89
Wald χ^2 (11)		813.79***
Scale Parameter		0.1957

*$p < 0.10$ (two-tailed tests)   **$p < 0.05$ ***$p < 0.01$

expected increase of 4,242 arrests (aggregated across all the states and all the years in our sample), which means 223 more arrests per year on average. In comparison, most of the states, 61 percent of our state-level observations, report fewer than 220 arrests. The total number of 4,242 is greater than the total number of arrests in any state in our sample other than California in 1998; it is equal to all of the arrests for five states (Alaska, Montana, New Hampshire, North Dakota, and South Dakota) for the nineteen-year time span we observe. The president has the power to change the enforcement behavior of DEA field agents if he or she maximizes his or her attention in his or her public rhetoric to the war on drugs.

Figure 5.2 shows the dot plot of the estimated impacts of the president maximizing his or her drug war rhetoric at the state level. Not surprisingly, the largest impacts given the hypothetical offered here are for California, New York, and Texas. There is a gap in the estimated impacts between these three states and the next several, which include Florida, Pennsylvania, Illinois, and Ohio. The estimated impacts for several of the states are marginal, namely states with low populations

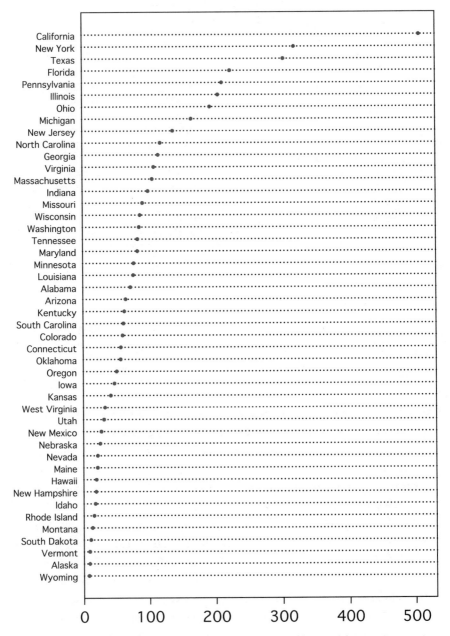

Figure 5.2. Expected Additional DEA Arrests, Assuming the President Maximizes Drug Rhetoric

like Wyoming, Alaska, Vermont, and South Dakota. Given the nature of the dependent variable as an incidence rate, of course, the impacts depend explicitly on population.

We also addressed a second hypothetical: a movement by the president from a low level of drug rhetoric (the first quartile or 25th percentile of the rhetoric variable's distribution, or 3.2) to a high level (the third quartile or 75th percentile, or 13.5). Figure 5.3 shows that the impact of this shift, which really represents a moderate increase in the amount of drug rhetoric by the president, is about half that of the first hypothetical. The ranking of the impact across the states, however, is roughly the same: California, New York, and Texas show the largest impact, while less populous states would experience lower impacts.

To be sure, presidential rhetorical leadership is not the only external signal that sways DEA enforcement. Policy signals emanating from Congress (for example, hearings on drug issues) also changed DEA enforcement activities. The magnitude of that influence actually exceeds that of presidential rhetoric. Still, executive rhetoric has a statistically significant and substantively important influence on the implementation agendas of the DEA offices located across the country.

We find few other effects for external policy cues on DEA policy outputs. We fail to observe DEA responsiveness to local opinion, expressed either as citizens' perceptions on the extent of the drug problem or state political elite ideology. National media attention also has no bearing on DEA enforcement activities.

We do find important effects for other pathways of executive influence: staffing, presidential appointments, and forfeiture incentives. First, a common criticism of agencies is that they do not readily respond to changes in executive political preferences. We find that implementation moves as the DEA administrator changes. In table 5.1, the dichotomous variables indicating the tenure of respective DEA administrators suggest that enforcement fell during Bensinger's tenure, increased during Lawn's time, and rose during the terms of Bonner and Constantine; when we account for forfeiture in table 5.2, we find that the sign of Bensinger's effect remains negative and significantly different from zero, but we lose confidence in the Lawn effect and the sign of the Bonner effect is now negative. Taken together, the evidence here is that during Bensinger's time DEA produced fewer cases (as described in chapter 3).

Second, the drug forfeiture amendments to the federal criminal code in the mid-1980s led to increased enforcement activity in the country's DEA offices. These amendments to the criminal code were part of Ronald Reagan's heavily promoted law-and-order legislative agenda, and they provided field agents with

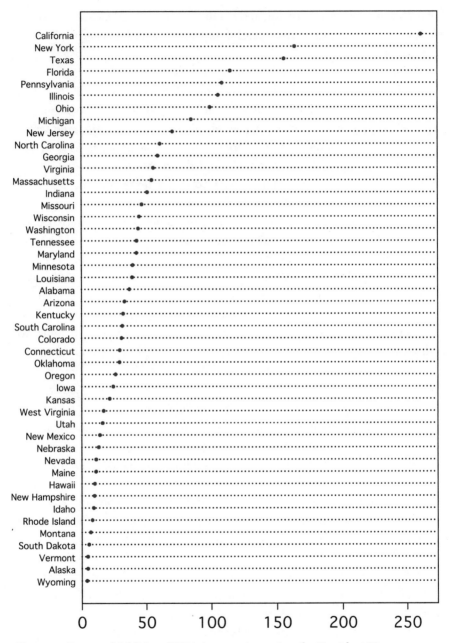

Figure 5.3. Expected Additional DEA Arrests, Assuming the President Uses
Moderate Drug Rhetoric

tangible incentives to pursue an enforcement-oriented approach to the narcotics problem. Finally, staffing increases in the agency are strongly associated with higher arrests, suggesting that enforcement outputs are responsive to personnel capabilities.

Discussion

Our findings reveal prima facie evidence that the president can use his or her public rhetoric both to shape the policy agenda and to change the behavior of field agents. Public rhetoric transmits policy signals, helps enforcement agents make sense of their role in government, and guides future action.

This approach is a marked departure from past ways of thinking about the power of presidential rhetoric, where the focus has been on mobilizing public sentiment or gaining leverage with Congress. Rhetoric can have an additional role—until now, a largely understudied one—if the president seeks to expand his or her opportunities to change how large, dispersed federal bureaucracies implement the law. DEA agents represent the front line in the war on drugs. Given the sequential nature of the criminal justice system, DEA agents stand as powerful gatekeepers: their enforcement decisions decide what cases enter the system and affect the range of decisions that other actors (like prosecutors) encounter when working downstream from the decision to charge. In the chapters that follow, we examine whether we can observe this effect for other actors, who are perhaps more insulated from political overseers and thus independent, and who also implement the president's policy agenda.

We want to emphasize, though, the importance of this vignette alone for our evolving understanding of the state's power to enforce its laws in large, diverse democracies with varying preferences and political divisions. Presidents always struggle with their ability to gain control over unwieldy bureaucracies. Narcotics control, as a policy arena, only makes that problem worse. Difficulties in monitoring action come from location, and the temptations for an agent to look the other way must be enormous. Kaufman's famous forest ranger suffered from this problem when deciding whether to cut timber; how can the problem not be worse in the case of narcotics interdiction? Indeed, the stories told in chapter 3 only serve to emphasize how many presidents found it difficult to administer the narcotics control agencies; even the FBI wanted no part of the DEA's business because it did not trust its own agents to resist the temptations.

But presidents dating back to Nixon understood the power that could come with a DEA, although they may not all have seen it as having the same purpose. The presumption, it seems, has been that having an agency like it is better than not having one, but overseeing it is another question altogether. The models shown in this paper may not lay those fears entirely to rest, but they certainly provide some hope. Presidential agenda-setting shaped the agency's behavior in predictable ways; the impact is significant within the parameters of what the agency actually could do. The normative side of this is left untested, since we do not know whether the social benefits of responsiveness to the bully pulpit outweigh its costs. In the case of the DEA, we have identified the impact of a mechanism of the administrative presidency, the social value of which will always depend on the president's preferences.

CHAPTER SIX

For the People

*The U.S. Attorneys and the Impact of Executive Signals
on Prosecutorial Priorities*

The U.S. Attorneys, vital to the executive branch's war on drugs, are relatively understudied by social scientists. The Attorneys are the primary prosecutorial arm of the federal government. They are also the primary field agents of the U.S. Department of Justice (DOJ) and handle virtually all prosecutions in the federal courts. Prosecutorial discretion exercised by the offices of the U.S. Attorneys across the nation represents the last in a sequence of policy judgments that shape the street-level implementation of programs such as the war on drugs (Whitford 2002). Given their unique place in the American bureaucracy, the relative lack of scholarly attention given to these key agents of policy implementation is remarkable. While other federal agencies investigate and process case information about narcotics violations, the final decision to prosecute is by and large restricted to the U.S. Attorneys.

The U.S. Attorneys were created by the Judiciary Act of 1789 as part of the structure of inferior courts and support personnel in the early Republic, and they have endured as the focal point for the civil and criminal prosecution of violations of federal laws. Since their inception, the U.S. Attorneys have historically prosecuted the nation's laws in a largely unfettered environment. While there have been a number of attempts to increase oversight of their activities, the net result is that they have tended to live lives of "splendid isolation" (Seymour 1975). As the most authoritative account of the U.S. Attorneys' activities notes, the "legacy of this early independence . . . helps produce a degree of autonomy and independence from the department perhaps unmatched by any other field service in the federal government" (Eisenstein 1978, 11). This extensive autonomy and discretion are perhaps best explained by Rabin, who contends:

> The authority of the federal prosecutor has been expressly designated by Congressional mandate that: "except as otherwise provided by law, each U.S. Attorney, within his district, shall—(I) Prosecute for all offenses against the United States. . . ." On its face, this language seems to establish an absolute duty requiring U.S. Attorneys to prosecute every criminal violation of federal law. Read literally, then, Congressional intent is violated regularly in every U.S. Attorney's office in the country. While no commentator has ever suggested that the statutory mandate be taken literally, it is easier to proclaim the inevitability of federal prosecutorial discretion than to rationalize it. (Rabin 1971, 1072–1073)

Thus, while the U.S. Attorneys are responsible for the prosecution of all offenses, they enjoy premium discretion in both initiating and declining cases (Eisenstein 1978; Perry 1998). This discretion extends to both criminal and civil jurisdiction but is especially noticeable in criminal cases, since many civil cases involve defending the interests of the United States (Seymour 1975).

There are ninety-four Attorneys, one in each federal judicial district. Eighty-nine are scattered across the United States in contiguous districts; the remaining five are located in Puerto Rico, the Virgin Islands, the Canal Zone, the Northern Mariana Islands, and the District of Columbia. Each state has at least one Attorney, and no district's boundaries cross a state line. Each Attorney oversees a staff of assistant U.S. Attorneys (AUSAs), who are career bureaucrats and are assigned to the district by the DOJ.

The U.S. attorney general is formally charged with supervision of the ninety-four U.S. Attorneys and, by extension, the AUSAs. This management authority is exercised in part through the Executive Office for United States Attorneys (EOUSA), located in the Department of Justice. However, the critical powers of appointment and removal of Attorneys rest solely with the president. Appointment typically occurs with senatorial courtesy (upon the advice and consent of rest of the Senate) and creates a bond between the appointee and the senators from the state within which the district lies. Presidents concentrate on selection, because removal has traditionally been quite rare due to the local standing of individual Attorneys and the roles of senators in the appointment process. Indeed, the process of their appointment (from the district in which they will practice) shows exactly how strong their local ties—as opposed to their dependence on national constituencies—can be.

The President and His or Her Prosecutors: Agenda Responsiveness or Splendid Isolation?

Given their dispersed location, history of independence, multiple means of prosecutorial discretion, and limited number of available supervision mechanisms, the U.S. Attorneys represent a hard test for executive influence on the bureaucracy through public rhetoric. We also believe that there is not always policy consensus at even the higher levels of the DOJ about the direction of the war on drugs. In *Main Justice*, McGee and Duffy recount the reaction of some officials at DOJ headquarters when statistics suggested that the enforcement-oriented approach was not stemming the tide of drug sales or related violence:

> To those outside the law enforcement community, it might seem an ironic, even heretical notion, but to many of the career lawyers and prosecutors inside Main Justice it was an article of faith that solving the nation's drug problem could not be accomplished by prosecutions and jail sentences alone. [Jack] Keeney, [David] Margolis and other Criminal Division lawyers had long since reached a conclusion they thought was self-evident: Education, rehabilitation and improving the grim lot of those most prone to drug addiction ought to become national priorities. "Education and fixing the underlying conditions that lead people to take drugs," Margolis asserted, "that's what's needed. Anyone who thinks that drug enforcement is primarily a law enforcement issue, they're smoking wacky tabacky." (McGee and Duffy 1996, 42–43)

These attitudes toward the war on dugs, however, stood in stark contrast to the policy signals emanating from the Oval Office and the Capitol, and officials at Main Justice understood the discrepancy: "Like David Margolis and Jack Keeney, [Janet] Reno understood the importance of prevention efforts in slowing the nation's galloping drug epidemic. Prevention was not a popular idea with politicians, however. As much as those at Main Justice believed in it, their overseers in the White House and Congress emphasized enforcement. Sadly, one came at the expense of the other" (McGee and Duffy 1996, 48).

Geographical distance between Washington and the field-level prosecutors naturally would amplify any lack of policy consensus in the halls of Main Justice. U.S. Attorneys and AUSAs often come from the localities in which they work and likely share the core beliefs and views of the local population on salient public issues. A local area whose citizens are strongly against an enforcement-dominated approach to the narcotics problem could spawn U.S. Attorneys and AUSAs that share these local views and have ideological beliefs at odds with the enforcement-based approach of recent presidential administrations.[1]

A president who seeks to promote a policy must also struggle with getting his or her field-level prosecutors to adopt those policy priorities; through the U.S. Attorneys, the DOJ wields extraordinary power to influence the direction of everyday American life. As McGee and Duffy explain, "The enforcement of criminal federal law is a primary means by which each administration carries out its domestic policy agenda. For that reason, the Justice Department has become one of the big prizes of every presidential campaign" (McGee and Duffy 1996, 8).

But can presidents establish and maintain consensus with such a dispersed and independent set of agents as the U.S. Attorneys? Does public rhetoric offer a viable policy tool for the president, as in the case of the DEA? Presidential rhetoric promoting the war on drugs has taken different forms: planned remarks, discussions with reporters on the drug war as an administration priority, and also "town hall" situations where the president talks directly with citizens or school-children about the dangers of drug use. Throughout the war on drugs, however, presidents have explicitly directed statements to the U.S. Attorneys as chief government prosecutors.

For instance, in 1987, Reagan again noted the role of the U.S. Attorneys in a public radio address: "Much of what we do at the Federal level is aimed at choking off the supply of illegal drugs. With the assistance of Vice President Bush, we're continuing to make tremendous progress in seizing drugs crossing our borders; with the Customs Service and the Coast Guard working more closely together, we'll seize even more. We arrest drug traffickers and send them to prison. With the Drug Enforcement Administration, FBI, and the U.S. Attorneys working more closely together, we'll be even tougher on those who traffic in drugs."[2] In 1990, President George H. W. Bush directly addressed the drug war in a meeting with federal, state, and local prosecutors:

Please be seated. And please take off your coats. I mean, it's a little warm out here in the Rose Garden. Well, thank you, Attorney General Thornburgh, and U.S. attorneys, State attorneys general. I see our Director of the FBI here, and local district attorneys and other law enforcement officials. I am just delighted to have this opportunity to welcome our nation's prosecutors to the White House. I know that you spent the morning over at Justice with Dick Thornburgh. I just got briefed on that—discussing the legal changes that we need to help you do your jobs more effectively. And I know that other subjects are preoccupying all of us these days, but I repeat today what I said last week: Drugs and violent crime remain a top priority.[3]

As suggested by these quotations and demonstrated in figure 4.9 in chapter 4, presidents have expended time and effort endorsing the drug war through their public speeches. But do the splendidly isolated Attorneys and AUSAs listen? Later in this chapter, we offer and test our central hypothesis that the presidential use of the bully pulpit did change how the U.S. Attorneys prosecuted drug crimes. Specifically, we claim that as the composition of presidential statements regarding narcotics increased, the narcotics composition of the U.S. Attorneys' caseloads also increased.

However, as we discussed in chapter 2, the president may have at his or her disposal tools of management other than public rhetoric. Perhaps foremost among these tools is the power of personnel management, namely appointment and termination of agency actors. In recent years, a series of events commonly referred to as the "fired U.S. Attorneys scandal" provides us with a point of illumination on the utility and limits of this alternative means of controlling agency discretion and policy direction. In the section that follows, we briefly examine this affair and the lessons it offers for executive policy management.

Testing Prosecutorial Independence: The Fired U.S. Attorneys Scandal

As outlined previously, conventional wisdom dictates that prosecutors and, more specifically, U.S. Attorneys work in "splendid isolation." In other words, they act with little formal oversight and have historically been protected from the pressures of political machinations in their decision making. There is good reason to believe that this aphorism is accurate. While U.S. Attorneys legally serve "at the pleasure of the president," it has customarily been the case that, outside of the normal turnover that occurs when a new president takes office, the Attorneys are rarely fired or asked to resign during their natural term (four years or, in the case of a two-term president, eight years).

A recent study of the U.S. Attorneys indicates that from 1981 to 2006 there were fifty-four U.S. Attorneys who left office before completion of their normal term. Of these departures, it can be presumed that forty-six were not due to termination or forced resignation: eighteen left to become federal judges or magistrates, six left for positions in the executive branch, four sought elective office, seventeen left for positions in either state government or the private sector, and one died. Of the rest, the premature departures of only five were verifiably due to either dismissal by the President (two) or compelled resignation (three); information was not available for the remaining three departures (Scott 2007). Furthermore, these five severances do not appear to have been based on political or ideological discord with the administration but rather had to do with the personal conduct of the Attorneys at issue (for instance, criminal charges for inappropriate case disclosure; grabbing a television reporter by the throat; or resignation amid accusations of biting an exotic dancer on the arm; see Scott 2007, 6). In sum, such departures from the office have been the rare exception to the rule during this study's time frame, and there is little anecdotal evidence to suggest that this time period is unique in this regard.

It is against this backdrop of U.S. Attorney independence and job security that Americans came to hear about the rapid-fire termination of a palpable number of U.S. Attorneys during the second term of President George W. Bush.[4] We believe that this affair provides a valuable set of insights on the parameters of presidential overhead control of federal prosecutorial direction. We do not endeavor to set forth a comprehensive account of the actions that transpired or the investigations that followed; such treatments are already plentiful (for instance, Rozell and Sollenberger 2008). We do believe that this politically volatile episode illustrates well the problematic nature of an executive's use of strong-arm personnel tactics with a governmental entity that many feel is quite appropriately independent and nonpolitical in its decision making.

By the time that the Attorney firings scandal presented itself to the nation in early 2007, the Bush administration had already developed a reputation for pushing the boundaries of presidential power in order to promote the administration's ideological agenda. Consequently, the administration's decision to begin purging Justice Department personnel in its second term might have been reasonably anticipated. Accounts of the incident suggest that the firings had their origin in an initial suggestion by White House counsel Harriet Miers that all of the U.S. Attorneys be replaced at the beginning of Bush's second term (Harriger 2008). Ultimately, the Justice Department, under newly appointed attorney general Alberto Gonzales, undertook a more modest revamping of U.S. Attorneys. A smaller number of the Attorneys were identified as being problematic to the administration's partisan and ideological goals through what most would now acknowledge was a politicized review process and were consequently terminated toward the end of 2006. Participating in these termination decisions were Gonzales; Miers; Bush's deputy chief of staff, Karl Rove; Gonzales's chief of staff, D. Kyle Sampson; and the Deputy Director of the Executive Office for U.S. Attorneys, Monica Goodling, along with a handful of other key players. Of course, all of the fired Attorneys were Bush appointees.

Particularly visible in this purging of the Justice Department was the termination of David Iglesias, the U.S. Attorney for the New Mexico federal judicial district and a staunch Republican. Allegations arose that his termination was based, at least in part, on his refusal to initiate voter fraud cases against Democratic interests and to accelerate indictments of prominent Democrats right before the 2006 election (Solomon 2008). Similar allegations have been made regarding the dismissal of Carol Lam, the prominent U.S. Attorney for the Southern District of California, as well as some of the other fired Attorneys (Cohen 2007).[5]

One might reasonably ask, why would the administration do such a thing? Surely the ire of the Senate would be brought to bear in any confirmation proceeding for their replacements, thus undercutting any initial ideological or partisan gain obtained by the dismissal. While this reasoning may have obtained in previous years, something changed in the U.S. Attorney selection process during the second Bush administration that provided a novel opportunity for reshaping the Department of Justice. In 2006, Congress's reauthorization of the USA PATRIOT Act included a provision that changed the way that interim U.S. Attorneys were handled. Previously, the attorney general could only make an interim appointment for 120 days. When this time ran out, the relevant U.S. District Court Judge would appoint an Attorney until such a time as the president and the Senate came to a decision on a permanent one. The new provisions of the PATRIOT Act took federal judges, and for that matter the Senate, out of the equation. When a vacancy occurred, the attorney general could simply appoint a new U.S. Attorney indefinitely (Rozell and Sollenberger 2008, 319). Under this new process, the prospect of purging the DOJ of Attorneys who were not toeing the administration line and replacing them with new ones (all while bypassing the Senate) became attractive.

While the administration's actions seemed to fly underneath the radar for a few months, questioning by the media eventually prompted members of Congress to bring this strategic purging of the Attorneys to the national agenda. Hearings were called in which Congress pressed relevant DOJ officials for details and explanations for the dismissals. Initial attempts by officials to play down the actions as an "overblown personnel matter" failed, and the administration attempted to keep the peace by promising to attend to the matter in a responsive fashion. But it soon became apparent that the relevant officials would adopt an evasive posture and that the White House would not challenge them.

The hearings involving Attorney General Gonzales were particularly pointed, but it was probably the testimony of Monica Goodling that caused the most trouble for the White House, as her answers demonstrated inconsistencies in the stories of the other relevant DOJ officials and confirmed that a line had been crossed in politically based DOJ hiring (Harriger 2008; McKay 2008; Rozell and Sollenberger 2008). In the storm of this controversy, the nation witnessed contempt of court charges against Miers and Rove for not complying with subpoenas to testify (these were not enforced by the DOJ), consternation over Bush's repeated and questionable invocations of executive privilege, a lawsuit filed by House Democrats requiring Miers and Rove to testify, and a full-blown investigation of potential politically based DOJ hiring by Justice Department inspector Glenn Fine. In time, Gonzales, Goodling, Sampson, and other key players in the scandal would resign their positions.

The Bush administration's new attorney general, former federal judge Michael Mukasey, did not inspire new confidence in the Department when he announced that no charges would be pursued against former DOJ actors, despite the findings in Fine's investigation report that politically biased hiring had been rampant in the DOJ, not only for the Attorneys but for career bureaucrats as well. Indeed, reports suggested that political litmus tests were even used in hiring DOJ interns (Lichtblau 2008b). Commented Mukasey on the findings, "Not every wrong, or even every violation of the law, is a crime" (Lichtblau 2008a).

To say that the administration's attempt to strong-arm U.S. Attorney decision making through personnel changes did not pay off would be an understatement. Beyond the hearings, subpoenas, and resignations it incurred, the administration did not even get to make much use of the new executive-friendly appointment provisions of the PATRIOT Act. Congress reacted quickly to the scandal and in

2007 passed the Preserving the United States Attorney Independence Act, which essentially restored the process to how it worked before the PATRIOT Act changes. While it is true that most of the new appointments remained in place, the political fallout for the incursion into U.S. Attorney independence is evident.

Even before the results of Fine's investigation into DOJ personnel practices were made public, a majority of citizens polled on the matter believed that the firings were politically motivated rather than based on performance criteria. A majority of citizens polled also disapproved of the way Gonzales had handled the issue and felt that Bush's invocation of executive privilege (so that members of his administration would not have to testify) was made in order to cover up the reasons for the firings rather than to preserve the Constitution's separation of powers between Congress and the presidency (Cohen and Agiesta 2007). The administration did not fare any better in the media. David Iglesias, who has penned a popular book on his experiences in the scandal, has become a media darling, and more of the fired Attorneys have come forward with their accounts of the scandal. Their accounts of the affair, coupled with op-ed pieces critical of the administration's politicization of the DOJ, certainly did not help the public standing of an executive already running low in the polls; nor did they help a party seeking to retain the White House in the 2008 presidential election.

It is clear that strong-arm hiring and firing tactics will not likely be viable, on balance, as a means of influencing the U.S. Attorneys. The country simply is not amenable to the idea of politicizing federal prosecutors. The historical tradition of splendid isolation for these government officials is too deeply seated in our understandings of good government to allow such maneuverings by the executive.

So, how does the president get these field-level prosecutors to get on board with his or her policy vision, to follow his or her set of priorities? First, we must recognize that there are limits to what a president can reasonably hope to accomplish in influencing the Attorneys. Attempting to influence specific prosecutions for partisan gain is simply ill-advised and illegitimate. However, presidents can perhaps get dispersed federal prosecutors to get on board with their set of policy priorities as a more general matter. The U.S. Attorneys live and work in local environments that have competing influences and pressures to focus on certain matters (immigration, white-collar crime, or election fraud, for instance) depending on local concerns. These local pressures (as well as the personal priorities of any given Attorney) may not always comport with the president's preferences as to how federal prosecutors focus their time and energies. However, if the president can, using the power of the bully pulpit, begin to win the hearts and minds of these dispersed and splendidly isolated administrators of justice, then he or she may be able to gain policy leverage in the manner in which they implement the nation's laws.

Research Design

So, can the president use a more nuanced means of influencing the policy priorities of the U.S. Attorneys? Below, we examine this proposition through analysis of federal prosecutors' prioritizations of their caseloads. In assessing the influence of presidential agenda signals on the policy making of the U.S. Attorney offices, our units of analysis are the eighty-nine U.S. Attorney district offices spread across the country, from 1981 to 1993.[6] We examine two dependent variables. Both are caseload composition measures, measured as a percentage, for narcotics and drugs crime prosecutions. The first measure is the composition of *cases handled* that are drug-related; the second is the composition of *cases concluded*. For the U.S. Attorneys, these represent two different thresholds of effort. When a U.S. Attorney receives a possible prosecutorial action, it becomes a *matter* (a referral not immediately declined but considered further for possible criminal prosecution) once an AUSA spends an hour or longer considering or working on the action. A *case* is a matter that a U.S. Attorney decides to prosecute through a court action; this threshold is passed when a significant document is filed in court (this category does not include affairs conducted before a United States Magistrate, such as misdemeanors).

For bookkeeping, the EOUSA notes that a case is *handled* when it is dealt with at the court stage at any point during the recording year. A case is *concluded* when it is administratively recorded as disposed of by the district court during a given year. These last two thresholds are converted to a percentage basis—the percent of cases either handled or concluded that are drug-related—by federal fiscal year. Our two measures of the composition of the U.S. Attorneys' caseload were obtained from the EOUSA internal administrative files, both in paper and electronic form. Our data for this analysis are limited to the 1981 to 1993 because in 1994, the EOUSA stopped publishing the office-specific case data broken down by topic. The data before 1981 also lack the same granularity.

Our primary hypothesis is that the drug composition of the U.S. Attorneys' caseload—in terms of either cases handled or concluded—increases when the drug policy composition of the president's public rhetoric increases. These dependent variables provide two glimpses of how the Attorneys implement public policy. Clearly, case conclusion costs more than case handling because it depends on how the federal district courts process the cases the Attorneys handle. Both dependent variables are measured in percentage terms on a federal fiscal year basis and cover the fiscal years 1981 to 1993. Figures 6.1 and 6.2 display the cross-sectional distributions of composition of the U.S. Attorneys' caseload for cases handled and concluded over our time frame.

Our primary independent variable is the degree to which the presidential statements refer to narcotics. Since each president operates with a similar finite schedule for activities (such as speeches and appearances), this measure provides compositional information on the presidents' prioritization of drug policy in their domestic agendas as well as information on the perceptions that policy implementers might hold regarding relative executive policy priorities. This measure and the other independent variables (except where otherwise noted) are recorded on a calendar year basis (1980–1992); the dependent variables are recorded on a fiscal year basis. The variables are matched to the dependent variables to provide a natural half-year lag. This clarifies the direction of causality to a degree.

While our central concern is with the role of presidential policy signals, we recognize that the U.S. Attorneys prosecute potential violations of public laws based on a number of factors, with presidential policy signals being only one potential

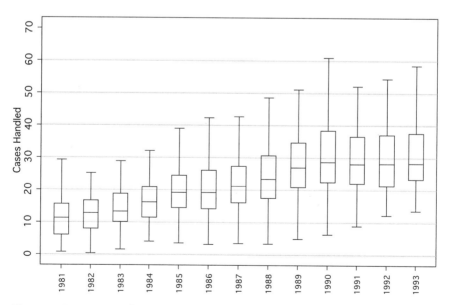

Figure 6.1. Percentage of Drug Cases, U.S. Attorney Cases Handled

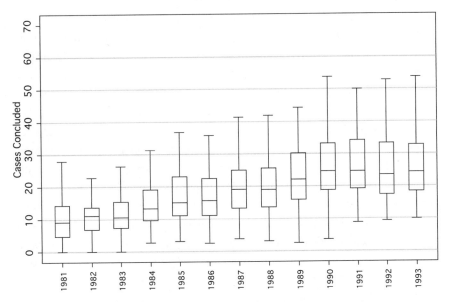

Figure 6.2. Percentage of Drug Cases, U.S. Attorney Cases Concluded

consideration. We include a collection of alternate mechanisms to represent local, national, and personal inputs into the prosecutorial process.

First, we recognize that the U.S. Attorneys' discretion may depend on the way
in which cases are referred by investigating agencies at the national, regional, or
state and local levels. To control for the increase in referrals due to changing investigation practices, we include the percentage of matters handled by the U.S.
Attorney that are drug-related. As noted, matters are recorded when the U.S. Attorney or AUSA spends at least one hour considering charges in a potential case.
Our expectation is that the relationships between neither case handling nor conclusion are one-to-one with matter handling. A percentage of matters become
cases; a percentage of cases are concluded. The effects of presidential policy signaling will occur at the margin.

Given the nature of the prosecutorial process, we include two measures of the
internal dynamics of the U.S. Attorney's office processing cases in a given district
and year. One captures aspects of how teams of AUSAs process cases. The second
captures the effects of leadership by the U.S. Attorney herself in guiding the local
office. The first measure is the number of staff (full-time equivalent, FTE) located
in the U.S. Attorney's office in a given year (logged to account for high skew).

While the processing measure is compositional in nature, it is likely that the drug case composition will increase with increases in staff. One reason is the substantial hours necessary to bring a case to completion; the second is the strong link between the number of FTE AUSAs and the population of the district. More important, we include the party of the president nominating the U.S. Attorney serving in a given year. The nomination process means that the president's identity signals the party affiliation of the U.S. Attorney in the vast number of cases. If the Attorney has control over the office's processing of cases, we expect that Democratic Attorneys (coded 1; otherwise 0) process a smaller composition of drug cases than Republican Attorneys during this time period. While the position of the Attorney frequently switches with changes in presidential administration, a number of Democratic Attorneys (mainly located in the South) served throughout the Reagan administration.

We also recognize that presidential policy signals are not the only external cues that may factor into the U.S. Attorneys' prosecution of cases, and we accordingly account for other potential national and localized influences on the prosecutorial process. The specific influences that we assess parallel those factors posited and explained in more detail in chapter 5 on the DEA. Detailed measurement descriptions for all independent variables are provided in appendix B.

We begin by acknowledging that in a system of separated powers and multiple political principals, field agents may also react to congressional attention to a policy area. We therefore test the hypothesis that the U.S. Attorneys' agenda is positively influenced by congressional attentiveness to drug policy issues. We also include two measures of ideology or public opinion, which, due to the Attorneys' dispersed location and the nature of their constraints on prosecution, are local. Public opinion may be influential because of the Attorneys' external options in local or regional politics (Perry 1998), the perception that their legitimacy depends on public support (Warren 1993), the role of local juries in determining "win rates" in court, or events and attitudes the Attorneys encounter in everyday life. The first of these measures allows us to test the proposition that the U.S. Attorneys react to regional public sentiment on the importance of the drug problem. Our second measure of local ideology captures a broader "liberal-conservative" dimension, the institutional (elite) ideology of the state where the district is located (Berry et al. 1998). We hypothesize that prosecutors in districts with liberal elites produce a lower drug composition. Last, we account for substantial change in society's general concern with drug policy issues by including the number of mentions in the *New York Times* (Baumgartner and Jones 1993). If media changes affect the Attorneys, then we expect that the drug composition of the Attorneys' workload increases as the relative number of mentions rise.

Results and Discussion

We estimate two models: the first examines cases handled and the second cases concluded. Our independent variables include the presidential signals measure, the referrals control, and the remaining six local, national, and internal covariates. Our data are for the eighty-nine U.S. Attorneys in the fifty states for the calendar years 1980 to 1992 (federal fiscal years 1981 to 1993). To account for the panel data, we estimate each model as a set of generalized estimating equations (GEE), as explained in more detail in chapter 5.[7] Tables 6.1 and 6.2 present the two models.

First, for both case handling and conclusion, clear accounting relationships exist between the matters referred to the office and the two dependent variables. In prosecuting the war on drugs, the U.S. Attorneys were constrained in what

Table 6.1.   GEE Estimates for the Narcotics Composition
of the U.S. Attorney Cases Handled

Variables	Coefficient	SE
Matters Handled	0.5095	0.0538***
Presidential Rhetoric	0.1367	0.0317***
Congressional Hearings	−0.0037	0.0076
Local Priority Opinion	0.0424	0.0345
Local Institutional Ideology	0.0061	0.0122
Press Coverage	69.1475	30.6679**
U.S. Attorney Staff Capacity	2.6667	0.7167***
U.S. Attorney's Party	−1.3358	0.4239***
Post-Forfeiture Period	1.0397	0.6579
Constant	4.6716	2.6569*
Observations		1157
Link Function		Identity
Family		Gaussian
Working Correlation Matrix		AR(1)
ρ		0.83
Wald χ^2 (9)		287.27***
Scale Parameter		69.2002

*$p < 0.10$ (two-tailed tests)   **$p < 0.05$ ***$p < 0.01$

Table 6.2. GEE Estimates for the Narcotics Composition
of the U.S. Attorney Cases Concluded

Variables	Coefficient	SE
Matters Handled	0.6819	0.0727***
Presidential Rhetoric	0.2152	0.0366***
Congressional Hearings	−0.0034	0.0110
Local Priority Opinion	0.0860	0.0448*
Local Institutional Ideology	0.0004	0.0144
Press Coverage	9.2588	44.7186
U.S. Attorney Staff Capacity	1.4748	0.7085**
U.S. Attorney's Party	−1.1032	0.5755*
Post-Forfeiture Period	1.5963	0.7926**
Constant	0.2605	3.0051
Observations		1157
Link Function		Identity
Family		Gaussian
Working Correlation Matrix		AR(1)
ρ		0.64
Wald χ^2 (9)		323.40***
Scale Parameter		63.4652

*$p < 0.10$ (two-tailed tests) **$p < 0.05$ ***$p < 0.01$

they could accomplish in court by what was brought to them by referring agencies. In both situations (cases handled and cases concluded), the offices handled and concluded cases with less than perfect efficiency. In other words, they exercised discretion by screening many cases from the pool of referrals. It is evident that the implementation of the war on drugs involved the exercise of significant prosecutorial discretion.

Given this discretion, we find evidence that the prosecutors were responsive to presidential policy signals: the drug composition of the Attorneys' caseloads was higher when presidential statements emphasized drug policy; the caseload composition was lower when statements fell. The magnitude of the effect is higher for case conclusion, suggesting a stronger role for presidential signaling in the latter context. Together, the results from the two equations indicate dual effects: presidential policy signals shift bureaucratic attention at early and late stages, and these signals are most effective at the most costly last stage.[8]

As in the case of the DEA, we consider a hypothetical to describe the magnitude of that effect. The hypothetical is the president's choice between making no statements and maximizing his or her attention to the war on drugs. What would be the total impact of that choice? We calculated the expected proportion of drug cases handled (drug cases as a percentage of all cases handled) at the U.S. Attorney's district level when presidential rhetoric was at its minimum (zero) and when it was at its maximum (twenty), holding all other variables constant at their means.[9] We also calculated the same proportion for drug cases concluded (drug cases as a percentage of all cases concluded). We then calculated the number of expected drug cases handled and concluded for each district in each year of our data, given the total number of cases handled and concluded (also held constant). The total impact across our sample for a president who chooses to maximize his or her public rhetoric on the war on drugs was an expected increase of 20,302 cases handled (or 1,562 per year on average). As a way of comparison, 99 percent of our district-level observations report fewer than 1,562 drug cases handled in a given year. The only districts larger than this were observations from South Florida, Eastern New York, and South Texas. The total number is larger than the total number of drug cases handled for South Florida, the district with the largest total (18,851) for the thirteen-year time span we observe.

Figure 6.3 extends this hypothetical by showing the impact of the president's rhetoric at level of the individual U.S. Attorney's district. We estimate the impact of the president maximizing rhetoric—the shift from not talking about drugs to taking the highest level of attention shown in the data included here—by calculating how the total additional number of drug cases will be distributed across the 89 judicial districts (which are contiguous with the U.S. Attorneys' offices). The figures that show district-level impact have been ordered so that we observe the descending expected differences in the total number of cases handled (in these figures) or concluded (presented below) for the greatest and smallest impacts.

Specifically, the largest expected differences in the total number of cases under these two scenarios occur for the usual suspects: the Southern district of Florida, the Southern district of Texas, the Southern district of New York, and the Central district of California. These districts collectively would experience the largest expected shifts. Other districts have smaller expected impacts: for example, New Hampshire, the Eastern district of Oklahoma, Delaware, the Middle district of Louisiana. Of course, these differences have to do with the additional differences, across districts, in the total number of cases handled, given that our dependent variable is the proportion of the caseload that is composed of narcotics cases. The single greatest impact, in the Southern district of Florida, is expected to be almost 1,200.

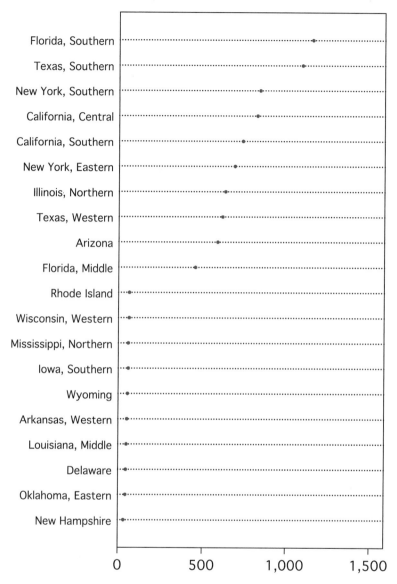

Figure 6.3. Expected Additional U.S. Attorney Cases Handled, Assuming the President Maximizes Drug Rhetoric

Figure 6.4 extends the logic experiment by considering a second hypothetical: the impacts of the shift in the president's rhetoric from a moderate level (the first quartile of the distribution) to another moderate level (the third quartile). Since the change in the independent variable is smaller in this case, the district-level impacts are also smaller—less than half the impacts seen in the first hypothetical

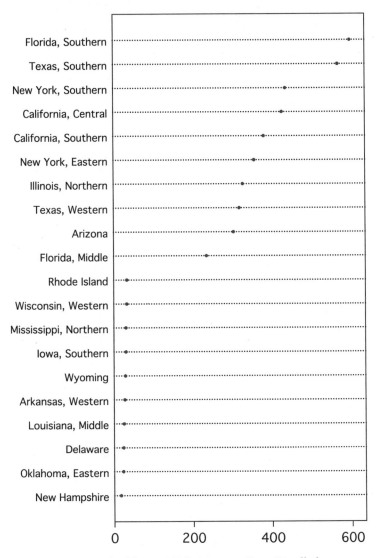

Figure 6.4. Expected Additional U.S. Attorney Cases Handled, Assuming the President Uses Moderate Drug Rhetoric

in figure 6.3. We still observe the greatest impacts in the case of two districts (in Florida and Texas), and we still observe the same rapid change in the expected differences from high levels toward small numbers (for most districts).

We also assessed the first hypothetical, of the president maximizing his or her rhetoric, in the case of the proportion of cases concluded that were drug cases. The total impact across our sample was an expected increase of 16,263 cases concluded (1,251 per year on average). That average amount is larger than every district-level observation but one: South Texas in FY 1990 (1,321). The total number is twice as large as the total number of drug cases concluded for any district; again, the closest contender is South Texas, which concluded 6,608 drug cases during the thirteen-year time span we observed.

Figure 6.5 shows the estimated impact in terms of the expected additional number of cases concluded across the eighty-nine judicial districts given the change from no rhetoric to the maximum level observed in the data. What this shows is that one specific district—the Southern district of Texas—is expected to have the highest number of cases concluded. This district-specific estimate shows part of the different behavior among the U.S. Attorneys in terms of cases handled and cases concluded—that while rhetoric may have a large impact on cases handled in one district, it can have a greater impact on cases concluded in a second. This is because the U.S. Attorneys have different production functions for these two different observables of their prosecutorial discretion. Moreover, we see in figure 6.5 a big difference between the impact on the Southern district of Texas and the next cluster of five—two California districts, and one each from Texas, New York, and Florida. Another dropoff occurs from these five to the next grouping of two, and a third from those two to a cluster of seven. One aspect of this exercise is to show that the impact of presidential rhetoric can be different in different districts even though our statistical models estimate a single coefficient. These differences come from the various baselines that operate across the districts; our estimates of the impacts reflect these baselines, although to be clear, our model also accounts directly for them through the use of the GEE estimator.

Finally, figure 6.6 shows the results from our second hypothetical, this time carried out for the U.S. Attorneys' case conclusion behavior. This figure shows the impact of a shift in presidential rhetoric from the first quartile of the independent variable's distribution to its third quartile—essentially, the movement through 50 percent of the observed levels of rhetoric presidents engaged in during the time period under study in this book. We again see a decrease in the overall impact, given the smaller change in independent variable, but the same rank order.

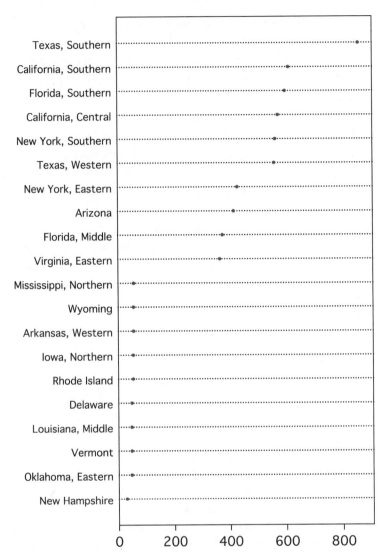

Figure 6.5. Expected Additional U.S. Attorney Cases Concluded, Assuming the President Maximizes Drug Rhetoric

However, the Attorneys do not implement policy in a vacuum dominated only by the president. Our results also show roles for local public opinion, national press coverage, and two internal considerations, staffing and Attorney's party. Specifically, the Attorneys shifted the composition of their caseload in regions where drugs are considered to be a pressing public concern. They also shifted it

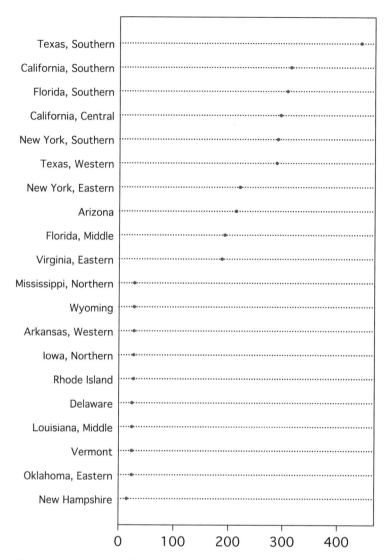

Figure 6.6. Expected Additional U.S. Attorney Cases Concluded, Assuming the President Uses Moderate Drug Rhetoric

over time in relation to national press coverage of narcotics-related issues. Internally, districts with more staff members had a greater drug composition to their caseload and, as anticipated, Republican U.S. Attorneys had a greater composition of drug prosecutions. Finally, the cases concluded model provides some evidence that forfeiture law changes prompted increased Attorney attention to drug cases. While these results complement the findings on presidential policy signals, the presidential finding is robust to changes in the model specification. The presidential statements variable is positive and significant regardless of the other local, national, or internal controls included.

While the past two decades have brought many changes to law enforcement and legal theory, since 1798 the U.S. Attorneys have remained the primary prosecutorial mechanism in federal law enforcement. These results reveal the content and practice of their prosecutorial discretion—discretion that dictates whether and when broad changes in crime policy, like the war on drugs, have real impact. The practice of this prosecutorial discretion is surprisingly political. U.S. Attorneys respond not only to local opinion and the national media but are also seriously affected by rhetoric from the Oval Office.

When considered along with the effects in the case of the DEA, we see strong and clear evidence for an executive effect in the president's use of rhetoric to send policy signals and set the national policy agenda. By going beyond traditional notions of presidential influence on the public agenda, the media, and Congress, these results reveal a direct mechanism the president wields in shifting bureaucratic behavior. Fundamentally, presidents face substantial trials in gaining compliance with their desires for public policy, if only because of their inability to oversee personally the vast majority of policy agents located throughout the country and around the world. Rhetoric provides a direct mechanism for the managerial influence of the president. Furthermore, its use is unlikely to incur the type of political fallout that the administration of George W. Bush experienced in its attempt to adjust U.S. Attorney policy making through strong-arm, politicized personnel maneuvers.

The power of the president to shift bureaucratic attention by signaling his or her policy priorities is real and substantial. In chapters 5 and 6 we demonstrate that the presidential use of rhetoric is consistent with his or her motivation for managerial control of the federal bureaucracy: presidential policy signals adjust the relative attention of unelected, dispersed field agents. The utility of this rhetorical means of managerial control suggests that rhetoric plays a role well beyond shifting the public agenda or influencing the media or Congress. Because of the wide discretion bureaucrats wield, rhetoric offers a substantial—and direct—route for presidential influence on federal field agencies. What may be surprising is how powerful this route actually is.

Discussion

The splendid isolation of the U.S. Attorneys has long been a topic of interest for students of prosecution. As James Eisenstein recounted in his *Counsel for the United States,* "Framed and hanging on the wall of most U.S. Attorneys' offices is a quotation from a Supreme Court opinion of the 1930s commenting on their duties: 'The United States Attorney is the representative not of an ordinary party to a controversy, but of a sovereignty whose obligation to govern impartially is as compelling as its obligation to govern at all; and whose interest, therefore, in criminal prosecution is not that it shall win a case, but that justice will be done'" (Eisenstein 1978, 26). The shape of federal prosecution, and of the role of the state in public and private lives, is driven by the discretionary choices made by the U.S. Attorneys. They collectively are the conscience of Mancur Olson's "bandit"—the state that must decide how to tie its own hands so that it does not abuse the trust of its people (Olson 1993).

This chapter shows the degree to which presidents help shift, through subtle means, the attention and the behavior of those who operate in splendid isolation. As in the case of the DEA, this vignette shows a powerful role for the bully pulpit in stories of the administrative presidency. The president pursues low-dimensional strategies like public rhetoric because they can pay off in many different arenas. Of course, this also means that presidential speech is like a "loaded gun" waiting to go off, in that one does not know what target it will hit. But the long-run impact of that speech, wielded carefully, has value for presidents seeking to control field agents, making discretionary choices scattered across the country.

The Attorneys also show us how agents of the state are affected by these kinds of public pronouncements when they help shape a public understanding of what should be done. The U.S. Attorneys face many competing influences—at a minimum, the wide array of agencies that bring them cases for prosecution in the federal courts. The ethics of prosecution would call for balancing impartiality and justice in all such situations. We know in the case of the DEA that presidential rhetoric flowed into the cases they brought to the federal prosecutors. We now know that given that universe of cases from which to select, the prosecutors also reflected the president's attention to narcotics in how they selected cases for consideration.

Prosecution of federal crimes by the U.S. Attorneys is the end of a long chain of events that represent the outcome of the policy process. The Attorneys' choices help solidify, or possibly mitigate, all those choices. At one time, presidents worried that quite a few U.S. Attorneys held views (fed by a prominent social construction) that wholly undermined important national priorities, as when U.S. Attorneys in the South failed to prosecute violations of the Voting Rights Act (see Eisenstein 1978). Presidents were left with only a few ways to keep that from happening, such as the centralization of prosecution at the Department of Justice.

Presidents have the option of doing that in the case of the war on drugs, but they do not have to. We find instead that presidents rely on (and build) social constructions that are almost as powerful as those held in southern communities when those U.S. Attorneys failed to implement the VRA.

Our next vignette moves from the federal level to the local. The U.S. Attorneys are field agents of the president; do presidential rhetorical strategies affect the behavior of those who do not report directly to the president?

CHAPTER SEVEN

Taking It to the States

Testing the Limits of Presidential Influence
and State Drug Enforcement

W e have demonstrated how the president's public rhetoric can change how federal agents and prosecutors implement policy. Both the field enforcement agents who serve as the front line in the war on drugs and the federal prosecutors in their "splendid isolation" reacted to presidential policy signals by adjusting their workloads. These findings exist even after we account for a broad range of other potential causes of federal enforcement performance. While presidents largely use public rhetoric as a tool in their efforts to define politics and set the policy agenda, presidential rhetoric is also useful for presidents struggling to manage how their subordinates implement policy. When policy is carried out by dispersed and largely autonomous field agencies, the ability of executives to extend their influence over policy through public statements holds significance for presidential leadership. We claim that presidents have this influence because of their unique role as the only national executive and the only politician who serves a single national constituency. For field agents and prosecutors, presidential statements serve to simplify a complex implementation environment in which what they ought to do is never very clear. In drug war politics, the presidents can build their statements on a social construction of policy's role in protecting people from threats like narcotics. Presidential statements help field agents and prosecutors make sense of their world.

Does the effect of presidential rhetoric traverse the federal-state divide in narcotics policy? Are presidential policy signals effective at changing how state actors implement policy? In chapter 3 we focused on the federal government's role in the war on drugs and crime fighting in general. While these efforts are generally more prominent in the media and have a higher public profile, the last four decades have shown that state and local governments continue to implement most criminal justice policy in the nation. Most policy in the war on drugs is carried out by the states. Does the president's ability to influence how policy is implemented carry over to the local level?

In this chapter we examine when and how presidents have been involved in policymaking in narcotics at the state level and ask whether the president's rhetoric on narcotics influences state-level enforcement activity over which he or she has no formal oversight. Our analysis unfolds in three parts. First, we look at direct interactions between the executive branch and the states over drug policy and its implementation through active enforcement efforts and the setting of financial incentives. Second, we offer a theory of the mechanism through which presidents are able to influence state policy. Finally, we offer an empirical test of the claim that state-level enforcement responds to the president's policy signals about narcotics and discuss the implications of our findings for the long-term dynamics in how the president and the states interact.

New Federalism and the War on Drugs in the States

The states exercise extraordinary discretion in the substance and implementation of their criminal laws. Indeed, there are important differences among the states in terms of their legislation on narcotics as well as how they enforce these laws (Meier 1992). It was in this context that many considered Ronald Reagan's ascension to the White House as beginning a new era of federalism. The spirit of this claim is reflected in a speech he made during his first term as president to the Annual Convention of the National Association of Counties:

> We in this administration have taken another look at the Constitution and are applying it to the America of today. We will restore the 10th Amendment to the Constitution, which says that the Federal Government shall do only those things provided in the Constitution, and all other powers shall remain

with the States and with the people. For the first time in too many years, the Federal Government will recognize a limit on what it should do, how fat it can grow, and the power it can claim. With your help, we'll reverse the flow of power, sending it back to the localities.[1]

Reagan's "new federalism" reflected his core belief that important policy decisions are better left to local actors so that policies accurately reflect the values and norms of the local areas affected by those policies. This position was at the core of many deregulation initiatives and devolution efforts during his two terms in office. However, many argue that in criminal justice policy, his administration's actions ran counter to his general calls to return most policymaking responsibility to the states. In the 1960s and 1970s there was massive federal funding of broad-based state law enforcement efforts (the Law Enforcement Assistance Administration, for example), but in the 1980s the role for the federal government deemphasized broad-based funding for state agencies in favor of expanding federal activity in handling low-level, routine criminal offenses like larceny or low-level drug possession and sales (Heymann and Moore 1996, 107).

The federal government has wide-ranging authority under the Constitution's interstate commerce clause to become involved in areas of social and economic regulation customarily considered the province of state and local authorities. Some legal scholars describe this extended involvement as the "federalization" or "overfederalization" of run-of-the-mill state offenses, arguing that federal agencies should be involved in state and local law enforcement only where there is a historical national interest or special capability. Such situations include those where the federal government has a direct interest or that present a distinctly national concern; criminal enterprises that operate across state or national boundaries; crimes that are sophisticated, necessitating the federal government's comparative advantage in investigation and prosecution; or crimes in which there is state or local government corruption or in which the integrity of state government is questioned (Heymann and Moore 1996).

In contrast to these "guidelines," day-to-day federal involvement in relatively low-level drug offenses expanded dramatically in the 1980s and 1990s, including many that had historically been handled by state and local enforcement authorities and prosecutors. One example of federalization is when the Southern District of New York (under the direction of U.S. Attorney Rudolph Giuliani) began treating one day of the week as "federal day." On that day, citizens who had been arrested on a drug offense by state or local authorities were charged with a federal drug offense instead. State enforcement authorities and prosecutors remained involved in the case, but the ultimate convictions were federal, which meant stiffer sentences. This led to a flood of small drug cases in the federal courts and prison system (Brickey 1995). This federal strategy and those in other jurisdictions are reasons for the strong criticism of federalization of state criminal law and (specifically) narcotics policy. Even U.S. Supreme Court Chief Justice William Rehnquist warned that too much federal involvement into traditional state and local concerns would overwhelm an already overburdened federal justice system (Brickey 1995, 1136).

Along with hands-on involvement in routine drug cases, the federal government can change the shape of state and local narcotics policy through financial incentives. There are two main ways the federal government has used incentives to shape the states' narcotics policies: program-based grants and forfeiture rules.

First, program grants earmarked for narcotics enforcement have supported law-based approaches to controlling drug use on the state and local levels. Congress passed the well-known Edward Byrne Memorial State and Local Law Enforcement Assistance Program in 1986. Named after a rookie officer killed in a drug-related arrest, the program replaced the largely unfettered block grant programs under the defunct Law Enforcement Assistance Administration and required recipients to use funds on the war on drugs rather than broader criminal justice needs (Blumenson and Nilsen 1998). The Byrne funds led to the expansion of now abundant multi-jurisdictional drug task forces (MJDTFs), which serve to promote cooperative drug enforcement efforts among local, state, and federal entities. Their magnitude and range are staggering: collectively they are the highest-funded category among federal aid programs and annually receive about one-third of such federal funding (Blumenson and Nilsen 1998).[2] About one-fifth of local police participate in MJDTFs, and four-fifths of departments in cities with over 100,000 people are involved (O'Hear 2004). MJDTFs have shifted the federal war on drugs initiative and greatly expanded its street-level presence. Often these programs become self-funded, making them a cost-efficient way for presidents to extend their influence to the state and local policy arena. Critics claim that self-funding turns MJDTFs into self-perpetuating entities that lack accountability to their client populations and over which state officials have little meaningful oversight.

The second (and related) way the president's federal drug war gains the support and involvement of state and local enforcement actors is through forfeiture procedures and incentives. In general, forfeiture rules require that a person who fails to perform a legal obligation or who commits a crime must relinquish property or money without compensation. The latter situation is the main way that forfeiture impacts the war on drugs. Indeed, drug-related cases frequently feature self-funding from the proceeds obtained in forfeiture proceedings.

There was a long tradition of forfeiture of property with ties to criminal activity to the government in Europe before it was instituted in the United States. Until recently, its use was traditionally limited to the rare and exceptional case and so was generally out of favor. Modern drug forfeiture policies began during the Nixon administration as part of the federal government's broader law and order crusade. The administration argued that forfeiture would undermine the economics of the organized drug trade (Levy 1996). Congress passed legislation in 1970 that provided federal enforcement authorities with forfeiture powers, powers that expanded with the 1978 amendments to what became known as the Forfeiture Act (Vecchi and Sigler 2001; Williams 2002). These provisions allowed federal enforcement authorities to pursue both criminal forfeiture (*in personam*) and civil forfeiture (*in rem*) actions to combat the narcotics trade. Civil forfeiture proceedings were especially useful because they allowed authorities to proceed against property or the proceeds at issue without obtaining a conviction. Government must only show probable cause that the property is related to drug crimes; the burden of proof shifts to the property owner to counter the government's claim by a preponderance of the evidence or lose the property (Beckett 1997).

Despite these advantages, federal agencies did not use forfeiture much during the Ford and Carter years. In 1981 the General Accounting Office released a report, "Asset Forfeiture—A Seldom Used Tool in Combating Drug Trafficking," which prompted the Reagan administration and Congress to reassess existing forfeiture policies (Levy 1996). The 1984 Comprehensive Crime Control Act fixed some shortcomings of federal forfeiture law, expanded the scope of assets that could be forfeited (for example, real property), and adjusted the procedures that governed forfeiture. In 1984, changes were also made to the incentive structures of forfeiture policy that allowed federal enforcement agencies to retain funds deriving from forfeiture; the previous rule required that those assets be turned over to Treasury's General Fund (Blumenson and Nilsen 1998). Congress also introduced "equitable sharing" of forfeiture proceeds between the federal government and state and local enforcement authorities (Williams 2002).

At the same time the federal government amended forfeiture procedures, the states developed their own forfeiture statutes and policies. However, having few incentives for enforcement dampened state efforts at implementing forfeiture rules because most required that funds acquired via forfeiture be turned over to the state general fund or allocated to specific non-enforcement programs (like state education funding). Under the doctrine of equitable sharing, state agencies that allowed their forfeitures to be adopted (or turned over to the DOJ as federal forfeitures) received up to eighty percent of those funds, which could be used exclusively for state enforcement purposes (Blumenson and Nilsen 1998; Vecchi and Sigler 2001). State enforcement agencies were able to bypass state legal requirements to turn the funds over to non-enforcement budgets and keep the funds for their own purposes. This was a powerful incentive for state enforcement authorities to join the federal war on drugs (Benson, Rasmussen, and Sollars 1995).

Policy Consensus in a Time of State Resistance: The Potential for Presidential Rhetoric

Federal program grants and equitable forfeiture sharing provisions have caused states to move forward on federal criminal justice priorities. In addition to these incentives, the federal government can also change the flow of funds to states for other important programs (such as federal highway funds) when states fail to make progress on federal anti-drug policies like comprehensive drug testing in the criminal justice system or the creation of specialized drug courts (O'Hear 2004); this strategy parallels the annual certification of the interdiction efforts of foreign aid recipients. These inducements and programs, along with the potential for case-level federal involvement, paint a picture of significant involvement by the executive branch in subnational policymaking and implementation. The federal government's move into an area traditionally considered within the sphere of subnational governments begs the question of why presidents care about local policy implementation.

National policy initiatives, regardless of extent or scope, may not be as effective as policy partnerships with state and local authorities. Such partnerships provide a street-level presence that federal enforcement agencies cannot achieve on their own. Furthermore, such partnerships may validate the overall policy if consensus changes perceptions about the initiative's overall value. At a minimum, the president would prefer subnational authorities to adopt the character and intensity of his or her administration's law-and-order crusade.

We might expect that the incentives offered by the federal government would reduce the states' resistance to enforcement-oriented narcotics policy. The states might even match (if not exceed) federal efforts in the war on drugs: in making enforcement a priority, increasing the severity of punishment, and regulating a broad array of narcotics. Yet close examination of state policies shows that state and local governments have often moved away from a strong emphasis on enforcement and punishment, as the Carter administration did.

In 1977, Carter publicly announced his support for the decriminalization of marijuana, stating, "The National Commission on Marijuana and Drug Abuse concluded five years ago that marijuana use should be decriminalized, and I believe it is time to implement those basic recommendations."[3] This progressive proposal failed to gain momentum and was soon dropped, but eleven states had already decriminalized marijuana by 1977; in the same year a Gallup poll showed that 60 percent of Americans favored decriminalization (Meier 1994).[4] The federal approach to the narcotics problem shifted abruptly with Reagan's election, but few of these states recriminalized marijuana. Not amending those laws was largely a symbolic gesture, since these states (like others) consistently post large numbers of drug arrests. Decriminalization is just the tip of the iceberg in how some state and local governments depart from the emphasis on enforcement and punishment in federal drug policy.

In recent decades, state laws have been enacted that represent significant departures from the federal punitive approach even if they do not legalize or decriminalize drug use per se. Examples of such drug policy "reforms" include the diversion of nonviolent drug offenders from prison to drug treatment, the prohibition of racial profiling in police drug investigations, reductions in the collateral legal consequences of drug convictions (for example, disenfranchisement or qualification for public benefits), the deregulation of the sale and possession of sterile syringes, reform of the civil asset forfeiture laws to prevent abuses, and reduced sentences for certain nonviolent drug offenders (Piper et al. 2003).

The most well-known (and controversial) reforms are the medical marijuana initiatives. These laws vary from state to state, but they generally provide that qualified patients who would benefit from the use of marijuana may use it legally in accordance with regulatory guidelines. To date at least eleven states have passed effective medical marijuana laws (Eddy 2005; Thomas and Schmitz 2006).[5] Most medical marijuana laws were adopted through public referenda, but a number were enacted by state legislatures.

Drug policy reform proposals reflect a harm reduction approach and, on balance, have fared well in the state political arena. Generally, the electorate has not punished state or local politicians backing those reforms for being "soft on drugs" (Piper et al. 2003). One politician at the forefront of state drug policy reforms is

Gary Johnson, Republican governor of New Mexico from 1995 to 2003; in 1999 he became the highest-ranking American elected official to come out against the war on drugs and in favor of narcotics legalization and regulation. Johnson publicly debated federal drug czars Barry McCaffrey and Asa Hutchinson, arguing that "by no figment of the imagination is this something that we're winning. This is a war against ourselves" (Fecteau 2001). Johnson is perhaps the most recognized and fervent advocate of drug policy reforms, but he is not alone. A considerable number of state enforcement agents, prosecutors, judges, and elected representatives have publicly backed medical marijuana laws reform (Piper et al. 2003).

This divergence between the federal government's law-and-order agenda and drug policy reform in the states came to a head in the late 1990s when the DEA began arresting citizens whose drug activities were in compliance with state medical marijuana laws but violated federal narcotics provisions, most notably in California. DEA raids on medical marijuana suppliers and the accompanying arrests of suppliers and patient-users resulted in lawsuits brought by local governments as well as individuals. The U.S. Supreme Court eventually ruled in two cases. In *U.S. v. Oakland Cannabis Buyers' Cooperative* (2001), the Court overturned the Ninth U.S. Circuit Court of Appeals ruling that patients charged with federal marijuana trafficking charges could claim a medical necessity defense. The Court did not, however, invalidate state medical marijuana laws protecting patients and caregivers from state prosecution. In *Gonzalez v. Raich* (2005), the Court again overturned a Ninth Circuit ruling. The Ninth Circuit had held that application of the federal Controlled Substance Act to intrastate medical marijuana usage exceeded Congress's reach under the Commerce Clause. The Bush administration (through the solicitor general) filed an amicus brief opposing the Ninth Circuit's decision, and at least six states, including some with medical marijuana laws and some without, filed briefs supporting the decision. The Supreme Court disagreed with the states, holding that while the California medical marijuana activities at issue may have been contained within the state, they had enough of an influence on interstate commerce to fall under Congress's authority. The Court again declined to nullify state medical marijuana provisions, but the DEA was given a green light for future arrests of intrastate medical marijuana use under the federal statute (Eddy 2005).[6]

In sum, the litigation between local interests and the federal government over medical marijuana in California will not likely end any time soon. In a recent lower court case, a federal district court judge in California made serious inroads toward bringing the issue of federalism to a head in the heated legal debate over medical marijuana. In this case, *Santa Cruz v. Gonzales,* the county of Santa Cruz, along with a number of other named plaintiffs, filed suit against the federal government over its policy of raiding medical marijuana providers (in this case the Wo/Men's Alliance for Medical Marijuana), seizing marijuana, records, and other items and generally disrupting their activities. At the heart of the plaintiff's grievances was the idea that the federal government's practices were designed to force California to recriminalize medical marijuana by making implementation of its medical marijuana laws and attendant policy programs impracticable. The plaintiffs' complaint, seeking injunctive relief, declaratory relief, and damages, alleged, among other things, that the federal government's actions violated the Tenth Amendment to the Constitution, which provides that "the powers not delegated to the United States by the Constitution, nor prohibited by it to the states, are reserved for the States, respectively, or to the people." Judge Jeremy Fogel allowed the plaintiff's case to proceed, observing that while the Ninth Circuit has held that the terms of the federal Controlled Substances Act do not per se violate the Tenth Amendment, the alleged manner in which the federal government has implemented the Act in this context—threatening doctors and government officials who participate in the medical marijuana programs, targeting enforcement on medical marijuana users, and so on—could work to undercut the state's ability to discern legal from illegal marijuana use. This would work to make the state law unenforceable and, accordingly, would constitute a commandeering of the state legislative process in violation of the Tenth Amendment. While the ultimate outcome of this case is indeterminate, it sets the stage for a high-profile confrontation over the way states and the federal government deal with the drug issue.

Members of Congress have introduced a number of bills that would, in practical effect, shield citizens living in states with medical marijuana laws from federal enforcement and prosecution. None have passed to date. Conflicts between the federal government and state and local governments over medical marijuana are unlikely to be resolved anytime soon, in part because these skirmishes reflect deeper differences between the federal government's orientation toward enforcement and the preference of some states for reform. For example, the San Jose Police Department worked with federal agents for fifteen years, until the DEA executed a particularly contentious medical marijuana raid. After that, Police Chief William Lansdowne pulled his officers off of the DEA task force, explaining, "I think their [the DEA's] priorities are out of sync with local law" (Witt 2002). What has emerged from this conflict between state and federal authorities has been an uneasy armistice of sorts under which the federal authorities make raids and seize marijuana product but make few arrests. Samuels explains the situation in California: "In the past five years, an unwritten set of rules has emerged to govern Californians participating in the medical marijuana trade. Federal authorities do not generally bother arresting patients or doctors who write prescriptions. Instead the D.E.A. pressures landlords to evict dispensaries and stages periodic raids on them, either shutting them down or seizing their money and marijuana. Dispensary owners are rarely arrested, and patient records are usually left alone." This curious state of affairs has, perhaps ironically, led to a situation in which the raids and seizures keep marijuana prices high and the potency of the heirloom strains demanded by the upscale clientele who can afford them is much stronger than the street-level marijuana that was available twenty to thirty years ago (Samuels 2008, 50, 51).

Given the disconnect between federal objectives and the decriminalization approach of some states, presidents seeking consistency in enforcement-based narcotics policy have tried tools like joint task forces, forfeiture incentives, and conditional funding. Another available tool is the president's public rhetoric. Local authorities often account for what the president wants when they make and implement narcotics policy at the subnational level (Meier 1994). The executive branch is uniquely situated to sell an enforcement-oriented drug policy agenda to the states (O'Hear 2004). One reason is that the president's privileged access to the media offers a route to circumventing state or local government attempts to enforce policy views.

Why would state and local enforcement authorities respond to what the president says about narcotics policy? They are not accountable to the national executive, and the states often openly defy the president's policy views. The president lacks direct overhead control of state enforcement authorities, and his or her working relationship is certainly not analogous to his or her relationship with the U.S. Attorneys or the DEA. Yet we see important commonalities regarding how they might respond to the president's views. Generally, both federal and local agents respond to policy signals from a number of different political principals (or venues of influence), one of which is the president (Waterman, Rouse, and Wright 1998; Waterman and Rouse 1999). Neither group has much to gain by straying too far from the policy agendas of prominent principals; noncompliance comes with risk and uncertainty about how principals might respond. For example, a total lack of enforcement might bring federalization of local enforcement. Just as presidents see benefits in policy partnerships with state and local governments, politically those governments may see advantages in working with a partner perceived to carry a national mandate. Moreover, state officials may see policy cues from the presidency as more structured and cohesive than those from other, disjointed agenda-setters. There is an element of reinforcement: state officials already inclined to the president's policy agenda may reinforce those convictions by following his or her lead, and doing so may help them defend their original positions; this is made easier if the president can rely on an existing social construction of the narcotics problem.

Research Design

We address the hypothesis that state officials react to the president's public rhetoric by adjusting their enforcement activities. For the reasons we outlined above, we consider this case to be the hardest test of the effect of executive rhetoric on policy implementation in the case of the war on drugs. We test our hypothesis that presidential policy priorities shape state enforcement efforts using data on the drug composition of the state's annual total number of arrests measured from 1980 to 1998.[7] Figure 7.1 displays the cross-sectional distribution of the drug composition measured as the percentage of all arrests from 1980 to 2001.[8] This measure shows how the states and local authorities prioritize drug enforcement relative to other actions they could take. Figure 7.1 shows a slight trend in the drug composition of state-level arrests from 1987 on, and the cross-sectional variance across the states also increases over time. What explains this pattern?

In chapters 5 and 6, our primary explanatory variable was designed to reflect how the president makes the war on drugs a policy priority in his or her public speeches. This variable is the composition of total public statements by the president that make reference to narcotics. We also consider other competing causes of state-level enforcement. Our variables mirror those outlined in the previous two chapters. These considerations include the demand for enforcement (drug deaths), capacity (state-level staffing), other competing national policy signals (congressional hearings and media emphasis), local policy sentiment (state political elite ideology and regional public opinion on the importance of the drug problem), and forfeiture incentives (after the federal forfeiture amendments of 1984). Detailed descriptions of our variable measurements are in appendix C.

We also directly account for the role of reforms like decriminalization at the state level. As discussed in chapter 3, state marijuana laws trended toward partial decriminalization starting in the 1970s: Oregon in 1973; Alaska, California, Colorado, Maine, and Ohio in 1975; Minnesota in 1976; Mississippi, New York, and

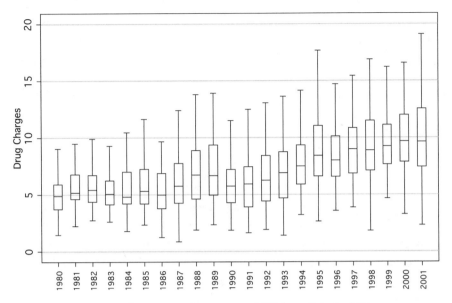

Figure 7.1. State Drug Charges as a Percentage of All State Criminal Charges

North Carolina in 1977; and, Nebraska in 1978 (DiChiara and Galliher 1994, 42).[9] A simple t-test shows that the drug composition of annual arrest totals on the state level is actually higher for those states with limited decriminalization in our data (7.4 instead of 7.2), although the difference is not significantly different from zero at conventional levels (t=0.801, Satterthwaite's df=307.911). The models we report below are robust to the inclusion of an intercept shift for those states with decriminalization in place during the years covered in our data.

We again employ generalized estimating equations (GEE) since our data are panels of states observed over a number of years. This approach yields parameter estimates that are uncontaminated by the effects of heteroskedastic and auto-correlated errors.[10]

Results and Discussion

Table 7.1 shows the results of our model. Again, we consider this implementation arena the toughest test for the power of presidential rhetoric to change the behavior of implementation agents. Yet we find that presidential rhetoric has a positive and significant effect on the percentage of arrests composed of narcotics cases.[11]

Table 7.1.   GEE Estimates for State Drug Enforcement

Variables	Coefficient	SE
Drug Deaths	0.2919	0.0630***
Presidential Rhetoric	0.0283	0.0124**
Congressional Hearings	−0.0774	0.0689
Local Priority Opinion	0.0617	0.0080***
Local Institutional Ideology	−0.0056	0.0042
Press Coverage	0.3464	0.0614***
Ln Full-Time Employees	1.4271	0.2391***
Decriminalization	−0.1669	0.4857
Post-Forfeiture Period	0.2812	0.1274**
Constant	−10.4802	2.2558***
Observations		905
Link Function		Identity
Family		Gaussian
Working Correlation Matrix		AR(1)
ρ		0.84
Wald χ^2 (9)		131.06***
Scale Parameter		6.5270

*p < 0.10 (two-tailed tests)   **p < 0.05   ***p < 0.01

Again, we offer a hypothetical to describe the magnitude of that effect. If the president chose between making no statements and maximizing his or her attention to the war on drugs, what would be the total impact of that choice? We calculated the expected proportion of drug arrests (drug arrests as a percentage of all arrests) at the state level when presidential rhetoric was at its minimum in the data (zero) and when it was at its maximum (twenty), all other variables being held at their means.[12] We then calculated the number of expected drug arrests for each state in each year of our data given the total number of arrests, also held constant. The total impact across our sample for a president who chooses to maximize his or her public rhetoric on the war on drugs was an expected increase of 735,633 arrests, or 38,717 more arrests per year on average. In comparison, 90 percent of our state-level observations report fewer than 34,090 drug arrests in a given year. The average number is roughly equal to the annual number of drug arrests in a moderately large state like Illinois or New Jersey; the total number is roughly equal to the total number of drug arrests for New Jersey for the nineteen-year time span under observation (818,646). The president's power to change the enforcement behavior of state and local enforcement authorities by maximizing his or her attention in his or her public rhetoric to the war on drugs is substantial.

Figure 7.2 shows the results of the first hypothetical: the comparison of two situations: one in which the president does not speak about drugs and one in which the president speaks about drugs at the highest levels recorded in our data in this book. We then estimate the number of expected drug arrests in each of these situations; Figure 7.2 shows the expected number (for each of the states) of additional cases associated with this shift in attention by the president. We see that the majority of the additional arrests would be in California, New York, and Texas and that these three states far and away would have more arrests than the next cluster. Interestingly, Florida is located in the next cluster, and would have about the same number of additional expected arrests as states like North Carolina and Virginia. It is important to stress that our estimates here depend on the total number of offenses recorded at the state level, since our dependent variable is the proportion of recorded offenses that are drugs-related.

The same pattern appears in figure 7.3, in which we explore the second hypothetical: that the president moves his or her rhetoric from a moderate position (the first quartile of the rhetoric variable's distribution) to another moderate position (the third quartile). This is the same thought experiment we carried out in the case of the U.S. Attorneys and the DEA's implementation of the war on drugs. Here, we observe a scaling down in the amount of expected additional arrests (by about half, from about 150,000 in the case of California to less than 80,000). We observe the same ranking across the states, with a shift from the top three through the majority of the states, finally ending with the lowest-ranked states. We expect few additional arrests for states like Vermont, the Dakotas, Wyoming, Montana, and Alaska. These states simply do not have the same number of offenses seen in the states at the top of figures 7.2 and 7.3. We emphasize, however, that while the impact is low for some states, that presidential rhetoric has any impact at this level is somewhat unexpected (and until now, not documented).

Moreover, policy signals from Congress and state political elites have no statistically significant effect on drug arrests. We do find that local public opinion on the drug problem and national media attention have somewhat stronger effects on states' prioritization of drug arrests. State and local enforcement authorities are especially attuned to their constituents' perceptions about the relative drug problem as well as the trends reported in the national media. State enforcement also responds to our measure of the baseline demand for enforcement (state per

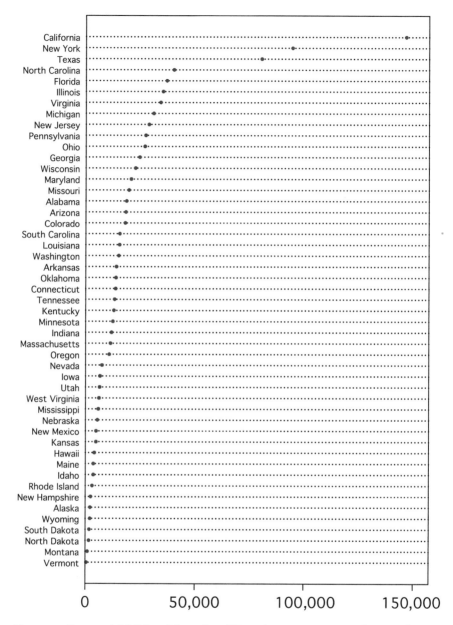

Figure 7.2. Expected Additional State-Level Drug Arrests, Assuming the President Maximizes Drug Rhetoric

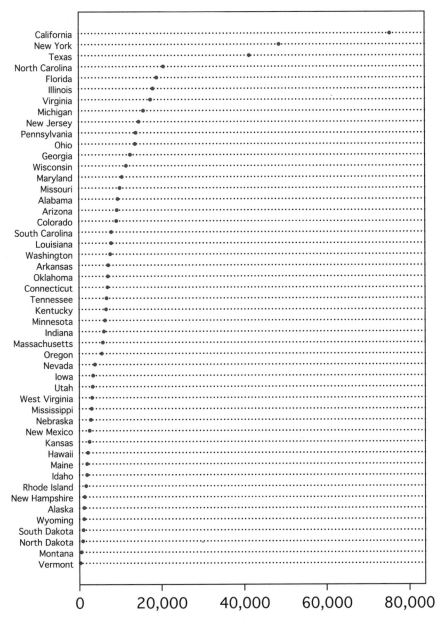

Figure 7.3. Expected Additional State-Level Drug Arrests, Assuming the President Uses Moderate Drug Rhetoric

capita drug deaths) as well as changes in personnel capabilities (staffing). Finally, the equitable sharing provisions of the 1984 legislative amendments produced an incentive structure that changed the states' drug enforcement priorities.

Discussion

Presidents encounter serious implementation hurdles if they try to change how state and local enforcement authorities carry out drug enforcement; given the broad lack of consensus about the federal government's approach to the war on drugs, this was to be expected. In this chapter we show that the president tries to use such tactics to change how states implement the war on drugs. We are mostly interested in whether the rhetorical techniques that worked with DEA agents and the U.S. Attorneys would also work on state and local actors over whom he or she has no formal overhead control. That there is a considerable effect for executive rhetoric reveals how effective this mechanism can be.

We find evidence of the feasibility of a rhetorical strategy for executive leadership in three discrete arenas of policy implementation. While other causes are more important in shaping the priorities of state and local enforcement authorities, that presidential rhetoric has a substantively consequential impact suggests the benefits of this strategy far outweigh its costs. This is especially so when one considers that the same strategy benefits a president wanting to influence politics, shape the national policy agenda, and even change what the DEA or the U.S. Attorneys believe they ought to do. All together, our findings in these three chapters suggest that even a president who cannot necessarily dictate the course of policy implementation can make important inroads toward setting the nation's policy agenda.

The responsiveness of state and local agents to presidential agenda-setting comes as somewhat of a surprise. The mechanisms of control that underpin the administrative presidency are often described in terms of the obligations that agents have with their principals (Brehm and Gates 1997; Miller and Whitford 2007). State-level officials have no formal obligation to follow the president's lead in the case of narcotics control policy, although presidents could use grants programs to create, in effect, an extended hierarchy that stretches to the states and local governments (Chubb 1985). Perhaps state-level organizations are more flexible and thus better able to respond to the winds of political change (Scholz and Wei 1986).

The simple answer in the vignette offered here is that state and local bureaucrats are susceptible to the same framing that presidents construct in the agenda-setting process and that also affects federal agents. To a degree, one consequence of this is that all three levels of field implementation move to the "beat of the same drummer." They all respond to a construction, offered by the president, that drugs are a main priority and worthy of costly effort in terms of arrests or prosecutions.

CHAPTER EIGHT

The Social Construction
of Presidential Agenda-Setting

Harry Truman had it right all along when he argued that the powers of the president boil down to the ability of an executive to persuade the other parts of government to do what he or she believes they "ought to have sense enough to do" anyway. There is little doubt that in order to be effective leaders, presidents need to make good policy choices. Their fundamental problem, however, is to get other actors who make or implement policy "on the same page." They would like some consensus as to what problems are important and what should be done to address them, and they hope that consensus gets them close to where they want the country to go.

If the president wants his or her policy priorities implemented, he or she must use all of the tools at his or her disposal to convince other relevant policy players that his or her policy vision and the path he or she has laid out toward that vision are consistent with being "responsible and effective." The president might be able to make some progress toward that goal by reorganizing agencies, appointing like-minded officials, or even offering financial incentives. However, even these tools may not be enough. Little in the design of our government, with its many actors and many agendas, gives the president much confidence that his or her actions alone can change policy and American society.

Our focus in this book is on how a president can advance his or her agenda for public policy by pressing his or her views about the importance of a policy issue and sending signals about potential solutions to social problems. Of course, part of what he or she does is help construct a social view or construction of those problems. But this social view, which in the case of narcotics goes back far in American history, also makes it possible for the president to make claims on the attention of those people who serve the government.

One aspect of the president's "going public" strategy is that his or her words have multiple audiences, that he or she can achieve many different goals in the same way. The evidence we assembled here shows that some key agents who implement narcotics policy listen when the president focuses his or her public rhetoric on that social problem and his or her policy solutions for handling it. The president will never be able to gain complete compliance through his or her use of public rhetoric. Yet the public signals he or she sends certainly influence the priorities of policy makers across government, and his or her gains (in terms of both politics and policy) in the war on drugs are real and substantial.

Presidential Leadership and American Public Policy: The Social Construction of Problems and Solutions

Most of what we know about the power of presidential rhetoric—and the reasons presidents take it so seriously—has come from studies that have focused on national institutions, the public, and the media. By and large our impressions of the president's place in American politics that come from these studies are that presidents are fairly weak in their ability to set the public agenda, if we think of setting the agenda in terms of changing what Congress, the courts, an average American, or the *New York Times* considers to be the policy priorities of our times (Edwards and Wood 1999).

We should not underestimate the importance of how the president—as the only politician elected by a national constituency—interacts with those other actors. Clearly, American politics and policy changes direction when these power brokers collectively agree that a specific social problem should be addressed by adopting a specific policy solution. But we should also accept that having influence over the "policy agenda" and exercising presidential leadership includes a much broader range of activities and dynamics.

Most policy is "made" on a day-to-day basis in the streets of the nation's cities and towns by unelected bureaucrats. In the case of narcotics, we would say that it is in the police departments, prosecutorial offices, and courts that the "rubber hits the road," that the agents of the state (both national and local) make real the policy inroads born in the stew of American politics. The extant literature on the "administrative presidency" demonstrates that executives can wield important influence through the avenues of administrative reorganization, rule-making, and appointment. We show that the president can also make a substantively significant difference in what these agents do with the power of the state when he or she makes use of the bully pulpit. The president uses the bully pulpit to influence how those agents perceive the importance of a social problem and what they can do about it. Because what the president says accentuates and builds on a social construction of that problem (and the target populations of state power) at the street level, the state's agents move from "can do" to "ought to do." The president helps make sense of their world and their role in wielding the power of the state, they help move the president's policy forward. This approach works for the president, too, because his or her influence extends beyond any limited influence on agenda-setting that he or she might have with other national institutions, the media, or the public.

The president is still only one voice among many players in the policy process. He or she cannot just impose his or her will on the agents of the state; they must be led in a careful manner. Executives strategically craft speeches and try to frame policy, and they use the cachet of the Oval Office to highlight a social problem and lend legitimacy to a way of attacking it. Presidents try to manipulate how other actors conceive of the problem and the set of potential solutions (Jacobs and Shapiro 2000).

In the war on drugs, presidents use symbolic rhetoric to position themselves as protectors of vulnerable populations (like children) and repudiators of threatening and disfavored target populations (such as drug addicts and drug kingpins). The social construction of the problem *as it is expressed in executive's policy messages* helps an agent understand who constitutes the set of relevant voices on policy and the set of acceptable responses to the problem. It is in this way, for example, that the perspectives of law enforcement and law-and-order solutions to the problem moved to the fore in the war on drugs while competing voices and responses (such as treatment initiatives or decriminalization) were marginalized.

But can the president's power of rhetoric and social construction be applied to areas other than narcotics policy? The short answer is, it depends. It is unlikely that presidents (or other leaders) can unilaterally paint the canvas of mainstream social construction of an issue or of the public's agenda through their public speechmaking. It is more realistic that presidents can only use public rhetoric to help facilitate social construction of issues and promote attention to a cause or social concern within certain parameters and under certain conditions. Further, presidents' words will almost certainly have competitors in the milieu of the social constructions of a given issue: Is it a problem worthy of public concern? If so, what is the range of appropriate solutions? Who are the groups affected and how are they to be perceived?

It is likely the case that presidents will find that some issues are more suitable for agenda setting and social construction through public rhetoric than others. While certain perennially core concerns such as the economy, foreign policy, and perhaps now, homeland security will always occupy a significant portion of the president's time, many less mandatory issues may vie for the president's rhetorical and social framing attention. Accordingly, the executive has a great degree of discretion in selecting policy issues for such treatment.

Social problems typically emerge in a series of critical phases or stages, along which they can drop from consideration as a serious social concern. Many behaviors that could arguably be deemed a social problem are familiar and well understood but are not identified as being worth serious public deliberation or concern. However, if they are repeatedly placed before the public conscience, then they gain recognition as a legitimate concern. If they pass this critical juncture, then problem redefinition may occur, during which target populations might be identified and solutions may be offered (Mullen, Pathe, and Purcell 2000). For instance, for many years the practices of driving under the influence and stalking were considered to be unfortunate but essentially inevitable social ills. While both were considered to constitute inappropriate behavior, neither was really the subject of serious public debate or concern, the subject of ordinary (not "political") conversation among citizens. However, in time, these issues gained prominence in the public conscience and were ultimately redefined as important crimes warranting stringent enforcement and punishment by the authorities. Perpetrators came to be regarded as serious criminals, and the victims of these crimes came to count for more. In short, the social construction of the issues evolved. To be sure, both issues had advocates and entrepreneurial promoters (for instance, Mothers Against Drunk Driving), but having such backing in no way guarantees social construction success for an issue.

Do presidents simply latch on to causes that have grassroots or media support? No, or at least not in a such a simplistic fashion. While it is hard to imagine a president spending capital and time to change the social construction of an issue in a way the public found abhorrent, as previously outlined, Jacobs and Shapiro (2000) make a strong case that politicians such as the president "don't pander" to public opinion. Instead, they carefully use their knowledge of public sentiment in framing and crafting their "sales pitch" for the policies that they do wish to promote. Inherent in this process is the social construction of target populations. Much as with social problems, the social construction of target populations involves characterizations or portrayals of the groups of people affected by policy (either positively or negatively) through the use of symbolic images, language, or narratives (Edelman 1988). As Schneider and Ingram explain, target groups generally fall into subgroups along dimensions of relative political power (weak or strong) and socially constructed status (positive or negative). For instance, businesses and the elderly are generally considered advantaged or politically powerful groups, as are unions and the cultural elite. However, the social construction of unions and the cultural elite is often negative, while businesses and the elderly traditionally have enjoyed a positive social construction. In similar fashion, children and the disabled both fall into the politically weak group but enjoy positive status, while criminals and communists are both politically weak and negatively perceived (Schneider and Ingram 1993, 336). Presidents, political animals that they are, must weigh the costs and benefits of any strategy of going public with these considerations in mind. While he or she may be able to use public rhetoric to help shape agency policy making, the viability of the endeavor and the potential collateral downsides might turn on how targeted populations are involved. The possible combination of targeted populations that may be involved, both those positively and negatively affected, present a continuum of the feasibility and wisdom of such a campaign of going public to affect bureaucratic policy making. Presidents (and other politicians) must be cognizant of not only the political strength of the subgroups involved but also the prevailing social construction of those subgroups.

For instance, the war on drugs presents a favorable combination of targeted populations since the costs are borne by a politically weak and negatively perceived subgroup (drug sellers and addicts) while the benefits are attributed to a group that enjoys a positive social construction (America's youth). Of course, implicit in this campaign is the social construction of these groups; in reality, both the sellers and users of illegal narcotics are frequently young people; hence there exists overlap between the beneficiary and problem target groups. Accordingly, political rhetoric often focuses on high-profile drug lords and dangerous heroin or crack addicts who must become thieves to support their habits. Decidedly less prominent in presidential public appeals on the drug problem are negative portrayals of college students experimenting with marijuana or tough talk about coming down hard on the neighbor's high school son who deals to his friends.

Just as social problems can be framed through social construction, so can targeted groups. Social constructions of targeted groups can be either restricted or expanded through the carefully crafted appeals of politicians. In the above example regarding the war on drugs, the group that is targeted as a threat is restricted to a traditionally negatively perceived set of types (hardcore users and drug lords). This makes the desired policy solution (enforcement) more palatable, as it excludes traditionally positively perceived groups (American youth). Alternatively, targeted groups can also be expanded to help promote the importance of a policy problem. For instance, as the target group that was perceived to benefit from AIDS research broadened over time to include hemophiliacs, children, and heterosexuals, this worked to make the social construction of the cause more positive. It is important to remember, however, that manipulating social constructions of problems or target groups is not necessarily easy; it presents an executive with its own set of parameters and challenges.

We might use this general framework to assess how advisable a campaign of going public might be for a president in promoting a given public policy initiative. As demonstrated in previous chapters, the agency environment and competing policy signals cast their own influences on outcomes. However, social construction considerations may also come into play. For example, if a president sought to increase civil rights enforcement by federal and state agencies by going public to promote the importance of equal rights, a number of target populations might be affected. Business is a politically powerful group and might resist such efforts to increase enforcement, as it could be costly for them. On the other hand, the beneficiaries of enforcement (for example, women, the disabled, or minority claimants) might also stand as a political force to be reckoned with. Since neither target population has an appreciable existing social construction advantage over the other, the president would need to craft his or her rhetoric carefully to cast the former group (business) in a negative light or in need of enforcement oversight, while placing the beneficiary group (claimants) in a more positive light through symbolic images, historical narrative, or personal stories. Presidents might also seek to constrict or expand the relevant target populations to accentuate the public profile of benefited groups and to focus on less popular regulated groups, especially egregious offenders or businesses that are already negatively perceived.

In contrast, an easier case for the president would be homeland security enforcement where the target of enforcement efforts are suspected terrorists or those who might be associated with suspected terrorists (both politically weak and negatively perceived) and the protected target group is essentially the rest of the country. Little presidential management or adjustment of existing social constructions would be necessary in this situation. As these examples reveal, presidents planning to go public in order to influence bureaucrats' implementation of policy will find that issues fall along a continuum of viability, depending on the existing social constructions of the issue and relevant target groups.

Target Populations, Policy Inequities, and the Collateral Consequences of the War on Drugs

Of course, presidents are strategic politicians and probably would not employ an approach of going public to setting the policy agenda and leadership if it did not pay dividends. Neither Ford nor Carter was able to scale back Nixon's war on drugs. Carter experienced significant backlash when he proposed the decriminalization of marijuana. But Reagan and Bush took up the mantle of the war on drugs in the 1980s and ratcheted up its intensity in terms of both rhetoric and enforcement—and the Republican Party occupied the White House for twelve years. In the 1990s Bill Clinton, not to be outdone in this matter, worked hard to undercut Republican claims that they were the law-and-order party by expanding the war on drugs and calling for 100,000 new police officers on the streets (Beckett 1997; Lichtblau 2004).

Since the advent of the war on drugs, it can be politically dangerous for a federal government politician, especially a president, to be perceived as soft on narcotics enforcement (Beckett 1997). Naturally, public appeals promoting the drug war and the escalation of narcotics enforcement would be largely untenable politically if the drug war, either in its social construction or its implementation, were to target directly populations that were being courted or were politically powerful (Yates and Fording 2005). We might imagine a quite different public reaction to the war on drugs if, hypothetically, DEA officials or state and local agents followed a president's public appeals and broke down front doors in the gated communities of suburbia and arrested the children of upper-middle-class voters. It is hard to see a president trying such a strategy, yet it is possible that it would actually be more effective at reducing drug use among the nation's youth.

This shows how strongly the political implications of the war on drugs are intertwined with the policy campaign's social construction and implementation. Beckett and Sasson suggest that the drug war is largely the product of political efforts to realign the electorate and to define social control, rather than social welfare, as government's primary responsibility (Beckett and Sasson 2000). Others go further and argue that public rhetoric concerning the drug war has allowed politicians (especially conservatives) to move away from past appeals identifying directly disfavored groups (like minorities), which are now off limits, to more euphemistic or "coded" appeals. Those appeals, on issues such as crime and drug abuse, may indirectly tap into similar prejudicial sentiments without threatening democratic ideals (Kinder and Sanders 1996; Beckett and Sasson 2000; Jacobs and Carmichael 2001).

The ultimate effectiveness of the drug war in alleviating drug abuse is zealously debated, and the issue is unlikely to be resolved any time soon (Tonry 1995; Bennett, DiIulio, and Walters 1996). Yet there truly are social consequences of the war on drugs. For instance, figure 8.1 shows the dramatic rise over time in the percentage of the federal prison population that is incarcerated for drug offenses. In 1980, drug offenders constituted less than 25 percent of federal prison inmates; by 1989 it had more than doubled; by 1994 it was just over 60 percent; by 2003, the level was holding steady at 55 percent.[1] Another way to consider the impact of the drug war is how the prison population of drug offenders has changed relative to "index" crimes (other serious, nondrug crimes). In 1980, the rate of drug-offense federal prisoners per 1000 index crimes was 23; by 1998, it was 94.[2] Between 1996 and 2002, the largest component of jail population growth was drug offenders.[3] Clearly, the war on drugs has changed the composition of those who serve time in federal prison. States have also experienced these shifts in their incarcerated populations, and while not as drastic as in the federal population, the effects are substantial enough that there has arisen a veritable cottage industry of publishing proposals to deal with the social burdens of incarceration (Parenti 2000; Dyer 2001; Wright 2003; Matlin and Reed 2005; Elsner 2006).

More important, we now understand that the significant effects of the drug war on the overall prison population have not been distributed equally among the nation's citizens. As in many American military endeavors, minorities, immigrants, and the poor have shouldered inordinate costs in the war on drugs. Usually these

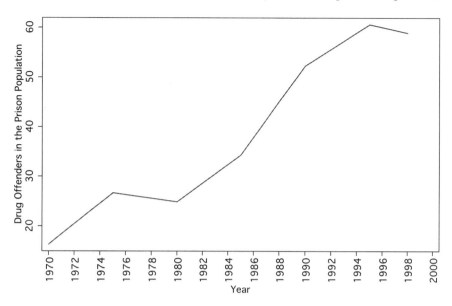

Figure 8.1. Percentage of the Federal Prison Population Incarcerated for Drug Offenses

groups bear the costs of war in the form of inequitable conscription and draft policies; in the war on drugs, the costs take the form of unequal enforcement and punishment (Yates, Collins, and Chin 2005). The effects are striking—in 1999, African Americans represented roughly 12.8 percent of the nation's population—but 35.2 percent of all drug offense arrests. In 2000 more African-American prisoners were incarcerated in the federal system for drug offenses than for all other offenses committed by African Americans combined.[4] Yet surveys show that minorities are generally no more likely to abuse narcotics than nonminorities and are less likely to abuse certain types of drugs than whites (Tonry 1995, 108–110). Immigrants also do not fare well when presidents have shifted emphasis to law and order. Around forty-eight thousand aliens were deported for criminal or drug violations from 1908 to 1980, but over thirty thousand alien removals were made on the basis of criminal or narcotics offenses from 1980 to 1989 alone.[5] As we might expect, one of the strongest criticisms of the drug war stems from these collateral consequences for disempowered target populations. One specific claim is that minorities are inordinately "taxed" for criminal justice policies since they are held to closer scrutiny and suffer disparate treatment (Kennedy 1997). What if the drug war was founded on an alternate rationale? Kennedy argues: "The war on drugs, although truly aimed against illicit narcotics, is conducted in a fashion that is negligently indifferent to the war's collateral damage to blacks. . . . If the war on drugs did to white communities what it is doing to black communities, white policymakers would long ago have called a truce in order to pursue some other, less destructive course" (1997, 351). Of course, one person's "negligent indifference" is another's "intentional bias." A part of our argument is that the social construction of the war on drugs is predicated on the nefarious "other" from which some favored group must be protected. While the president may not identify that other directly, it seems clear to many that the criminal justice system has done so.

What Lies Ahead

Whether one grades it as effective or ineffective, as equitable or inequitable, the war on drugs stands as one of the most ambitious presidential policy campaigns since World War II. The war on drugs probably has afforded recent presidents with valuable political leverage and has decisively captured the attention (if not the hearts and minds) of policymakers, the media, and the public. Will the drug war last as a hammer for presidents who want to rally broad support and demonstrate their strength as leaders? Will presidents want to use their power of the bully pulpit to promote this cause in the future, or will they turn the power of the pulpit to other, more advantageous issues? How far can presidents stretch the impact of public appeals to other topics that they find useful to make issues—and how far can they extend this power in getting public servants to do what they want?

The events of September 11, 2001, brought the drug war a competitor for national policy attention in the form of the war on terror. Of course, the Bush administration has worked to fold the war on drugs into anti-terrorism sentiment by using public service ads to link the two, a claim made easier by Afghanistan's historical role in opium production. But it remains to be seen whether the drug war campaign per se can retain its market share as a policy priority. In practical terms, the billions of dollars spent annually to fight terrorism will likely come from funds that were previously earmarked for the drug war. At a more fundamental level, terrorism represents for most Americans a different but more prominent and visceral fear in which it is necessary that the chief executive be involved. By contrast, over time many have come to consider narcotics use a matter better handled by citizens and communities without involving the central government (Lichtblau 2004).

It may also be that the standing social construction of the war on drugs will not resonate with policy makers and citizens in the same way it has in past years. The demographic profiles of high-ranking policy officials and citizen leaders continue to shift with time, and the attitudes of freethinking baby boomers who came of age in the more drug-amenable 1960s and 1970s increasingly have come to the political and social forefront. For instance, in 1986 only 8 percent of national survey respondents 50 years of age and over were in favor of marijuana legalization; in 2002 three times as many (24 percent) of the group age 50 and older favored legalization.[6] This does not constitute a majority, but it does show how dramatic the shift in attitude has been within this age group. Similarly, attitudes have shifted among the nation's young adults. In 1989 only 16.7 percent of college freshman favored legalization of marijuana; in 2002, 39.7 percent of freshman endorsed legalization.[7] Maybe mass opinion does not dictate policy outcomes, but it does reflect (to a certain degree) how the views of public officials who make policy may change and how the social environment within in which they work has changed. Presidents may come to find it less useful to prioritize the war on drugs in their policy rhetoric, and agency officials may find an enforcement-oriented approach to the drug problem less appealing. Bill Clinton's widely discussed failure to inhale and George W. Bush's "irresponsible" actions during his youth show how presidents have struggled to describe their individual experiences with narcotics in the middle of a campaign. Barack Obama's admission that he once used cocaine shows how far society has moved, even if he made those admissions well before he aspired to become president (Romano 2007). One indicator of the extent of that change is the response by Republican strategists that Obama's admission was not a "disqualifier" per se, since many baby boomers probably had tried marijuana (if not other illegal drugs) in the 1960s or 1970s and would have a higher tolerance for its past use among politicians.

Will presidents continue to lead agenda-setting and policy implementation through public appeals? Our focus in this book has been a single, though significant, policy initiative, yet our theoretical approach and the demonstrable sentiment of those who make policy in other issue areas (like Secretary of Treasury Don Regan) give us reason to believe that presidents are pretty good at identifying and promoting a social construction that supports their policy priorities. Presidents may be unable to find constructions that span or support issues on which they would like to change implementation so that it is closer to their preferences.

The president will not be able to force just any issue to the forefront, to make just any issue a policy priority for those who implement the law. But when presidents can effectively construct and manipulate social frames (Schneider and Ingram 1993) or otherwise provide clear and compelling signals among inconsistent perspectives (Zarefsky 2004) for those at the vanguard of policy, in those cases it is smart strategy for the president to do something as simple and as (relatively) costless as attempt to lead through focused public rhetoric.

What we cannot anticipate is whether the ability of presidents to lead policy— both how the agenda is set and how policy is implemented—through public rhetoric may change over time. Clearly, that Teddy Roosevelt was able to create a bully pulpit and change the role of the president (while constitutional powers remained static) shows that the milieu of American politics can change as the dynamics of public leadership evolve. In recent years, the advent of cable television and its vast array of choices for viewers has at least changed the president's power to lead through rhetoric and perhaps even "ended the golden age of presidential television" (Baum and Kernell 1999). The loss of their near-monopoly on television viewers has forced presidents to adapt their use of television for making pronouncements (the need to adapt only amplified by choice-driven satellite radio or internet-delivered video on demand).

Now presidents who want to set the policy agenda through public rhetoric must consider not only the social construction of issues and how their rhetoric benefits from and adds to that construction, they must struggle with how they fit those constructions into their own rhetoric. More important, they must also consider how rapidly the competitive market for ideas and attentions within which they work is changing. Presidents will have to be creative and tactical in getting their message across to the people who make policy happen. What aids their cause is that they have been pretty good at it so far.

Variables for Chapter 5

Variable	Description and Source
DEA Enforcement Effort (dependent variable)	The annual number of DEA arrests in a given state per 100,000 state citizens. *Source*: DEA, internal administrative files (various years).
Drug Deaths	The annual number of drug related deaths in a state, per 100,000 state citizens. *Source*: Center For Disease Control (Health and Human Services). *Website*: http://wonder.cdc.gov/wonder/data/mortSQL .html.
Presidential Rhetoric	The annual composition of the president's public statements dealing with the war on drugs—the ratio of paragraphs dealing with the problem of drugs to total pages multiplied by 100 (i.e., drug paragraphs per 100 pages of text). *Source*: *Public Papers of the Presidents of the United States* (U.S. Government Printing Office, various years).
Congressional Hearings	Congressional hearings on narcotics as a percentage of all congressional hearings. *Source*: Frank Baumgartner and Bryan Jones' Policy Agendas Project. *Website*: www.policyagendas.org.
Local Priority Opinion	Regional public demand—the percentage of respondents believing that "too little" resources are being spent to combat the drug problem. *Source*: National Opinion Research Center (General Social Surveys) *Criminal Justice Sourcebook* (various years).
Local Institutional Ideology	Ideology index of primary state political institutions. *Source*: Berry et al. (1998), updated.
Press Coverage	The annual percentage of stories in the *New York Times* related to the drug problem. *Source*: Frank Baumgartner and Bryan Jones' Policy Agendas Project. *Website*: www.policyagendas.org.

DEA Staff Capacity	The annual number of national full-time equivalent DEA staff. *Source*: DEA, internal administrative files (various years).
Post-Forfeiture Period	Dichotomous identifier for years following the 1984 Comprehensive Crime Control Act and related legislation. *Source*: Pub. L. No. 98-473 (1984).
DEA Administrator	Dichotomous identifier for the DEA administrator. *Source*: DEA organizational charts (various years). *Website*: www.dea.gov.

Descriptive Statistics for Variables

Variable	Obs	Mean	Std. Dev.	Min	Max
DEA Enforcement Effort	908	1.9515	0.6611	0.7547	3.6718
Drug Deaths	908	2.9264	1.6609	0.2102	11.1312
Presidential Rhetoric	908	8.0286	5.6663	0	20
Congressional Hearings	908	1.5707	0.7884	0.59	3.4
Local Priority Opinion	908	60.7280	5.5079	48	73
Local Institutional Ideology	908	51.1457	23.0994	0	97.9167
Press Coverage	908	0.7634	0.5142	0.1560	1.7308
DEA Staff Capacity	908	10.6681	0.0334	10.6206	10.7234
Post-Forfeiture Period	908	0.7555	0.4300	0	1

Variables for Chapter 6

Variable	Description and Source
Cases Handled (dependent variable)	Annual percentage of drug cases handled (brought to prosecution) out of all cases handled across 89 U.S. Attorney districts. *Source*: Executive Office of the U.S. Attorneys (EOUSA) internal administrative files, both in paper and electronic form (various years).
Cases Concluded (dependent variable)	Annual percentage of drug cases concluded (disposition recorded in court) out of all cases concluded across 89 U.S. Attorney districts. *Source*: Executive Office of the U.S. Attorneys (EOUSA) internal administrative files, both in paper and electronic form (various years).
Matters Handled	The annual number of U.S. Attorney referrals from investigating agencies that are not immediately declined. *Source*: Executive Office of the U.S. Attorneys (EOUSA) internal administrative files, both in paper and electronic form (various years).
Presidential Rhetoric	The annual composition of the president's public statements dealing with the war on drugs—the ratio of paragraphs dealing with the problem of drugs to total pages multiplied by 100 (i.e., drug paragraphs per 100 pages of text). *Source*: *Public Papers of the Presidents of the United States* (U.S. Government Printing Office, various years).
Congressional Hearings	Congressional hearings on narcotics as a percentage of all congressional hearings. *Source*: Frank Baumgartner and Bryan Jones' Policy Agendas Project. *Website*: www.policyagendas.org.
Local Priority Opinion	Regional public demand—the percentage of respondents believing that "too little" resources are being spent to combat the drug problem. *Source*: National Opinion Research Center (General Social Surveys) *Criminal Justice Sourcebook* (various years)

Local Institutional Ideology	Ideology index of primary state political institutions. *Source*: Berry et al. (1998), updated.
Press Coverage	The annual percentage of stories in the *New York Times* related to the drug problem. *Source*: Frank Baumgartner and Bryan Jones' Policy Agendas Project. *Website*: www.policyagendas.org.
U.S. Attorney Staff Capacity	The annual number of U.S. Attorney office staff across the 89 U.S. Attorney districts. *Source*: Executive Office of the U.S. Attorneys (EOUSA) internal administrative files, both in paper and electronic form (various years).
U.S. Attorney's Party	Partisan identification of the district's U.S. Attorney. *Source*: U.S. Department of Justice, Executive Office for United States Attorneys (USDOJ EOUSA), *Bicentennial Celebration of the United States Attorneys: 1789–1989* (Washington, D.C.: Executive Office for United States Attorneys, 1989). Updated by Yates and Whitford.
Post-Forfeiture Period	Dichotomous identifier for years following the 1984 Comprehensive Crime Control Act and related legislation. *Source*: Pub. L. No. 98-473 (1984).

Descriptive Statistics for Variables

Variable	Obs	Mean	Std. Dev.	Min	Max
Cases Handled	1157	22.8557	11.7564	0.4	66.2
Cases Concluded	1157	19.6917	11.6293	0	68.3
Matters Handled	1157	11.3163	7.5804	0	53.3
Presidential Rhetoric	1157	7.0283	6.0879	0.2811	19.7601
Congressional Hearings	1157	87.4615	31.9744	44	154
Local Priority Opinion	1157	61.3915	6.6425	35	73
Local Institutional Ideology	1157	52.4283	19.6474	4.4	95.0417
Press Coverage	1157	0.0072	0.0051	0.0016	0.0173
U.S. Attorney Staff Capacity	1157	2.9699	0.8229	0.7419	5.3279
U.S. Attorney's Party	1157	0.1815	0.3856	0	1
Post-Forfeiture Period	1157	0.6154	0.4867	0	1

Variables for Chapter 7

Variable	Description and Source
State Enforcement Effort (dependent variable)	The annual percentage of state drug arrests out of all arrests. *Source*: Federal Bureau of Investigation Uniform Crime Reports (various years). *Website*: www.fbi.gov.
Drug Deaths	The annual number of citizen drug related deaths in a state, per 100,000 state citizens. *Source*: Center For Disease Control (Health and Human Services). *Website*: http://wonder.cdc.gov/wonder/data/mortSQL .html.
Presidential Rhetoric	The annual composition of the president's public statements dealing with the war on drugs—the ratio of paragraphs dealing with the problem of drugs to total pages multiplied by 100 (i.e., drug paragraphs per 100 pages of text). *Source*: *Public Papers of the Presidents of the United States* (U.S. Government Printing Office, various years).
Congressional Hearings	Congressional hearings on narcotics as a percentage of all congressional hearings. *Source*: Frank Baumgartner and Bryan Jones' Policy Agendas Project. *Website*: www.policyagendas.org.
Local Priority Opinion	Regional public demand—the percentage of respondents believing that "too little" resources are being spent to combat the drug problem. *Source*: National Opinion Research Center (General Social Surveys) *Criminal Justice Sourcebook* (various years).
Local Institutional Ideology	Ideology index of primary state political institutions. *Source*: Berry et al. (1998), updated.
Press Coverage	The annual percentage of stories in the *New York Times* related to the drug problem. *Source*: Frank Baumgartner and Bryan Jones' Policy Agendas Project. *Website*: www.policyagendas.org.

Full-Time Employees   The annual level of state enforcement staffing per
                             100,000 citizens. *Source: Criminal Justice Sourcebook*
                             (various years).
Post-Forfeiture Period   Dichotomous identifier for years following the 1984
                             Comprehensive Crime Control Act and related
                             legislation. *Source*: Pub. L. No. 98-473 (1984).

Descriptive Statistics for Variables

Variable	Obs	Mean	Std. Dev.	Min	Max
State Enforcement Effort	905	6.8540	3.2017	0.8532	23.8685
Drug Deaths	905	2.8969	1.6744	0.2102	11.1312
Presidential Rhetoric	905	7.7867	5.7411	0	20
Congressional Hearings	905	1.5560	0.7869	0.59	3.4
Local Priority Opinion	905	60.6541	5.4983	48	73
Local Institutional Ideology	905	51.1720	22.8803	0	97.9167
Press Coverage	905	0.7458	0.5113	0.1560	1.7308
Full-Time Employees	905	8.9229	1.1102	6.5066	11.4329
Post-Forfeiture Period	905	0.7315	0.4434	0	1

Estimation Method

Our data analysis strategy is to model the causal relationships by using a version of generalized linear models, specifically generalized estimating equations, or GEE (Zeger and Liang 1986a, b). GEE is appropriate for situations such as this, in which we have created a panel data set covering the DEA regions over a series of years.* The primary advantages of the GEE approach are the availability of flexible error correlation structures, robust standard errors, and alternative distributional assumptions. This procedure is appropriate for the case of cross-section–dominant or time series–dominant data sets. Most importantly, this procedure yields parameter estimates that are uncontaminated by the effects of heteroskedastic and autocorrelated errors. Since we have repeated measures on the units of analysis, underlying (immeasurable or unmeasured) panel-specific effects can complicate the estimation of the common coefficients. Heteroskedasticity is also likely because each panel's variance may differ and there may be variation of scale among the units. The model here includes the calculation of the robust estimate of the variance to address this and also relaxes the independent-observations assumption for common units of analysis. Specifically, because GEE is a population-averaged estimator, it is similar to a random-effects approach, but population-averaged estimators specify a marginal distribution, so estimates are an average of the cluster-specific estimates. We also calculate Huber-White standard errors to address the population-averaged estimate's robustness.

The dependent variable may shift slowly in time if adjoining observations may be serially correlated. Specifically, in GEE estimation, n_i is the number of observations for a group, $\mathbf{R}$ is the within-group working correlation matrix (a square $\max\{n_i\} \times \max\{n_i\}$ matrix) for modeling the within-group correlation; $\mathbf{R}_{t,s}$ denotes the t,s element. For the GEE equivalent (population-averaged) of a random effects structure, $\mathbf{R}_{t,s}=1$ if $t=s$; otherwise, $\mathbf{R}_{t,s}=\rho$. For an AR(1) structure, $\mathbf{R}_{t,s}=1$ if $t=s$; otherwise, $\mathbf{R}_{t,s}=\rho^{|t-s|}$. In the final case, each model assumes that the error correlation structure is "unstructured," which simultaneously accounts for possible "stickiness"

---

* Models estimated with pooled cross-sectional time series frequently involve violations of OLS assumptions of homoskedasticity and uncorrelated error terms (Kmenta 1986; Greene 1993). While OLS estimates are unbiased in the presence of autocorrelation, these estimates are not efficient, and the variability of OLS coefficients contaminates tests of statistical significance.

in the dependent variable and immeasurable effects by making no specific assumption about the form of the error correlation structure. The only constraint is that the matrix's diagonal elements are 1: $\mathbf{R}_{t,s}=1$ if $t=s$; otherwise, $\mathbf{R}_{t,s}=\rho_{ts}$ (where $\rho_{ts}=\rho_{st}$). In the model here, the GEE specification includes a Gaussian distribution for the dependent variable and an identity link function (the canonical link for the Gaussian distribution).

Notes

CHAPTER THREE: A Presidential History of the War on Drugs

1. For example, in 1919 the Supreme Court affirmed in *Webb, et al. v. United States* (249 U.S. 96) and in 1920 in *Jin Fuel Moy v. United States* (920.SCT.612, 254 U.S. 189, 65 L. Ed. 214, 41 S. Ct. 98) that doctors had limited immunity under the Harrison Act. In 1922, the Supreme Court argued in *United States v. Behrman* that a doctor's prescription of cocaine for an addict constituted an unlawful "gratification of a diseased appetite for these pernicious drugs" (1922.SCT.177, 258 U.S. 280, 66 L. Ed. 619, 42 S. Ct. 303).

2. In 1927 the Division was transferred to the Bureau of Prohibition (the "Prohibition Unit").

3. The investigation also revealed connections between Levi Nutt (head of the Narcotic Division) and Rothstein. Also, the FNCB did little to regulate the domestic and international drug trade (Musto 1999, 203, 209).

4. Accounts of the FBN's activities include Anslinger's own *The Murderers: The Shocking Story of the Narcotic Gangs* (1962) and *The Protectors* (1964).

5. However, the Kennedy administration did support strong action with regard to pharmaceuticals. The events surrounding the use of thalidomide by pregnant women led to the Kefauver-Harris Amendment of 1962, which changed the process of approval and regulation of new drugs by the FDA.

6. Besteman describes a range of events regarding the growing demand for drug treatment that preceded the Kennedy Commission on Narcotics and Drug Abuse (Besteman 1990, 66).

7. Johnson addressed these trends in his message to Congress in March 1965 (Johnson 1965). To develop a strategy, he created the Commission on Law Enforcement and the Administration of Justice (the Katzenbach Commission), with an emphasis on uncovering the root causes of crime (E.O. 11236). The Law Enforcement Assistance Act of 1965 authorized the commission and provided funds for local enforcement. The commission asked for more funding for the War on Poverty and state and local law enforcement efforts; it also recommended reduced enforcement of narcotics control laws (Katzenbach 1967). The 1968 Omnibus Crime Control and Safe Streets Act greatly expanded the use of block grants to the states and local governments; it was administered by the Law Enforcement Assistance Administration (LEAA). On the history of the federal response to crime control, see O'Bryant and Seghetti (2002).

8. Available at www.presidency.ucsb.edu/ws/?pid=2126, accessed December 17, 2008.

9. Available at www.presidency.ucsb.edu/ws/index.php?pid=3590, accessed December 17, 2008.

10. See "Multi-Agency Force Halts Contraband," *Customs Today* 6, no. 3 (December 1969): 1, 12; and "The Customs Bureau: Making 'A Trip' More Difficult," *Government Executive* 1, no. 10 (December 1969): 2. For expanded views on Operation Intercept as a watershed event in the War on Drugs, see Shannon (1988) and Liddy (1998).

11. *Leary v. United States* (1969) SCT.1512, 395 U.S. 6, 89 S. Ct. 1532, 23 L. Ed. 2d 57. May 19, 1969.

12. The Act also led to revision of many state laws as the states sought consistency with the new schedule system (National Conference of Commissioners on Uniform State Laws 1970, 3; King 1972, 320). Some states chose to make their laws more punitive at this point (Rockefeller 1973). Other conferences for making state drug laws uniform followed (President's Commission on Model State Drug Laws 1993, 2).

13. Letter from Elvis Presley to Richard M. Nixon. Undated. Delivered to the White House on December 21, 1970. The event is well documented at "When Nixon Met Elvis," available at www.archives.gov/exhibits/when_nixon_met_elvis/letter.html, accessed December 17, 2008. For more information on this unusual episode, see Krogh (1994), Kirchberg and Hendrickx (1999), and Lowy (2001). Baum writes that Elvis inquired at the BNDD earlier, offered a $5,000 donation for a badge, and was thrown out (1996, 46).

14. Nixon, "Special Message to the Congress About the District of Columbia." April 7, 1971. Available at www.presidency.ucsb.edu/ws/?pid=2969, accessed December 17, 2008. Several agencies within HEW, including the National Institute for Mental Health, funded treatment, which led to conflict between agencies and between HEW and the administration. Rettig and Yarmolinsky (1995) describe federal support for and the regulation of methadone. Musto reports that a high-ranking BNDD staffer said "the bureau would hand out heroin if it thought that would cut crime" (1998).

15. Nixon, "Special Message to the Congress on Drug Abuse Prevention and Control," June 17, 1971. Available at www.presidency.ucsb.edu/ws/?pid=3048, accessed December 17, 2008.

16. The administration was hesitant to create a position of drug czar in negotiations with Congress over the legislation that created SAODAP (Musto and Korsmeyer 2002, 127). Anslinger might also be considered the first drug czar. The list of drug czars includes Jerome Jaffe, Myles Ambrose, Robert DuPont, Peter Bourne, Lee Dogoloff, Carlton Turner, Ian MacDonald, William Bennett, Robert Martinez, Lee Brown, Barry McCaffrey. George W. Bush named John P. Walters as director of the Office of National Drug Control Policy in 2001; he served the entire two terms.

17. In 1971 widespread reports suggested American soldiers were developing heroin addictions in Vietnam, with claims that 15 percent of 40,000 men were users. Nixon instituted "Operation Golden Flow" to address heroin use—testing by urinalysis

of those soldiers eligible for return; soldiers testing positive were provided detoxi-fication and treatment prior to their return (Baker 1972; Stanton 1976). Deputy Krogh's trip to Vietnam prompted his choice of Jaffe (Baum 1996, 50). Jaffe was se-lected to consolidate all federal programs under SAODAP. Nixon overruled military code that drug use was grounds for a dishonorable discharge. Congress never fully authorized treatment (no methadone), and the success rate was surprisingly high (Baum 1996, 62).

18. There are indications that corruption required CIA involvement in counterin-telligence operations. See Rockefeller Commission (1975, 233).

19. Interview with Egil Krogh, Public Broadcasting Service website for the *Front-line* show "Drug Wars." Available at www.pbs.org/wgbh/pages/frontline/shows/drugs/interviews/krogh.html, accessed December 17, 2008.

20. Eugene T. Rossides, assistant Treasury secretary, and his deputy, G. Gordon Liddy, were responsible for all law-enforcement activities and were brought into con-flict with others like Mitchell at DOJ. Under Myles J. Ambrose, Customs started to take the lead in enforcement efforts that BNDD should have controlled; Rossides also argued for a new agency that would gather together federal, state, and local assets (Baum 1996, 60). He brought expanded the use of Internal Revenue Service tax au-dits and collection against suspected drug dealers. These efforts increasingly brought Treasury into conflict with the BNDD and Mitchell. Ambrose and Liddy often sought support from Krogh (Epstein 1977). Liddy joined the White House domestic policy team in June 1971.

21. Interestingly, Mitchell was left out of the process: he was unaware of the reor-ganization until its announcement on television (Baum 1996, 68).

22. ODALE was the beginning of a modern law enforcement organization for dealing with the post-1960s narcotics crisis. Assets involved included BNDD per-sonnel; the Immigration and Naturalization Service; the U.S. Marshals Service; the DOJ Tax Division; the U.S. Attorneys; the IRS; Customs; and the Bureau of Alcohol, Tobacco, and Firearms; the Atomic Energy Commission; the Air Force; the Environmental Protection Agency; and the Interstate Commerce Commission. ODALE was given little access to resources (since it was formed by executive order, it had no Congress-appropriated funds), so all salaries and other costs were borne by other agencies. For example, most of the special prosecutors hired were em-ployed by the DOJ as "temporary consultants"; funds from the LEAA, although intended by Congress for local governments, were funneled through new local or-ganizations called "Research Associates" and then on to the strike forces (Epstein 1977).

23. Both quotations are from the transcript of the Public Broadcasting Service *Frontline* show "Drug Wars." Available at www.pbs.org/wgbh/pages/frontline/shows/drugs/etc/script.html, accessed December 17, 2008.

24. Interview with Myles Ambrose. Public Broadcasting Service website for the *Frontline* show "Drug Wars." Available at www.pbs.org/wgbh/pages/frontline/shows/drugs/interviews/ambrose.html, accessed December 17, 2008.

25. Nixon, "Message to the Congress Transmitting Reorganization Plan 2 of 1973 Establishing the Drug Enforcement Administration." March 28, 1973. Available at www.presidency.ucsb.edu/ws/?pid=4159, accessed December 17, 2008.

26. The benefits of the DEA were considered to be an end to the rivalries involving the BNDD and Customs and the FBI (responsible for organized crime); the creation of a focal point for state, local, and foreign governments; the existence of a single administrator to make the agency more accountable; the consolidation of drug enforcement operations; and momentum for coordinating all federal efforts related to drug enforcement (especially those outside DOJ). For a full description of the proposal, see Rachel (1982); see also Epstein (1977).

27. Rossides has said, "If not for Watergate, can you imagine what they would have done with the Drug Enforcement Agency?"—an indication of the power of the third-largest investigative agency (Epstein 1977).

28. Jaffe resigned in early 1973, and was replaced by DuPont. In an interesting illustration of Nixon's shifting priorities, SAODAP was ordered to vacate the White House annex it shared with BNDD in October 1973 to "make way for the energy crisis" (Epstein 1977).

29. Nixon, "Remarks at the First National Treatment Alternatives to Street Crime Conference," September 11, 1973. Available at www.presidency.ucsb.edu/ws/?pid=3958, accessed December 17, 2008.

30. Ford, "Message to the Congress on Legislative Priorities," September 12, 1974. Available at www.presidency.ucsb.edu/ws/?pid=4708, accessed December 17, 2008.

31. Ford, "Message to the Congress on Legislative Priorities," November 18, 1974. Available at www.presidency.ucsb.edu/ws/?pid=4566, accessed December 17, 2008.

32. Drug Abuse Office and Treatment Act Amendments of 1976. Public Law 94-237.

33. Ford, "Special Message to the Congress on a Proposed Appropriations Rescission for the Office of Drug Abuse Policy," July 1, 1976. Available at www.presidency.ucsb.edu/ws/?pid=6170, accessed December 17, 2008.

34. Nixon called for mandatory minimum sentences for heroin trafficking in the 1973 State of the Union Address. Congress did not act on that proposal; he called for it again in 1974 without effect. See Nixon, "State of the Union Message to the Congress on Law Enforcement and Drug Abuse Prevention," 1973; and "Special Message to the Congress Proposing Legislation To Control Drug Trafficking," 1974. Available at www.presidency.ucsb.edu/ws/?pid=4140 and www.presidency.ucsb.edu/ws/?pid=4361, accessed December 17, 2008.

35. Ford, "Special Message to the Congress on Drug Abuse," April 27, 1976. Available at www.presidency.ucsb.edu/ws/?pid=5875, accessed December 17, 2008.

36. Liddy suggested defoliation of marijuana fields during the planning stages for Operation Intercept (Baum 1996, 106).

37. After 1978, the parent movement had grown in power, and NORML and others were unable to convince other states to decriminalize possession (Baum 1996,

126). Oregon and Alaska voted to recriminalize possession of some small quantities of marijuana in 1989 and 1990 (Goode 1997, 48).

38. In March 1977, Carter reestablished the Strategy Council, created by the Drug Abuse Office and Treatment Act of 1972, to serve as the primary advisory committee for narcotics control policy; Bourne, as head of ODAP, was executive director of the council. Carter, "Office of Drug Abuse Policy Memorandum for the Heads of Certain Departments and Agencies," March 14, 1977. Available at www.presidency.ucsb.edu/ws/?pid=7174, accessed December 17, 2008.

39. Carter, "Drug Abuse Message to the Congress," August 2, 1977. Available at www.presidency.ucsb.edu/ws/?pid=7908, accessed December 17, 2008.

40. Carter, "Drug Abuse Message to the Congress," August 2, 1977.

41. See DEA, "A Tradition of Excellence: 1975–1980." Available at www.dea.gov/pubs/history/1975–1980.html, accessed December 17, 2008.

42. Paraquat, which is still one of the most commonly used herbicides, is a toxic chemical known for the damage it causes to a person's lungs, liver, and kidneys.

43. A 1978 HEW report indicated potential lung damage, but it is unclear whether that marijuana was harvestable. In 1979, the Center for Disease Control (as it was then called) announced a finding of no evidence of paraquat poisoning in the case of marijuana (Baum 1996, 127).

44. Interview with Peter Bourne, Public Broadcasting Service website for the *Frontline* show "Drug Wars." Available at www.pbs.org/wgbh/pages/frontline/shows/drugs/interviews/bourne.html, accessed December 17, 2008.

45. NBC Evening News, "Bourne Affair/Resignation," July 20, 1978. Summary available at the Vanderbilt Television News Archive, http://tvnews.vanderbilt.edu, accessed December 17, 2008. See also "The Wrong Rx for Peter Bourne." *Time*, July 31, 1978.

46. Bourne's resignation started a process that led to Stroup's resignation from NORML (Anderson 1981, ch. 18). American use of herbicides to control production in other countries continued.

47. The Act also implemented the Convention on Psychotropic Substances (signed in 1971) with a system for controlling amphetamines and barbiturates. Carter, "Psychotropic Substances Act of 1978 Statement on Signing S. 2399 Into Law," November 10, 1978. Available at www.presidency.ucsb.edu/ws/?pid=30148, accessed December 17, 2008.

48. "Marihuana: A Conversation with NIDA's Robert L. DuPont," *Science*, May 14, 1976, pp. 647–649.

49. Schuchard wrote under a pen name, Marsha Manatt. DuPont's last act as NIDA head was to give Schuchard a contract for writing the pamphlet; he considered her lack of scientific credentials "refreshing," and his successor, William Pollin, actively supported the pamphlet (Baum 1996, 122). *Parents, Peers, and Pot* is basically the government's official statement on marijuana and teenagers and historically the most-requested NIDA publication (Manatt 1979). On NIDA alterations to

the pamphlet text, see Massing (1998, 152). With the help of Sue Rusche, Schuchard formed Families in Action as the first national organization for fighting teenage drug use; later, Schuchard helped form the Parents' Resource Institute for Drug Education.

50. "White House Prepares War on Marijuana," *U.S. News and World Report,* May 21, 1979, p. 49.

51. While some states had decriminalized possession by this time, others increased penalties for possession. For example, a blue-ribbon commission in Texas led by H. Ross Perot was leading a "Texans' War on Drugs," with substantial assistance from Carlton Turner, a leading marijuana pharmacologist (Baum 1996, 128).

52. Reagan, "The President's News Conference," March 6, 1981, available at www .presidency.ucsb.edu/ws/?pid=43505, accessed December 17, 2008.

53. The initiative would lead in 1987 to the Partnership for a Drug-Free America, a nonprofit coalition that would run the third-largest American advertising campaign ever (Bennett and DiLorenzo 1992). Nancy Reagan's initiative became a genuine national phenomenon. For instance, schoolchildren in California formed the Just Say No Club movement, which went national and eventually had the fictional television character Punky Brewster as its honorary national chairperson; Mrs. Reagan also appeared on that primetime television show and others (Carmody 1985; Massing 1998, 174). In 1985, she held a conference of first ladies from nineteen countries to expand on her message of the role of volunteers in the war on drugs; a key speaker was Schuchard, representing the parent movement (Dillin 1985). On the role of Reagan's staff in managing Mrs. Reagan's rhetorical agenda on drugs, see Radcliffe (1985).

54. Carter's first attorney general, Griffin Bell, vetted the merger but instead set up three joint FBI-DEA task forces (Babcock 1981b). The merger was a difficult one: DEA agents were civil service, while FBI agents were "excepted" service. The DEA had a history of close cooperation with state and local officials unknown at the FBI, and the FBI's international profile was lower.

55. These amendments were included in the 1982 Department of Defense Authorization Act. The CIA was drafted by E.O. 12333. For more on the effects of military assistance in the war on drugs, see Reuter et al. (1988).

56. Later in 1989, Congress designated the DOD as the "single lead agency" in narcotics interdiction, according to the National Defense Authorization Act for Fiscal Years 1990 and 1991 (Hammond 1997).

57. One reason it probably would not have received approval was strong congressional oversight of the FBI and its operations during this time (see Jeffreys-Jones 2007, 209).

58. Reagan, "Radio Address to the Nation on Federal Drug Policy," October 2, 1982. Available at www.presidency.ucsb.edu/ws/?pid=43085, accessed December 17, 2008.

59. For more information on the rise and impact of the Medellín cartel, see Gugliotta (1989) and Strong (1995).

60. It would be difficult to overstate the importance of the cartel in framing the Administration's responses. By March 1982, Escobar had been elected to the Colombian Congress and was cultivating a "Robin Hood" persona in the Medellín slums. While he was later driven out of Congress, from that point on politics and narcotics (and terrorism) were bound together. At home, the seizure in early 1982 of 3,906 pounds of cocaine (with a wholesale value of over $100 million) raised awareness of the power of the Medellín cartel to assemble substantial resources for production and shipment.

61. Reagan, "Statement Announcing the Establishment of a Federal Anticrime Task Force for Southern Florida," January 28, 1982. Available at www.presidency.ucsb.edu/ws/?pid=42775, accessed December 17, 2008.

62. Reagan, "Remarks Announcing Federal Initiatives Against Drug Trafficking and Organized Crime," October 14, 1982. Available at www.presidency.ucsb.edu/ws/?pid=43127, accessed December 17, 2008.

63. Reagan, "Remarks on Signing Executive Order 12368, concerning Federal Drug Abuse Policy Functions," June 24, 1982. Available at www.presidency.ucsb.edu/ws/?pid=42671, accessed December 17, 2008.

64. Mullen served as interim administrator from July 10, 1981, to November 10, 1983. His appointment was held up due to an investigation of the FBI's role in background checks of Reagan appointees, which affected his role at the DEA (Thornton 1982b). He served as administrator until March 1, 1985.

65. Reagan, "Statement on Proposed Anticrime Legislation," May 26, 1982. Available at www.presidency.ucsb.edu/ws/?pid=42568, accessed December 17, 2008.

66. Reagan, "Radio Address to the Nation on Crime and Criminal Justice Reform," September 11, 1982; and Reagan, "Message to the Congress Transmitting Proposed Criminal Justice Reform Legislation," September 13, 1982. Available at www.presidency.ucsb.edu/ws/?pid=42952 and www.presidency.ucsb.edu/ws/?pid=42956, accessed December 17, 2008.

67. The exclusionary rule is a judicially created prophylactic rule that helps enforce the rights of U.S. citizens as set forth in the Bill of Rights. It provides a remedy for constitutional violations whereby evidence obtained by the government in violation of a citizen's constitutional rights cannot be used against them in a criminal trial. The rule was stated in its present form by the U.S. Supreme Court in *Weeks v. U.S.* (1914), in which the Court held that evidence obtained in violation of the Constitution by federal authorities should be excluded at trial. The Supreme Court later made the exclusionary rule applicable to state and local authorities via the Due Process clause of the 14th Amendment in *Mapp v. Ohio* (1961).

68. Reagan, "Memorandum Returning Without Approval a Bill Concerning Contract Services for Drug Dependent Federal Offenders," January 14, 1983. Available at www.presidency.ucsb.edu/ws/?pid=41310, accessed December 17, 2008.

69. Reagan, "Address Before a Joint Session of the Congress on the State of the Union," January 25, 1983. Available at www.presidency.ucsb.edu/ws/?pid=41698, accessed December 17, 2008.

70. Reagan, "Message to the Congress Transmitting Proposed Crime Control Legislation," March 16, 1983. Available at www.presidency.ucsb.edu/ws/?pid=41058, accessed December 17, 2008.

71. Reagan, "Radio Address to the Nation on Proposed Crime Legislation," February 18, 1984; "Radio Address to the Nation on Law Enforcement and Crime," July 7, 1984; and "Radio Address to the Nation on Congressional Inaction on Proposed Legislation," August 11, 1984. Available at www.presidency.ucsb.edu/ws/?pid=39541, www .presidency.ucsb.edu/ws/?pid=40135, and www.presidency.ucsb.edu/ws/?pid=40244. Accessed December 17, 2008.

72. 468 U.S. 897 (1984).

73. The House had started to construct an entirely different crime bill. In September, Congressman Dan Lungren (R-CA) attached a bill identical to the Senate one to an appropriations bill. The House voted under duress and passed what was essentially the president's bill (Baum 1996, 203).

74. The section that created the United States Sentencing Commission and sentencing guidelines for the federal courts is called the Sentencing Reform Act of 1984 (United States Sentencing Commission 2004, 5).

75. Reagan, "Interview With Southeast Regional Editors on Foreign and Domestic Issues," March 12, 1984. Available at www.presidency.ucsb.edu/ws/?pid=39626, accessed December 17, 2008.

76. Reagan, "Interview With Richard M. Smith, Morton M. Kondracke, Margaret Garrard Warner, and Elaine Shannon of Newsweek on the Campaign Against Drug Abuse," August 1, 1986. Available at www.presidency.ucsb.edu/ws/?pid=37699, accessed December 17, 2008.

77. Reagan, "Message to the Congress Transmitting Proposed Legislation to Combat Drug Abuse and Trafficking," September 15, 1986. Available at www.presidency.ucsb.edu/ws/?pid=36417, accessed December 17, 2008. Turner was the source of ideas regarding testing (Massing 1998, 183).

78. By 1983, forty-nine states had adopted mandatory minimums for drug possession (Musto 1999, 273).

79. A full discussion of disparities in arrests and incarceration rates for minorities is beyond the scope of this chapter. However, it is important to note two events in 1988 that focused attention to the racial aspects of the war on drugs. First, in 1988 the Los Angeles Police Department started Operation Hammer against the crack trade in South Central L.A., a strategy that had clear racial consequences (Davis 1990). Second, Attorney General Edwin Meese hired public relations firm Hill and Knowlton to alter the public perception of the war on drugs and its racial consequences (Epstein 1988). He also directed the U.S. Attorneys to prosecute upper-class and middle-class users selectively (Wisotsky 1992, 21).

80. "Drug Withdrawal," *Time*, January 19, 1987. Pollin left NIDA in 1985, to be replaced by Jaffe, former head of SAODAP. He found the administration to have little concern for treatment regimes: "They were still pretty much interested in PR

efforts—the Just Say No kind of thing—plus tough law enforcement" (quoted in Massing 1998, 180).

81. Bush, "Address to the Nation on the National Drug Control Strategy," September 5, 1989. Available at www.presidency.ucsb.edu/ws/?pid=17472, accessed December 17, 2008.

82. For a compilation of the events leading up to this, including the Bush administration's request for a bag of crack from the DEA and the DEA's sting operation, see Baum (1996, 287–289) and Reinarmen and Levine (1997, 23).

83. The annual document "Federal Strategy for Prevention of Drug Abuse and Drug Trafficking," though, dates back to 1973 pursuant to the Drug Abuse Office and Treatment Act of 1972.

84. The Thornburgh memo remained in force for most of the Clinton administration (in the form of the Reno Regulation) but ended with the McDade Amendment in 1999. On the power of the attorney general to limit the scope of discretion of the federal prosecutors, see Ely (2004).

85. Bonner earlier had lead the prosecution team against the executors of DEA Special Agent Camarena.

86. "Weed and seed" was in part a response to 1992 riots in Los Angeles.

87. There was a sense that ONDCP had become the dumping grounds for political supporters of the president.

88. Congress voiced discontent with the staff cuts at ONDCP (Merida 1993).

89. Congress passed the Comprehensive Methamphetamine Control Act of 1996 partly in response, tightening the control of precursor chemicals like pseudophedrine. A notable agreement with Wal-Mart followed in 1997 (DEA 2003b, 28).

90. The DEA was enjoined from revoking licenses in *Conant v. McCaffrey* (N.D. Cal. Sept. 7, 2000). By the end of 1982, thirty-one states had passed some kind of law addressing the use of medical marijuana. By the end of 2000, fourteen states had authorized or required a therapeutic regime program.

91. The main part of the increase came from the Violent Crime Reduction Program, which contributed an additional $220 million in FY 1997 to the DEA budget (U.S. DOJ 2002, 126). The Violent Crime Control and Law Enforcement Act of 1994 (P.L. 103-322) established the Violent Crime Reduction Program.

92. During the George W. Bush administration, the Federal Communications Commission would find that these buys violated payola laws.

93. An alternative view is that synthetic drugs accompany social upheaval, so their effects are inseparable from their causes (Jenkins 1999).

94. Bush, "Remarks Announcing the Nomination of John P. Walters To Be Director of the Office of National Drug Control Policy," May 10, 2001. Available at www .presidency.ucsb.edu/ws/?pid=45600, accessed December 17, 2008.

95. The DEA has also identified narcoterrorist interests in the domestic production and distribution of synthetic drugs like methamphetamine (DEA 2003b, 53).

CHAPTER FOUR: The Words of War

1. Our data are from the Centers for Disease Control and Prevention (Department of Health and Human Services). Changes to how these data are collected and assembled make it difficult to combine pre-1998 and post-1998 data. See "Compressed Mortality File" at the CDC website, available at http://wonder.cdc.gov/wonder/data/mortSQL.html, accessed December 18, 2008.

2. The inner fences appear at the points $Q_1 - 1.5 \times IQR$ and $Q_2 - 1.5 \times IQR$ where Q_1 and Q_2 are the first and second quartiles and IQR is the interquartile range.

3. See the appendices A–C for measurement details and description.

4. We note that our dependent variables are often constructed at the substate level (especially in the case of chapter 6). The Baumgartner-Jones *New York Times* variable is the best available on media coverage. We are unable to build that variable at the state level, and we cannot build it at the sub-state level. The fundamental problem in both cases is knowing the sampling frame: which papers to sample, and from those papers, what the universe of stories is. We would need both to build a more detailed measure of media attention to the War on Drugs.

5. Ronald Reagan, "Remarks Accepting the Presidential Nomination," August 23, 1984. Available at www.presidency.ucsb.edu/shownomination.php?convid=1, accessed December 18, 2008.

6. George Bush, "Acceptance Speech," August 18, 1988. Available at www.presidency.ucsb.edu/shownomination.php?convid=4, accessed December 18, 2008.

7. Michael Dukakis, "A New Era of Greatness for America: Michael S. Dukakis Accepting the Nomination for the Presidency of the United States," July 21, 1988. Available at www.presidency.ucsb.edu/shownomination.php?convid=10, accessed December 18, 2008.

8. William Clinton, "Acceptance Speech to the Democratic National Convention," July 16, 1992. Available at www.presidency.ucsb.edu/shownomination.php?convid=7, accessed December 18, 2008.

9. "First Clinton-Bush-Perot Presidential Debate," October 11, 1992. Available at www.presidency.ucsb.edu/showdebate.php?debateid=15, accessed December 18, 2008.

10. We note that the presidential statements variable and the hearings variable are correlated at 0.36. We also note the difficulty of addressing the additional question of causality in short time series like the ones analyzed here. To offer a level of evidence about the lack of causality, we estimated Granger causality tests after the estimation of a vector autoregression (VAR) model (Granger 1969; Hamilton 1994). Our tests show that we cannot reject the null hypothesis that either variable does not "Granger-cause" the other at any conventional significance level. Moreover, we have no difficulty including these variables as covariates in any of the models shown in chapters 5 through 7; the variance inflation factors from those regressions are well below levels of any concern; see below (Chatterjee and Hadi 2006).

11. Richard Nixon, "Radio Address about the State of the Union Message on Law Enforcement and Drug Abuse Prevention," March 10, 1973. Available at www.presidency.ucsb.edu/ws/?pid=4135, accessed December 18, 2008.

12. Gerald Ford, "Remarks at the Annual Conference of International Association of Chiefs of Police in Miami, Florida," September 27, 1976. Available at www.presidency.ucsb.edu/ws/?pid=6374, accessed December 18, 2008.

13. Jimmy Carter, "Drug Abuse Remarks on Transmitting a Message to the Congress," August 2, 1977. Available at www.presidency.ucsb.edu/ws/?pid=7907, accessed December 18, 2008.

14. Ronald Reagan, "Address to the Nation on the Campaign Against Drug Abuse," September 14, 1986. Available at www.presidency.ucsb.edu/ws/index.php?pid=36414, accessed December 18, 2008.

15. George H. W. Bush, "Remarks at an Antidrug Rally in Billings, Montana," July 20, 1990. Available at www.presidency.ucsb.edu/ws/index.php?pid=18693, accessed December 18, 2008.

16. William Clinton, "The President's Radio Address," March 1, 1997. Available at www.presidency.ucsb.edu/ws/index.php?pid=53808, accessed December 18, 2008.

17. William Clinton, "Remarks on the Zero Tolerance for Drugs in Prison Initiative," January 5, 1999. Available at www.presidency.ucsb.edu/ws/?pid=57610, accessed December 18, 2008.

18. George W. Bush, "Remarks on the Patriot Act in McLean, Virginia," June 10, 2005. Available at www.presidency.ucsb.edu/ws/?pid=63832, accessed December 18, 2008.

CHAPTER FIVE: Presidential Policy Leadership and Federal Enforcement

1. Interview with Robert Stutman, Public Broadcasting Service website for the *Frontline* show "Drug Wars." Available at www.pbs.org/wgbh/pages/frontline/shows/drugs/interviews/stutman.html, accessed December 19, 2008.

2. Ronald Reagan, "Remarks at a White House Ceremony Honoring Law Enforcement Officers Slain in the War on Drugs." April 19, 1988. Available at www.presidency.ucsb.edu/ws/?pid=35698 accessed December 19, 2008.

3. The DEA also has five international field divisions, but we do not focus on them.

4. See Personal DEA communication in response to Freedom of Information Act request (#06-0104-F): "However, in reference to the DEA staffing information you requested, DEA is unable to respond because no information is readily retrievable for the time period indicated and because the records sought may reveal information that could jeopardize DEA's security. Finally, we have no records which illustrate the changes that have occurred in DEA's Divisions."

5. We report data from 1980 to 1998 due to restrictions in data availability for a key independent variable; namely, the data coverage is conditional on the availability

of our main independent variable that serves as a control variable: the mortality data for drugs deaths. This measure appears in each model. We are unable to improve our coverage of this variable. For this reason, our figures in chapter 4 are often more inclusive, but our statistical models are smaller.

6. We investigated alternative proxies such as citizen self-reported use in surveys and annual emergency room admissions for drug overdose (Meier 1992). Those measures were unavailable either at the state level or for our extended time frame of analysis.

7. We are able to independently estimate only the effects for Bensinger, Lawn, Bonner, and Constantine due to collinearity. When we also estimate an intercept shift for forfeiture, we can only independently estimate fixed effects for Bensinger, Lawn, and Bonner.

8. Models estimated with pooled cross-sectional time series frequently involve violations of OLS assumptions of homoskedasticity and uncorrelated error terms (Kmenta, 1986; Greene, 1993). While OLS estimates are unbiased in the presence of autocorrelation, these estimates are not efficient, and the variability of OLS coefficients contaminates tests of statistical significance.

We do not need to estimate models that involve the Beck and Katz correction for the Parks GLS (general least squares) procedure. The Beck and Katz correction is important to improve the estimator when there are many fewer panel units than there are time periods per panel (for example, 10–20 panels and 10–40 periods). Our data are "wide" in the sense that there are either 50 or 89 cross-sectional units and fewer than 20 time periods per panel. We also note that the Beck-Katz correction is specific to GLS and does not apply to the GEE estimator that we use in this book. For more information, see Beck and Katz (1995).

9. We have no difficulty including these variables as covariates in any of the models shown in chapter 5; the variance inflation factors from those regressions are well below levels of any concern (Chatterjee and Hadi 2006).

10. We note two possible methodological concerns here. The first is the possibility that rhetoric is endogenous with arrests—that the president talks more about the war on drugs when law enforcement officials are more active. The second issue is the possibility that the effect of presidential rhetoric decays with time—that if the president speaks in this year, that speech has effects in this year and the next (and possibly beyond that).

In this chapter, we estimate the contemporaneous effects of speech on the DEA. We account for both possible endogeneity and decay in the construction of our data. Our data contain natural lags in the case of the DEA and the U.S. Attorneys; this is because our output variables (DEA arrests and cases processed by the Attorneys) are measured on a federal fiscal year basis, while presidential rhetoric is measured on a calendar-year basis. This clarifies the direction of the effect of rhetoric on outcomes and helps address decay.

Our focus in this book is on the contemporaneous effect of speech on policy outputs, which flows from the long-held view that rhetoric's impact decays quickly (Edwards 2003). We addressed the possible decay function by reestimating models by the "Arellano-Bond" linear dynamic panel data estimator with up to two lags in each independent variable and up to two lags in the dependent variable; robust standard errors (Arellano and Bond 1991). This model is a complex exercise for assessing the robustness of the claims we make here about the effects of rhetoric on policy outputs. The model shows evidence for both contemporaneous and lagged effects for rhetoric on policy outputs in the case of the DEA.

This shows that the claims we are making here are robust to the use of other models that allow for a range of ways for rhetoric to cause outputs. Tables 5.1 and 5.2 are fairly simple possible models. They also present underestimates (in other words, "lower bounds") of the impact of the president on policy implementation in the war on drugs.

11. Marginal effects are calculated accounting for the log transformation of the dependent variable. The estimated marginal effect is calculated as $d(\ln y)/dx$.

CHAPTER SIX: For the People

1. In chapter 7, on state enforcement in the war on drugs, we outline the differences that exist among states regarding attitudes toward the war on drugs and related drug policy reforms that have been enacted.

2. Ronald Reagan, "Radio Address on Drug Abuse and Trafficking," May 30, 1987. Available at www.presidency.ucsb.edu/ws/index.php?pid=34347, accessed December 20, 2008.

3. George H. W. Bush, "Remarks to Federal, State, and Local Prosecutors," September 12, 1990. Available at www.presidency.ucsb.edu/ws/index.php?pid=18821, accessed December 20, 2008.

4. Different accounts of the firings provide varying totals of the actual number of fired Attorneys, depending on the time frame considered. A frequently cited number was seven.

5. Careful readers will recall that Lam was the U.S. Attorney praised by Bush in his public speech outlined in chapter 4.

6. Our EOUSA data for this analysis are limited to 1981 to 1993 because in 1994, the EOUSA stopped publishing the office-specific case data broken down by topic, publishing only national aggregates thereafter. The data before 1981 also lack the same granularity.

7. We have no difficulty including these variables as covariates in any of the models shown in chapter 6; the variance inflation factors from those regressions are well below levels of any concern (Chatterjee and Hadi 2006).

8. Again, we note the two possible methodological concerns here of endogeneity of rhetoric and case processing, and a decay effect of presidential rhetoric over time. The models shown in tables 6.1 and 6.2 show the contemporaneous effects of speech on the U.S. Attorneys. As with the DEA, we account for both possible endogeneity and decay in the construction of our data. Our data contain natural lags in the case

of the U.S. Attorneys since our output variables (cases processed) are measured on a federal fiscal year basis, while presidential rhetoric is measured on a calendar-year basis.

We went beyond our focus on the contemporaneous effect of speech on policy outputs (largely supported in the past, e.g., Edwards 2003) and addressed the possible decay function by reestimating by the "Arellano-Bond" linear dynamic panel data estimator with up to two lags in each independent variable, and up to two lags in the dependent variable; robust standard errors (Arellano and Bond 1991). The model shows evidence for both contemporaneous and lagged effects for rhetoric on policy outputs in the case of the U.S. Attorneys for the case handling variable. The only case in which we do not find both contemporaneous and lagged effects is the "cases concluded" data exercise for the U.S. Attorneys. Our claims are largely robust to the use of other models that allow for a range of ways for rhetoric to cause outputs. Tables 6.1 and 6.2 are still simple possible models, but they also represent underestimates (lower bounds) of the impact of the president on policy implementation in the war on drugs.

9. The estimated marginal effect is calculated as dy/dx.

CHAPTER SEVEN: Taking It to the States

1. Ronald Reagan, "Remarks at the Annual Convention of the National Association of Counties in Baltimore, Maryland," July 13, 1982. Available at www.presidency.ucsb.edu/ws/?pid=42727, accessed December 20, 2008.

2. In 1991 the Byrne program provided $139 million to fund 881 MJDTFs with amounts ranging from $111,000 to over $23 million (Blumenson and Nilsen 1998, 43).

3. Jimmy Carter, "Drug Abuse Message to the Congress," August 2, 1977. Available at www.presidency.ucsb.edu/ws/?pid=7908, accessed December 20, 2008.

4. "Decriminalized" is not a precise legal standard. The states used different legal approaches for marijuana possession and use. However, they shared a common core in that possession of small amounts of marijuana did not constitute a jailable offense. Possession of marijuana was not legal but typically only carried a penalty of a small fine.

5. How many states have viable or "effective" medical marijuana laws? At least thirty-six states have or have had laws deemed favorable to medical marijuana use but do not necessarily protect patients from state-level criminal penalties for cultivation, possession, or use of medical marijuana. For instance, Maryland essentially decriminalized medical marijuana; patients face arrest and a $100 fine but no incarceration. However, some do not consider this to be effective decriminalization, since it does not protect a full range of protections; for example, cultivation is not addressed and there is no protection from arrest. It has been described as a "workable" law (Thomas and Schmitz 2006).

6. In a related case, *Conant v. Walter* 309 F.3d 629(2002), the Ninth Circuit upheld a group of California physicians' challenge (injunction) to the Clinton administration's threat to revoke their licenses and cut off Medicaid and Medicare funding if they

recommended marijuana to patients pursuant to California's medical marijuana law. In 2003, the Bush administration appealed the case to the U.S. Supreme Court, which declined review; it stands as prevailing precedent in the Ninth Circuit.

7. As noted in chapter 5, we report data from 1980 to 1998 due to restrictions in data availability for our main independent variable that serves as a control: the mortality data for drugs deaths. This measure appears in each model, but we are unable to improve our coverage of this variable. Our figures in chapter 4 are often more inclusive, but our statistical models are smaller.

8. Our regression analysis time frame is limited due to lack of data for some of our independent variables after 1998.

9. Oregon and Alaska voted to recriminalize possession of some small quantities of marijuana in 1989 and 1990, respectively (Goode 1997, 48).

10. We have no difficulty including these variables as covariates in any of the models shown in chapter 7; the variance inflation factors from those regressions are well below levels of any concern (Chatterjee and Hadi 2006).

11. We note the same two possible methodological concerns in the case of the states of endogeneity of rhetoric and arrests, and a decay effect of presidential rhetoric over time. The model shown in table 7.1 shows contemporaneous effects for speech on the behavior of the states. Unlike in the cases of the DEA and the U.S. attorneys, where we accounted for possible endogeneity and decay by using natural lags from output variables measured on a federal fiscal year basis and rhetoric measured on a calendar-year basis, in this section our data in the cases of the states also account for potential endogeneity, although we remain interested in contemporaneous effects. Specifically, our variables are both measured on a calendar-year basis, but the data for state-level outcomes are not released to the public (including the president) until after the calendar year; the president cannot know the state-level outcomes when allocating his rhetoric.

We then followed the approach in chapters 5 and 6 to address the possible decay function by reestimating by the "Arellano-Bond" linear dynamic panel data estimator with up to two lags in each independent variable, and up to two lags in the dependent variable; robust standard errors (Arellano and Bond 1991). That model shows evidence for both contemporaneous and lagged effects for rhetoric on policy outputs in the case of the states. This means that table 7.1 shows underestimates (lower bounds) of the impact of the president on policy implementation in the war on drugs.

12. The estimated marginal effect is calculated as dy/dx.

CHAPTER EIGHT: The Social Construction of Presidential Agenda-Setting

1. Bureau of Justice Statistics, U.S. Department of Justice, *Sourcebook of Criminal Justice Statistics*, 2000 and 2004 editions. Index crimes include the violent crimes of murder and nonnegligent manslaughter, forcible rape, robbery, and aggravated assault and the property crimes of burglary, larceny-theft, and motor vehicle theft. See "Persons under Correctional Supervision," *Sourcebook of Criminal Justice Statistics*, 2000

edition, available at www.albany.edu/sourcebook/pdf/sb2000/sb2000-section6.pdf, accessed December 21, 2008.

2. Bureau of Justice Statistics, U.S. Department of Justice, "Sourcebook of Criminal Justice Statistics," 2000 edition. Index crimes include the violent crimes of murder and nonnegligent manslaughter, forcible rape, robbery, and aggravated assault and the property crimes of burglary, larceny-theft, and motor vehicle theft. See "Persons under Correctional Supervision," *Sourcebook of Criminal Justice Statistics,* 2000 edition.

3. "Criminal Offenders Statistics," Bureau of Justice Statistics, U.S. Department of Justice. Available at www.ojp.usdoj.gov/bjs/crimoff.htm, accessed December 21, 2008.

4. Bureau of Justice Statistics, U.S. Department of Justice, Sourcebook of Criminal Justice Statistics, 2000 edition.

5. Yates, Collins, and Chin (2005), citing Immigration and Naturalization Service, U.S. Department of Justice, *1997 Statistical Yearbook of the Immigration and Naturalization Service,* 167.

6. See: "Attitudes toward Legalization of the Use of Marijuana," *Sourcebook of Criminal Justice Statistics,* 2003 edition, available at www.albany.edu/sourcebook/pdf/t268.pdf, accessed December 21, 2008.

7. See "College Freshman Reporting that Marijuana Should Be Legalized," *Sourcebook of Criminal Justice Statistics,* 2005 edition, available at www.albany.edu/sourcebook/pdf/t2902005.pdf, accessed December 21, 2008.

Bibliography

Abrams, Jim. 1994. "GOP Vows to Reshape Clinton's Drug Policy." *Chicago Sun-Times.* December 25, p. 31.

Anderson, Oscar E., Jr. 1958. *The Health of a Nation: Harvey W. Wiley and the Fight for Pure Food.* Chicago: University of Chicago Press.

Anderson, Patrick. 1981. *High in America: The True Story behind NORML and the Politics of Marijuana.* New York: Viking.

Anderson, Susan Heller, and David W. Dunlap. 1986. "New York Day by Day." *New York Times.* July 10, B3.

Anslinger, Harry J. 1962. *The Murderers: The Shocking Story of the Narcotic Gangs.* New York: Farrar, Straus, and Cudahy.

———. 1964. *The Protectors.* New York: Farrar, Straus, and Giroux.

Arellano, Manuel, and Stephen Bond. 1991. "Some Tests of Specification for Panel Data: Monte Carlo Evidence and an Application to Employment Equations." *Review of Economic Studies* 58:277–297.

Babcock, Charles R. 1981a. "DEA Head Bensinger Ousted from Post by Administration." *Washington Post.* June 17, A5.

———. 1981b. "FBI Man's Move to DEA Stirs Concern." *Washington Post.* June 19, A11.

Bailey, Michael, Lee Sigelman, and Clyde Wilcox. 2003. "Presidential Persuasion on Social Issues: A Two Way Street?" *Political Research Quarterly* 51:49–59.

Baker, S. L. 1972. "U.S. Army Heroin Abuse Identification Program in Vietnam: Implications for a Methadone Program." *American Journal of Public Health* 62:857–860.

Barrett, A. W. 2004. "Gone Public: The Impact of Going Public on Presidential Legislative Success." *American Politics Review* 31:1–33.

Baum, Dan. 1996. *Smoke and Mirrors: The War on Drugs and the Politics of Failure.* Boston: Little, Brown.

Baum, Matthew, and Samuel Kernell. 1999. "Has Cable Ended the Golden Age of Presidential Television?" *American Political Science Review* 93:1–16.

Baumgartner, Frank, and Bryan D. Jones. 1993. *Agendas and Instability in American Politics.* Chicago: University of Chicago Press.

Beck, Neal, and Jonathon N. Katz. 1995. "What to Do (and Not to Do) with Time-series Cross-section Data." *American Political Science Review* 89:634–647.

Beckett, Katherine. 1994. "Setting the Public Agenda: 'Street Crime' and Drug Use on American Politics." *Social Problems* 41:425–447.

———. 1997. *Making Crime Pay: Law and Order in Contemporary American Politics*. New York: Oxford University Press.

Beckett, Katherine, and Theodore Sasson. 2000. *The Politics of Injustice: Crime and Punishment in America*. Thousand Oaks, CA: Pine Forge Press.

Belenko, Steven R. 2000. *Drugs and Drug Policy in America: A Documentary History*. Westport, CT: Greenwood Press.

Bennett, James T., and Thomas J. DiLorenzo. 1992. *Official Lies: How Washington Misleads Us*. Alexandria, VA: Groom Books.

Bennett, William J. 1992. *The De-Valuing of America: The Fight for Our Culture and Our Children*. New York: Summit Books.

Bennett, William J., John DiIulio, and John Walters. 1996. *Body Count: Moral Poverty . . . And How to Win America's War on Crime and Drugs*. New York: Simon and Schuster.

Bennis, W. G., and G. Nanus. 1985. *Leaders*. New York: Harper and Row.

Benson, Bruce, David Rasmussen, and David Sollars. 1995. "Police Bureaucracies, Their Incentives, and the War On Drugs." *Public Choice* 83:21–45.

Berry, William D., Evan J. Ringquist, Richard C. Fording, and Russell L. Hanson. 1998. "Measuring Citizen and Government Ideology in the American States, 1960–93." *American Journal of Political Science*. 42(1): 327–348.

Bertram, Eva, Morris Blachman, Kenneth Sharpe, and Peter Andreas. 1996. *Drug War Politics: The Price of Denial*. Berkeley: University of California Press.

Besteman, Karst. 1990. "Federal Leadership in Building the National Drug Treatment System." In *Treating Drug Problems*, ed. Dean R. Gerstein and Henrick J. Harwood. Washington, D.C.: National Academy Press.

Blumenson, Eric, and Eva Nilsen. 1998. "Policing For Profit: The Drug War's Hidden Economic Agenda." *University of Chicago Law Review* 65:35–114.

Bonnie, Richard J., and Charles H. Whitbread III. 1970. "The Forbidden Fruit and the Tree of Knowledge: An Inquiry into the Legal History of American Marijuana Prohibition." *Virginia Law Review* 56(6): 971–1203.

Brace, Paul, and Barbara Hinckley. 1992. *Follow the Leader: Opinion Polls and the Modern Presidents*. New York: Basic Books.

Brehm, John, and Scott Gates. 1997. *Working, Shirking, and Sabotage: Bureaucratic Response to a Democratic Public*. Ann Arbor: University of Michigan Press.

Brickey, Kathleen. 1995. "Criminal Mischief: The Federalization of American Criminal Law." *Hastings Law Journal* 46:1135–1174.

Bridenball, Blaine, and Paul Jesilow. 2005. "Weeding Criminals or Planting Fear: An Evaluation of a Weed and Seed Project." *Criminal Justice Review* 30(1): 64–89.

Calvert Institute for Policy Research. 2005. "Calvert News May 2005 The 'War on Drugs': A Reconsideration after Forty Years." May 1. Available at www .calvertinstitute.org/main/pub_detail.php?pub_id=147, accessed December 17, 2008.

Cameron, Charles M. 2000. *Veto Bargaining: Presidents and the Politics of Negative Power*. Cambridge, UK: Cambridge University Press.

Canes-Wrone, Brandice. 2004. "The Public Presidency, Personal Approval Ratings, and Policy Making." *Presidential Studies Quarterly* 34:477–492.

———. 2006. *Who Leads Whom?* Chicago: University of Chicago Press.

Canes-Wrone, Brandice, and Scott de Marchi. 2002. "Presidential Approval and Legislative Success." *Journal of Politics* 64:491–509.

Carlson, Peter. 2005. "Exhale, Stage Left." *Washington Post*, January 4, C5.

Carmody, John. 1983. "Now Here's the News." *Washington Post.* October 13, D9.

———. 1985. "Now Here's the News." *Washington Post.* February 22, E9.

Cassell, Clark. 1984. *President Reagan's Quotations.* Washington, D.C.: Braddock Publications.

Cater, Douglas. 1959. *The Fourth Branch of Government.* Boston: Houghton Mifflin.

Chatterjee, Samprit, and Ali S. Hadi. 2006. *Regression Analysis by Example.* 4th ed. New York: Wiley.

Chubb, John E. 1985. "The Political Economy of Federalism." *American Political Science Review* 79(4): 994–1015.

Clark, Peter A. 2000. "The Ethics of Medical Marijuana: Government Restrictions vs. Medical Necessity." *Journal of Public Health Policy* 21(1): 40–60.

Cobb, Roger, and Charles Elder. 1971. "The Politics of Agenda-Building: An Alternative Perspective For Modern Democratic Theory." *Journal of Politics* 33: 892–915.

Cockburn, Alexander, and Jeffrey St. Clair. 1998. *Whiteout: The CIA, Drugs, and the Press.* New York: Verso.

Cohen, Adam. 2007. "Why Have So Many U.S. Attorneys Been Fired? It Looks a Lot Like Politics." *New York Times.* February 26.

Cohen, Jeffrey E. 1995. "Presidential Rhetoric and the Public Agenda." *American Journal of Political Science* 39:87–107.

———. 1997. *Presidential Responsiveness and Public Policy-Making.* Ann Arbor: University of Michigan Press.

Cohen, Jeffrey, and David Nice. 2003. *The Presidency.* New York: McGraw-Hill.

Cohen, Jeffrey, and Richard Powell. 2005. "Building Public Support from the Grassroots Up: The Impact of Presidential Travel on State-Level Approval." *Presidential Studies Quarterly* 35:11–27.

Cohen, Jon, and Jennifer Agiesta. 2007. "Poll: Most Say Politics Motivated U.S. Attorney Firings." *Washington Post.* April 16.

Cohen, M. D., J. G. March, and J. P. Olsen. 1972. "A Garbage Can Model of Organizational Choice." *Administrative Science Quarterly* 17(1): 1–25.

Cook, Timothy E. 1993. *Governing with the News: The News Media as a Political Institution.* Chicago: University of Chicago Press.

Corwin, Edward S. 1957. *The President: Office and Powers 1787–1957,* 4th ed. New York: New York University Press.

Cyert, R. M., and J. G. March. 1963. *A Behavioral Theory of the Firm.* 2nd ed. Malden, MA: Blackwell Publishers.

Davenport-Hines, Richard. 2002. *The Pursuit of Oblivion.* New York: W.W. Norton.

Davis, Kenneth Culp. 1969. *Discretionary Justice: A Preliminary Inquiry.* Baton Rouge: Louisiana State Press.

Davis, Mike. 1990. *City of Quartz: Excavating the Future in Los Angeles.* London: Verso.

DEA [Drug Enforcement Administration]. 2003a. "Drug Enforcement Administration: A Tradition of Excellence, 1973–2003, Part I." Washington, D.C.: DEA. Available at www.dea.gov/pubs/history/history_part1.pdf, accessed December 17, 2008.

———. 2003b. "Drug Enforcement Administration: A Tradition of Excellence, 1973–2003, Part II." Washington, D.C.: DEA. Available at www.dea.gov/pubs/history/history_part2.pdf, accessed December 17, 2008.

DiChiara, Albert, and John F. Galliher. 1994. "Dissonance and Contradictions in the Origins of Marihuana Decriminalization." *Law and Society Review.* 28(1): 41–78.

Dillin, John. 1985. "White House Stresses Citizen Volunteers in Its Battle Against Drugs." *Christian Science Monitor.* April 26, p. 44.

Doig, Jameson W., and E. Hargrove. 1987. "Leadership and Political Analysis." In *Leadership and Innovation: A Biographical Perspective on Entrepreneurs in Government,* ed. Jameson W. Doig and E. Hargrove. Baltimore: Johns Hopkins University Press.

Dolan, Chris J. 2005. "United States' Narco-Terrorism Policy: A Contingency Approach to the Convergence of the Wars on Drugs and Against Terrorism." *Review of Policy Research* 22(4): 451–471.

Domestic Council Drug Abuse Task Force. 1975. *White Paper on Drug Abuse: A Report to the President from the Domestic Council Drug Abuse Task Force.* Washington, D.C.: U.S. Government Printing Office.

Dougherty, Philip H. 1983. "Advertising: Drug Drive Outlined to First Lady." *New York Times.* October 12, D22.

Downs, Anthony. 1967. *Inside Bureaucracy.* Little, Brown.

Druckman, James, and Justin Holmes. 2004. "Does Presidential Rhetoric Matter? Priming and Presidential Approval." *Presidential Studies Quarterly* 34:755–778.

Duffy, Brian. 1986. "War on Drugs: More Than a 'Short-Term High'?" *U.S. News and World Report.* September 29, p. 28.

Dunworth, Terence, and Gregory Mills. 1999. "National Evaluation of Weed and Seed." National Institute of Justice: Research in Brief. June 1999.

DuPont, Robert L. 1971. "Profile of a Heroin Addiction Epidemic." *New England Journal of Medicine* 285:320–324.

Durant, Robert F. 1992. *The Administrative Presidency Revisited: Public Lands, the BLM, and the Reagan Revolution.* Albany: State University of New York Press.

Durant, Robert F., and William G. Resh. Forthcoming. "The Presidency and the Bureaucracy." In *Oxford Handbook of the American Presidency.* Oxford, UK: Oxford University Press.

Dyer, Joel. 2001. *The Perpetual Prisoner Machine: How America Profits from Crime.* Boulder, CO: Westview Press.

Eddy, Mark. 2005. "Medical Marijuana: Review and Analysis of Federal and State Policies." Congressional Research Service Report For Congress.

Edelman, Murray. 1988. *Constructing the Political Spectacle*. Chicago: University of Chicago Press.

Edwards, George C. 2003. *On Deaf Ears: The Limits of the Bully Pulpit*. New Haven: Yale University Press.

———. 2007. *Governing by Campaigning: The Politics of the Bush Presidency*. New York: Pearson Longman.

Edwards, George C., and Stephen Wayne. 1994. *Presidential Leadership: Politics and Policy Making*. New York: St. Martin's Press.

Edwards, George C., and B. Dan Wood. 1999. "Who Influences Whom? The President, Congress, and the Media." *American Political Science Review* 93(2): 327–344.

Eisenstein, James. 1978. *Counsel for the United States: U.S. Attorneys in the Political and Legal Systems*. Baltimore: Johns Hopkins University Press.

Eisner, Marc Allen, and Kenneth J. Meier. 1990. "Presidential Control versus Bureaucratic Power: Explaining the Reagan Revolution in Antitrust." *American Journal of Political Science* 34(1): 269–287.

Elsner, Alan. 2006. *Gates of Injustice: The Crisis in America's Prisons*. New York: Prentice Hall.

Elwood, William. 1994. *Rhetoric in the War on Drugs: The Triumphs and Tragedies of Public Relations*. Westport, CT: Praeger.

Ely, Amie N. 2004. "Prosecutorial Discretion as an Ethical Necessity: The Ashcroft Memorandum's Curtailment of the Prosecutor's Duty to 'Seek Justice.'" *Cornell Law Review* 90(1): 237–278.

Epstein, Aaron. 1988. "Meese Seeks Positive PR on Drug War." *Atlanta Journal-Constitution*. May 14.

Epstein, Edward Jay. 1977. *Agency of Fear: Opiates and Political Power in America*. New York: Putnam.

FDA [Food and Drug Administration]. 1981. "The Story of the Laws behind the Labels, Part III, 1962 Drug Amendments." *FDA Consumer*. June 1981.

Fecteau, Loie. 2001. "CNN Lets Drug Foes Go at It." *Albuquerque Journal*. March 22. Available at www.mapinc.org/newscsdp/v01/n503/a03.html, access December 17, 2008.

Feldman, Martha S., and James G. March. 1981. "Information in Organizations as Signal and Symbol." *Administrative Science Quarterly* 26(2): 171–186.

Fesler, James W. 1949. *Area and Administration*. Tuscaloosa: University of Alabama Press.

Fine, Terri Susan. 1994. "Interest Groups and the Framing of the 1988 Democratic and Republican Party Platforms." *Polity* 26:517–530.

Finkelman, Paul. 1993. "The Second Casualty of War: Civil Liberties and the War on Drugs." *Southern California Law Review*. 66:1389–1452.

Flemming, Roy B., John Bohte, and B. Dan Wood. 1999. "Attention to Issues in a System of Separated Powers: The Macrodynamics of American Policy Agendas." *Journal of Politics* 61:76–108.

Forbes, Daniel. 2000. "Prime-time Propaganda." Salon.com. January 13. Available at http://archive.salon.com/news/feature/2000/01/13/drugs/index.html, accessed December 17, 2008.

Friedman, Milton. 1953. "The Methodology of Positive Economics." *Essays in Positive Economics*. Chicago: University of Chicago Press.

Galliher, John F., and Allynn Walker. 1977. "The Puzzle of the Social Origins of the Marihuana Tax Act of 1937." *Social Problems* 24(3): 367–376.

Gamarekian, Barbara. 1980. "Smoothing Mrs. Reagan's Way into the White House." *New York Times*. December 5, B12.

Gfroerer, Joseph C., and Marc Brodsky. 1992. "The Incidence of Illicit Drug Use in the United States, 1962–1989." *British Journal of Addiction* 87:1345–1351.

Gfroerer, Joseph C., Li-Tzy Wu, and Michael A. Penne. 2002. "Initiation of Marijuana Use: Trends, Patterns, and Implications." Department of Health and Human Services. Substance Abuse and Mental Health Services Administration. Office of Applied Studies. July 2002.

Goldberg, Peter B. 1980. "The Federal Government's Response to Illicit Drugs, 1969–1978." In *The Facts About Drug Abuse*. Drug Abuse Council. New York: Free Press.

Goldberg Peter B., and James V. DeLong. 1972. "Federal Expenditures on Drug-Abuse Control." In *Dealing with Drug Abuse: A Report to the Ford Foundation*. Ford Foundation.

Gooberman, Lawrence A. 1974. *Operation Intercept: The Multiple Consequences of Public Policy*. Pergamon Press.

Goode, Erich. 1970. *The Marijuana Smokers*. New York: Basic Books.

———. 1997. *Between Politics and Reason: The Drug Legalization Debate*. New York: St. Martin's Press.

Goode, Erich, and Nachman Ben-Yahuda. 1994. *Moral Panics: The Social Construction of Deviance*. London: Blackwell.

Granger, Clive W. J. 1969. "Investigating Causal Relations by Econometric Models and Cross-Spectral Methods." *Econometrica* 37:424–438.

Green, Bruce A., and Fred C. Zacharias. 2008. "The 'U.S. Attorneys Scandal' and the Allocation of Prosecutorial Power." *Ohio State Law Journal* 69(2): 187–254.

Greene, William H. 1993. *Econometric Analysis*. Englewood Cliffs, NJ: Prentice Hall.

Gugliotta, Guy. 1989. *Kings Of Cocaine: Inside The Medellín Cartel—An Astonishing True Story of Murder, Money, and International Corruption*. New York: Simon and Schuster.

Hale, Jon F. 1995. "The Making of the New Democrats." *Political Science Quarterly* 110(2): 207–232.

Hamilton, James D. 1994. *Time Series Analysis*. Princeton: Princeton University Press.

Hammond, Matthew Carlton. 1997. "The Posse Comitatus Act: A Principle in Need of Renewal." *Washington University Law Quarterly* 75(2): 953–984.

Hammond, Thomas H., and Jack H. Knott. 1996. "Who Controls the Bureaucracy? Presidential Power, Congressional Dominance, Legal Constraints, and Bureaucratic Autonomy in a Model of Multi-Institutional Policy-Making." *Journal of Law, Economics, and Organization* 12(1): 119–166.

Hanson, Norwood Russell. 1958. *Patterns of Discovery: An Inquiry into the Conceptual Foundations of Science.* Cambridge University Press.

Harriger, Katy J. 2008. "Executive Power and Prosecution: Lessons from the Libby and the U.S. Attorney Firings." *Presidential Studies Quarterly* 38(3): 491–505.

Hart, John. 1995. "President Clinton and The Politics of Symbolism: Cutting the White House Staff." *Political Science Quarterly* 110(3): 385–403.

Heymann, Phillip, and Mark Moore. 1996. "The Federal Role in Dealing with Violent Street Crime: Principles, Questions, and Cautions." *Annals of the Academy of Political and Social Science* 543:103–115.

Hill, Kim Quaile. 1998. "The Policy Agendas of the President and the Mass Public: A Research Validation and Extension." *American Journal of Political Science* 42:1328–1334.

Hoffman, Karen. 2004. "Review: On Deaf Ears: The Limits of the Bully Pulpit." *Journal of Politics* 67:293.

Inciardi, James A. 1986. *The War on Drugs: Heroin, Cocaine, Crime, and Public Policy.* Mountain View, CA: Mayfield Publishing.

Jacobs, David, and Jason Carmichael. 2001. "The Politics of Punishment across Time and Space: A Pooled Time-Series Analysis of Imprisonment Rates." *Social Forces* 80:61–91.

Jacobs, Lawrence, and Robert Shapiro. 2000. *Politicians Don't Pander: Political Manipulation and the Loss of Democratic Responsiveness.* Chicago: University of Chicago Press.

Jeffreys-Jones, Rhodri. 2007. *The FBI: A History.* Lexington: University Press of Kentucky.

Jenkins, Philip. 2000. *Synthetic Panics: The Symbolic Politics of Designer Drugs.* New York: NYU Press.

Johnson, Lyndon B. 1965. "Special Message to the Congress on Law Enforcement and the Administration of Justice." March 8. Available at www.presidency.ucsb.edu/ws/?pid=26800, accessed December 17, 2008.

Johnson, Timothy R., and Jason Roberts. 2004. "Presidential Capital and the Supreme Court Confirmation Process." *Journal of Politics* 66:663–683.

Jones, Bryan D., and Frank Baumgartner. 2005. *The Politics of Attention: How Government Prioritizes Problems.* Chicago: University of Chicago Press.

Katzenbach, Nicholas deB. 1967. *The Challenge of Crime in a Free Society: A Report by the President's Commission on Law Enforcement and the Administration of Justice.* February. U.S. Government Printing Office.

Kaufman, H. 1960. *The Forest Ranger: A Study in Administrative Behavior.* Baltimore: Johns Hopkins University Press.

Kennedy, Randall. 1997. *Race, Crime, and the Law.* New York: Random House.

Kernell, Samuel. 1986. *Going Public: New Strategies of Presidential Leadership.* Washington, D.C.: CQ Press.

————. 1993. *Going Public: New Strategies of Presidential Leadership.* 2nd ed. Washington, D.C.: CQ Press.

————. 1997. *Going Public: New Strategies of Presidential Leadership.* 3rd ed. Washington, D.C.: CQ Press.

Kiewet, Roderick, and Matthew McCubbins. 1991. *The Logic of Delegation: Congressional Parties and the Appropriations Process.* Chicago: University of Chicago Press.

Kinder, Donald, and Lynn Sanders. 1996. *Divided By Color: Racial Politics and Democratic Ideals.* Chicago: University of Chicago Press.

King, Rufus G. 1953. "Narcotics Bureau and the Harrison Act: Jailing the Healers and the Sick." *Yale Law Journal* 62(5): 736–749.

————. 1972. *The Drug Hang-Up.* New York: W.W. Norton.

Kingdon, John. 1984. *Agendas, Alternatives, and Public Policies.* New York: Harper Collins.

Kirchberg, Connie, and Marc Hendrickx. 1999. *Elvis Presley, Richard Nixon, and the American Dream.* Jefferson, NC: McFarland.

Kmenta, Jan. 1986. *Elements of Econometrics.* New York: Macmillan.

Kozel, Nick, Robert L. DuPont, and Barry Brown. 1972. "Narcotics and Crime: A Study of Narcotic Involvement in an Offender Population." *International Journal of the Addictions* 7(3): 443–450.

Krogh, Egil. 1994. *The Day Elvis Met Nixon.* Bellevue, WA: Pejama Press.

Kuhn, Thomas S. 1962. *The Structure of Scientific Revolutions.* Chicago: University of Chicago Press.

Labaton, Stephen. 1993. "Surgeon General Suggests Study of Legalizing Drugs." *New York Times.* December 8, A23.

Lee, Henry. 1963. *How Dry We Were.* Englewood Cliffs, NJ: Prentice-Hall.

Levy, Leonard. 1996. *A License to Steal: The Forfeiture of Property.* Chapel Hill: University of North Carolina Press.

Lewis, Neil A. 1993. "White House Seeks To Combine F.B.I. with Drug Agency." *New York Times.* August 19.

Lichtblau, Eric. 2004. "For Voters, Osama Replaces the Common Criminal." *New York Times.* July 18.

————. 2008a. "Mukasey Won't Pursue Charges in Hiring Inquiry." *New York Times.* August 12.

————. 2008b. "Report Assails Political Hiring in Justice Department." *New York Times.* June 25.

Liddy, G. Gordon. 1998. *Will: The Autobiography of G. Gordon Liddy.* New York: St. Martin's.

Lieberman, Robert. 1995. "Social Construction (Continued). "*American Political Science Review* 89(2): 437–441.

Light, Paul C. 1999. *The President's Agenda: Domestic Policy Choice from Kennedy to Carter.* 3rd ed. Baltimore: Johns Hopkins University Press.

Lowy, Jonathan. 2001. *Elvis and Nixon.* New York: Crown.

Manatt, Marsha. 1979. *Parents, Peers, and Pot.* Superintendent of Documents, U.S. Government Printing Office, Washington, D.C. 20402 (Stock No. 017-024-00941-5); National Clearinghouse for Drug Abuse Information.

Manderson, Desmond. 1999. "Symbolism and Racism in Drug History and Policy." *Drug and Alcohol Review* 18(2): 179–186.

Majone, Giandomenico. 1992. *Evidence, Argument, and Persuasion in the Policy Process.* New Haven: Yale University Press.

March, James G., and Johan P. Olsen. 1989. *Rediscovering Institutions: The Organizational Basis of Politics.* New York: Simon and Schuster.

Massing, Michael. 1998. *The Fix.* New York: Simon and Schuster.

Matlin, David, and Ishmael Reed. 2005. *Prisons: Embracing New America: From Vernooykill Creek to Abu Ghraib.* Berkeley, CA: North Atlantic Books.

McGee, James, and Brian Duffy. 1996. *Main Justice: The Men and Women Who Enforce the Nation's Criminal Laws and Guard Its Liberties.* New York: Simon and Schuster.

McKay, John. 2008. "Train Wreck at the Justice Department: An Eyewitness Account." *Seattle Law Review* 31:265–296.

Meier, Kenneth. 1992. "The Politics of Drug Abuse: Laws, Implementation, and Consequences." *Western Political Quarterly* 45:41–69.

———. 1994. *The Politics of Sin: Drugs, Alcohol, and Public Policy.* Armonk, NY: M. E. Sharpe.

Merida, Kevin. 1993. "Senate Panel Questions Cuts and Accounting at White House." *Washington Post.* April 23.

Miller, Gary J. 1992. *Managerial Dilemmas: The Political Economy of Hierarchy.* Cambridge: Cambridge University Press.

Miller, Gary J., and Andrew B. Whitford. 2007. "The Principal's Moral Hazard: Constraints on the Use of Incentives in Hierarchy." *Journal of Public Administration Research and Theory* 17(2): 213–233.

Moe, Terry. 1987. "An Assessment of the Positive Theory of Congressional Dominance." *Legislative Studies Quarterly* 12:475–520.

———. 1989. "The Politics of Bureaucratic Structure." In *Can the Government Govern?* ed. Paul E. Peterson and John E. Chubb. Washington, D.C.: Brookings Institution.

Morone, James. 2003. *Hellfire Nation: The Politics of Sin in American History.* New Haven: Yale University Press.

Muir, William K. 1992. *The Bully Pulpit: The Presidential Leadership of Ronald Reagan.* San Francisco: Institute for Contemporary Studies.

Mullen, Paul, Michelle Pathe, and Rosemary Purcell. 2000. *Stalkers and Their Victims.* Cambridge: Cambridge University Press.

Murphy, John. 2005. "The IRA and the FARC in Colombia." *International Journal of Intelligence and Counterintelligence* 18(1): 76–88.

Musto, David F. 1972. "The History of the Marihuana Tax Act of 1937." *Archives of General Psychiatry* 26:101–108.

——. 1998. "Just Saying 'No' Is Not Enough." *New York Times*. October 18. Available at www.nytimes.com/books/98/10/18/reviews/981018.18mustot.html, accessed December 17, 2008.

——. 1999. *The American Disease: Origins of Narcotics Control*. 3rd ed. New York: Oxford University Press.

Musto, David F., and Pamela Korsmeyer. 2002. *The Quest for Drug Control: Politics and Federal Policy in a Period of Increasing Substance Abuse, 1963–1981*. New Haven: Yale University Press.

National Conference of Commissioners on Uniform State Laws. 1970. *Preface to Final Report, Uniform Controlled Substances Act, National Conference of Commissioners on Uniform State Laws*. Chicago, IL, August.

Nelson, Michael. 1989. *Congressional Quarterly's Guide to the Presidency*. Washington, D.C.: CQ Press.

Neustadt, Richard E. 1960. *Presidential Power: The Politics of Leadership*. New York: John Wiley and Sons.

Nixon, Richard. 1967. "What Has Happened to America?" *The Reader's Digest*. October, 49–54.

Noll, Roger G. 1985. *Regulatory Policy and the Social Science*. Berkeley: University of California Press.

O'Bryant, JoAnne, and Lisa Seghetti. 2002. "Crime Control: The Federal Response." Issue Brief for Congress. Congressional Research Service. The Library of Congress.

O'Hear, Michael. 2004. "Federalism and Drug Control." *Vanderbilt Law Review* 789–882.

Olson, Mancur. 1993. "Dictatorship, Democracy, and Development." *American Political Science Review* 87(3): 567–576.

ONDCP [Office of National Drug Control Policy]. 2007. "National Drug Control Strategy, 2007." Washington, D.C.: The White House. Available at www.whitehousedrugpolicy.gov/publications/policy/ndcs07/ndcs07.pdf, accessed December 17, 2008.

Owen, Frank. 2008. *No Speed Limit: The Highs and Lows of Meth*. New York: St. Martin's Griffin.

Pacula, Rosalie Liccardo, Jamie F. Chriqui, Deborah A. Reichmann, and Yvonne M. Terry-McElrath. 2002. "State Medical Marijuana Laws: Understanding the Laws and Their Limitations." *Journal of Public Health Policy* 23(4): 413–439.

Parenti, Christian. 2000. *Lockdown America: Police and Prisons in the Age of Crisis*. New York: Verso.

Pear, Robert. 1981. "Plan to Merge FBI and Drug Agency Pressed." *New York Times*. July 12, p. 1.

Perry, H. W., Jr. 1998. "United States Attorneys—Whom Shall They Serve?" *Law and Contemporary Problems* 61(Winter): 129.

Pious, Richard M. 1996. *The Presidency*. Neeham Heights, MA: Allyn and Bacon.

Piper, Bill, Matthew Briggs, Katherine Huffman, and Rebecca Lubot-Conk. 2003. *State of the States: Drug Policy Reforms, 1996–2002*. New York: Drug Policy Alliance.

Pomper, Gerald. 1980. *Elections in America: Control and Influence in Democratic Politics*. New York: Dodd, Mead and Co.

Pound, Edward T. 1982. "FBI Director to Take Over Key Role in Narcotics Cases." *New York Times*. January 22, A12.

President's Commission on Model State Drug Laws. 1993. *Executive Summary, President's Commission on Model State Drug Laws*. Washington, D.C.: The White House. December.

President's Commission on Organized Crime. 1986. *America's Habit: Drug Abuse, Drug Trafficking, and Organized Crime*. Washington, D.C.: U.S. Government Printing Office.

Pressman, Jeffrey L., and Aaron Wildavsky. 1984. *Implementation: How Great Expectations in Washington Are Dashed in Oakland*. 3rd ed. Berkeley: University of California Press.

Rabin, Robert. 1971. "Agency Criminal Referrals in the Federal System: An Empirical Study of Prosecutorial Discretion." *Stanford Law Review* 24:1036–1091.

Rachel, Patricia. 1982. *Federal Narcotics Enforcement: Reorganization and Reform*. Boston: Arbor.

Radcliffe, Donnie. 1980. "Nancy Reagan, and Conduct Unbecoming: The Code of the New First Family: Nancy Reagan's Code." *Washington Post*. November 21, F1.

———. 1981. "The First Lady at Second Genesis." *Washington Post*. July 14, C6.

———. 1985. "Surprised for Nancy Reagan: A Nicaraguan Appeal at Drug Abuse Talks." *Washington Post*. October 22, B1.

Ratcliffe, R. G., and Bennett Roth. 2000. "Campaign 2000; Drugs, Both Good and Bad, Dominate Campaign Trail." *Houston Chronicle*. October 7, A21.

Regan, Donald T. 1988. *For The Record: From Wall Street to Washington*. New York: Harcourt Brace Jovanovich.

Reinarmen, Craig, and Harry Gene Levine. 1997. *Crack in America: Demon Drugs and Social Justice*. Berkeley: University of California Press.

Rettig, Richard A., and Adam Yarmolinksy, eds. 1995. *Federal Regulation of Methadone Treatment*. Institute of Medicine.

Reuter, Peter H., Gordon Crawford, Jonathan Cave, Patrick Murphy, Don Henry, William Lisowski, and Eleanor Sullivan Wainstein. 1988. *Sealing the Borders: The Effects of Increased Military Participation in Drug Interdiction*. Santa Monica, CA: RAND.

Riker, William H. 1986. *The Art of Political Manipulation*. New Haven: Yale University Press.

Rockefeller, Nelson. 1973. *Annual Message to the New York State Legislature*. January 3. *Annotated List and Indexes of the New York State Legislative Documents Series, 1919–1976*. 1986. Compiled by Robert Allan Carter. Volume VII, Annual Reports of Permanent State Agencies, the Legislature and the Courts, and Annual Message of the Governor / Annual Reports of Public Authorities, Semi-Official State Agencies, State and Private Institutions, Schools and Private Organizations. Albany: University of the State of New York.

Rockefeller Commission. 1975. *Report to the President by the Commission on CIA Activities within the United States.* Washington, D.C.: U.S. Government Printing Office.

Romano, Lois. 2007. "Effect of Obama's Candor Remains Unseen." *Washington Post.* January 3, A1.

Roosevelt, Theodore. 2005. "The President as Steward of the Public Interest." In *Thinking about the Presidency,* ed. Gary L. Gregg II. Lanham, MD: Rowman and Littlefield.

Rosellini, Lynn. 1981. "First Lady Tells Critics: 'I am Just Being Myself.'" *New York Times.* October 13, A20.

Rossiter, Clinton. 1960. *The American Presidency.* New York: Harcourt Brace.

Rozell, Mark J., and Mitchel A. Sollenberger. 2008. "Executive Privilege and the U.S. Attorneys Firings." *Presidential Studies Quarterly* 38(2): 315–328.

Russell, George. 1985. "Mexico Slowdown on the Border." *Time.* March 4.

Rydell, C. Peter, and Susan S. Everingham. 1994. *Controlling Cocaine: Supply versus Demand Programs.* Drug Policy Research Center. Santa Monica, CA: RAND.

Samuels, David. 2008. "Dr. Kush: How Medical Marijuana Is Transforming the Pot Industry." *The New Yorker.* July 28, pp. 49–61.

Schlesinger, Arthur M., Jr. 1973. *The Imperial Presidency.* Boston: Houghton Mifflin.

Schlosser, Eric. 2003. *Reefer Madness.* Boston: Houghton Mifflin.

Schmidt, Susan. 2000. "Young, Rural, Addicted—and Ignored; As Heroin Expands Its Reach, Drugs Are on the Back Burner in Presidential Race." *Washington Post.* October 10, A10.

Schneider, Anne, and Helen Ingram. 1993. "Social Construction of Target Populations: Implications for Politics and Policy." *American Political Science Review* 87:334–347.

Scholz, John T., and Feng Heng Wei. 1986. "Regulatory Enforcement in a Federalist System." *American Political Science Review* 80(4): 1249–1270.

Scholz, John T., and B. Dan Wood. 1998. "Controlling the IRS: Principals, Principles, and Public Administration." *American Journal of Political Science* 42(1): 141–162.

Scott, Kevin M. 2007. "U.S. Attorneys Who Have Served Less than Full Four-year Terms, 1981–2006." *Congressional Research Service Report for Congress.* February 22.

Segal, Bernard, ed. 1986. *Perspectives on Drug Use in the United States.* New York: Haworth Press.

Selznick, Philip. 1957. *Leadership in Administration: A Sociological Interpretation.* Evanston, IL: Row, Peterson.

Seymour, Whitney North, Jr. 1975. *United States Attorney.* New York: William Morrow.

Shannon, Elaine. 1988. *Desperados: Latin Drug Lords, U.S. Lawmen, and the War America Can't Win.* New York: Viking.

Sharp, Elaine B. 1992. "Agenda Setting and Policy Results: Lessons from Three Drug Policy Episodes." *Policy Studies Journal* 20:538–551.

Shellow, Robert, ed. 1976. *Drug Use and Crime: Report of the Panel on Drug Use and Criminal Behavior*. Washington, D.C.: National Technical Information Service.

Shull, Steven A., and David Garland. 1995. "Presidential Influence Versus Agency Characteristics in Explaining Policy Implementation." *Policy Studies Review* 14:49–70.

Simon, Jonathan. 2007. *Governing through Crime: How the War on Crime Transformed American Democracy and Created a Culture of Fear*. New York: Oxford University Press.

Sloman, Larry Ratso. 1998. *Reefer Madness: The History of Marijuana in America*. New York: St. Martin's Press.

Solomon, Deborah. 2008. "The Prosecutor: Questions for David Iglesias." *New York Times Magazine*. May 25.

Spillane, Joseph F. 2002. *Cocaine: From Medical Marvel to Modern Menace in the United States, 1884–1920*. Baltimore: Johns Hopkins University Press.

Stanton, M. D. 1976. "Drugs, Vietnam and the Vietnam Veteran: An Overview." *American Journal of Drug and Alcohol Abuse* 3:557–570.

Steinert, Heinz. 2003. "The Indispensable Metaphor of War: On Populist Politics and the Contradictions of the State's Monopoly of Force." *Theoretical Criminology* 7(3): 265–291.

Stinchcombe, Arthur L., Rebecca Adams, Carol A. Heimer, Kim Lane Schepple, Tom W. Smith, and D. Garth Taylor. 1980. *Crime and Punishment in America: Changing Attitudes in America*. San Francisco: Jossey-Bass.

Stone, Deborah. 2002. *Policy Paradox: The Art of Political Decision Making*. Revised ed. New York: W.W. Norton.

Strong, Simon. 1995. *Whitewash: Pablo Escobar and the Cocaine Wars*. London: Macmillan.

Taft, William Howard. 2005. "The President Constrained by the Constitution." In *Thinking about the Presidency*, ed. Gary L. Gregg II. Lanham, MD: Rowman and Littlefield.

Thomas, Chuck, and Richard Schmitz. 2006. *State-By-State Medical Marijuana Laws: How to Remove the Threat of Arrest*. Washington, D.C.: Marijuana Policy Project.

Thornton, Mary. 1982a. "FBI to Take Major Role in Drug Enforcement." *Washington Post*. January 22, A13.

———. 1982b. "More Boy Scout Leader than Drug Agent? New DEA Chief Struggles to Raise Morale." *Washington Post*. October 18, A11.

———. 1991. *The Economics of Prohibition*. Salt Lake City: University of Utah Press.

Tonry, Michael. 1995. *Malign Neglect: Race, Crime, and Punishment in America*. New York: Oxford University Press.

Truman, David B. 1940. *Administrative Decentralization: A Study of the Chicago Field Offices of the United Slates Department of Agriculture*. Chicago: University of Chicago Press.

Tulis, Jeffrey K. 1987. *The Rhetorical Presidency.* Princeton, NJ: Princeton University Press.

———. 2004. "Review: On Deaf Ears: The Limits of the Bully Pulpit." *Perspectives on Politics* 2:838.

United States Department of Justice. 2002. "Budget Trend Data: 1975 Through the President's 2003 Request to the Congress." Budget Staff, Justice Management Division, Spring. Available at www.usdoj.gov/jmd/budgetsummary/btd/1975_2002/btd02tocpg.htm, accessed December 17, 2008.

United States Sentencing Commission. 1997. *Special Report to the Congress: Cocaine and Federal Sentencing Policy.* Washington, D.C.: U.S. Government Printing Office.

———. 2004. *Fifteen Years of Guidelines Sentencing: An Assessment of How Well the Federal Criminal Justice System Is Achieving the Goals of Sentencing Reform.* Washington, D.C.: U.S. Sentencing Commission.

Valentine, Douglas. 2004. *The Strength of the Wolf: The Secret History of America's War on Drugs.* New York: Verso.

Vecchi, Gregory, and Robert Sigler. 2001. *Assets Forfeiture: A Study of Policy and Its Practice.* Durham, NC: Carolina Academic Press.

Walters, Ronald W. 1990. "Party Platforms as Political Process." *PS: Political Science and Politics* 23: 436–438.

Warren, Kenneth F. 1993. "We Have Debated Ad Nauseam the Legitimacy of the Administrative State—But Why?" *Public Administration Review* 53:249–254.

Waterman, Richard W. 1989. *Presidential Influence and the Administrative State.* Knoxville: University of Tennessee Press.

Waterman, Richard, and Amelia Rouse. 1999. "The Determinants of the Perceptions of Political Control of the Bureaucracy and the Venues of Influence." *Journal of Public Administration Research and Theory* 9:527–569.

Waterman, Richard, Amelia Rouse, and Robert Wright. 1998. "The Venues of Influence: A New Theory of Political Control of the Bureaucracy." *Journal of Public Administration Research and Theory* 8:13–38.

Weick, Karl E. 1995. *Sensemaking in Organizations.* Thousand Oaks, CA: Sage.

Weiner, Tim, and Ginger Thompson. 2001. "Mexico Seeks Closer Law Enforcement Ties With Wary U.S." *New York Times.* April 11, A2.

Weiss, Janet A., and Sandy Kristin Piderit. 1999. "The Value of Mission Statements in Public Agencies." *Journal of Public Administration Research and Theory* 9:193–224.

Whitford, Andrew B. 2002. "Bureaucratic Discretion, Agency Structure, and Democratic Responsiveness: The Case of the United States Attorneys." *Journal of Public Administration Research and Theory* 12(1): 3–27.

Will, George F. 2000. "The Real Enemy in the Drug War." *Washington Post.* January 18, A21.

Williams, Howard. 2002. *Asset Forfeiture: A Law Enforcement Perspective.* Springfield, IL: Charles Thomas.

Wilson, James Q. 1978. *The Investigators: Managing FBI and Narcotics Agents.* New York: Basic Books.

———. 1989. *Bureaucracy: What Government Agencies Do and Why They Do It.* New York: Basic Books.

Wilson, James Q., and George Kelling. 1982. "Broken Windows: The Police and Neighborhood Safety." *The Atlantic Monthly.* March, pp. 1–11.

Wilson, Woodrow. 2005. "The Presidency and the Power of Public Opinion." In *Thinking About the Presidency,* ed. Gary L. Gregg II. Lanham, MD: Rowman and Littlefield.

Wisotsky, Steven. 1986. *Breaking the Impasse in the War on Drugs.* New York: Greenwood Press.

———. 1992. "A Society Of Suspects: The War on Drugs and Civil Liberties." Cato Policy Analysis No. 180.

Witt, Louise. 2002. "Bush's Reefer Madness." Salon.com, November 5. Available at http://dir.salon.com/story/news/feature/2002/11/05/drugwar, accessed December 17, 2008.

Wood, B. Dan, and Jeffrey Peake. 1998. "The Dynamics of Foreign Policy Agenda Setting." *American Political Science Review* 92:173–184.

Wood, B. Dan, Chris T. Owens, and Brandy M. Durham. 2005. "Presidential Rhetoric and the Economy." *Journal of Politics* 67:627–645.

Wood, B. Dan, and Richard W. Waterman. 1994. *Bureaucratic Dynamics: The Role of Bureaucracy in a Democracy.* Boulder, CO: Westview Press.

Wright, Paul. 2003. *Prison Nation: The Warehousing of America's Poor.* New York: Routledge.

Yates, Jeff, Todd Collins, and Gabriel J. Chin. 2005. "A War on Drugs or a War on Immigrants? Expanding the Definition of 'Drug Trafficking' in Determining Aggravated Felon Status for Noncitizens." *Maryland Law Review* 64:875–909.

Yates, Jeff, and Richard Fording. 2005. "Politics and State Punitiveness in Black and White." *Journal of Politics* 67:1099–1121.

Yates, Jeff, and Andrew Whitford. 2005. "Institutional Foundations of the President's Issue Agenda." *Political Research Quarterly* 58:577–585.

Yates, Jeff, Andrew Whitford, and William Gillespie. 2005. "Agenda Setting, Issue Priorities, and Organizational Maintenance: The U.S. Supreme Court, 1955 to 1994." *British Journal of Political Science* 35:369–381.

Zarefsky, David. 2004. "Presidential Rhetoric and the Power of Definition." *Presidential Studies Quarterly* 34(3): 607–619.

Zeger, S. L., and K. Y. Liang. 1986a. "Longitudinal Data Analysis for Discrete and Continuous Outcomes." *Biometrics* 42:121–130.

———. 1986b. "Longitudinal Data Analysis Using Generalized Linear Models." *Biometrika* 73:13–22.

Zeger, S. L., K.-Y. Liang, and S. L. Albert. 1988. "Models for Longitudinal Data: A Generalized Estimating Equation Approach." *Biometrics* 44:1049–1060.

Zernicke, Paul H. 1994. *Pitching the Presidency: How Presidents Depict the Office*. Westport, CT: Praeger.

Zorn, Christopher J. W. 2001. "Generalized Estimating Equation Models for Correlated Data: A Review with Applications." *American Journal of Political Science* 45:470–490.

Index

Page numbers followed by *f* refer to figures; those followed by *t* refer to tables.